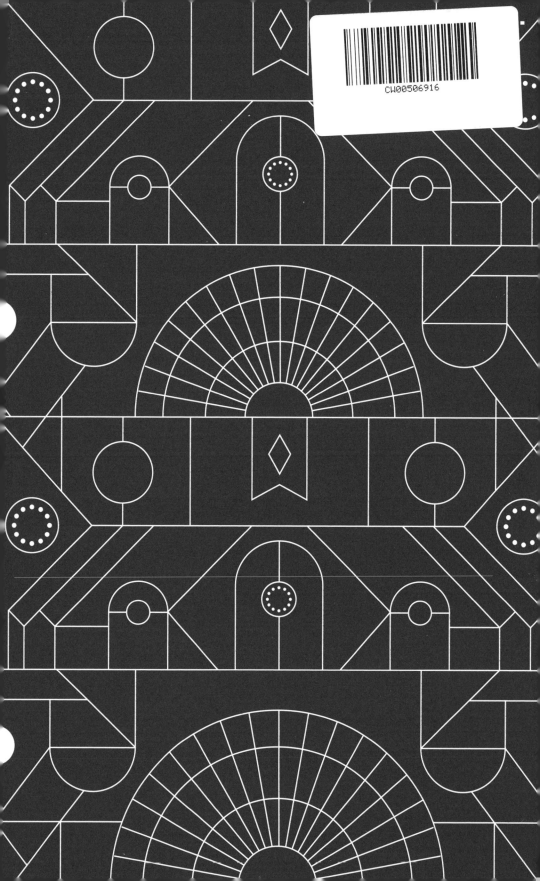

Spaceships Over Glasgow

Spaceships Over Glasgow

Mogwai, Mayhem and Misspent Youth

Stuart Braithwaite

WHITE
RABBIT

First published in Great Britain in 2022 by White Rabbit,
an imprint of The Orion Publishing Group Ltd
Carmelite House, 50 Victoria Embankment
London EC4Y 0DZ

An Hachette UK Company

10 9 8 7 6 5 4 3 2 1

A CIP catalogue record for this book is
available from the British Library.

ISBN (Hardback) 978 1 4746 2412 1
ISBN (Export Trade Paperback) 978 1 4746 2413 8
ISBN (eBook) 978 1 4746 2415 2
ISBN (Audio) 978 1 4746 2416 9

Typeset by Input Data Services Ltd, Somerset

Printed in Great Britain by Clays Ltd, Elcograf S.p.A.

www.whiterabbitbooks.co.uk
www.orionbooks.co.uk

To Elisabeth Elektra, Kate Braithwaite and Victoria Braithwaite for all the love and support and Dominic, Martin and Barry for getting on all the stages with me

Contents

Part One
Stargazing

1.

The Ubiquitous Telescope

I wasn't born into music.

I arrived on this earth on 10 May 1976 in William Smellie Hospital in Lanark, Scotland, the second child of Catherine and John Braithwaite after my big sister, Victoria, who was born three years earlier. My mum was an NHS GP and my father was Scotland's only telescope maker.

My mum, the oldest of five children, was the daughter of George and Janet Peck, a native of the island of Lewis, the largest of the group of islands known as the Outer Hebrides, off the north-west coast of Scotland. George was a fisherman and merchant seaman who had served in the Second World War as part of the Arctic convoys, and later in life held the role of lighthouse keeper of the Tiumpan Head Lighthouse, a stone's throw from Flesherin, the village where he'd lived his whole life. He had married Janet Trainer of Strathaven, Lanarkshire after a whirlwind, weeks-long romance in the middle of the war. My mum was brought up in the two-bedroom house that my grandad built with his own hands overlooking the Minch, the sea that separates the main-land from the island. Upon finishing high school in Stornoway, my mum Kate (as she's known) was accepted to study medicine at the University of Aberdeen. After graduating she went on to serve as a family doctor in the industrial Lanarkshire town of Hamilton. It was at a party in Hamilton where she met my dad, native Hamiltonian John Braithwaite.

My dad's route to becoming Scotland's only telescope maker is probably worthy of a book in itself. My grandfather Bill Braithwaite left his native Hamilton, and indeed Scotland, as a young man to fight Franco's fascists along with many others in the International Brigades in Spain. He returned intact to Scotland but his efforts against the fascism that Hitler brought would prove less robust. My grandad lost his leg in an explosion during the Second World War and had to make do with a tin leg for the rest of his life. He'd played in goal for the local team Hamilton Academicals as a teenager, and upon seeing his now one-legged pal, a friend of my grandad quipped, 'At least you'll still get a game for Accies, Bill.' Scottish humour can be dark.

After the war Bill Braithwaite became an engineer of scientific instruments, working at the telescope and binocular shop run by Arthur Frank in the Saltmarket area of Glasgow's Merchant City. It was here that my dad would work every Saturday as a teenager, helping his father and learning the craft that would define his life. My dad studied economics at the University of Strathclyde in Glasgow, even representing it on the TV quiz show *University Challenge*. He took no joy from numbers, however, and sneaked into the astronomy lectures instead. He was always obsessed with the stars and had a lifelong disdain for capitalism and the greed that it breeds. After he left university, my dad got a job in England at the arms company Avimo, designing sights for military helicopters. Something of a hippy at heart, my dad decided he didn't fancy a future as part of the military–industrial complex and returned to Scotland. He went on to have a variety of jobs, such as running a very early computer system for the famous Templeton Carpet Factory at Glasgow Green, to working at a steel company in Coatbridge. It was during this period that he met my mum.

After a short while staying in the flat above the surgery where my mum worked across from the bus station in Hamilton, they bought a rather dishevelled house near the village of Law in South Lanarkshire. They married in 1970 and, in 1973, my sister Victoria was born. The flat in Hamilton being a wee bit pokey, they moved to an extremely dilapidated house in the countryside near Law. Their place was a bit of a health hazard, with holes in the walls and suchlike. My dad was a lifelong campaigner for Scottish independence and an active member of the still some-what underground Scottish National Party, after having left the Labour Party due to its refusal to back nuclear disarmament. The extra space provided room for him to set up a printing press in an outbuilding, which he used to make seemingly endless posters and flyers to boost the independence cause. I still recall the piles of day-glo posters with Prime Minister Margaret Thatcher carica-tured as Dracula, with Scotland's oil dripping from her fangs. It was in this ramshackle environment that the family lived when I came along in May 1976, at the start of a summer that was to bring with it a record-breaking heatwave. My earliest memories are of playing with the hose in the garden, presumably trying to cool off in the decidedly un-Scottish baking sun. We stayed there for a year before moving to a house in Law. That house was in a Brookside-style cul-de-sac, the kind of place where everyone knows each other's business. One of my first memories of living there is of flying down the stairs and straight through a plate-glass door, yet somehow remaining unscathed. The impression that I was apparently invincible was one I would carry with me into my adult life.

We didn't stay there too long though. I don't think small town life particularly suited my folks.

When I was four my parents moved to the countryside and the Clyde Valley, a somewhat idyllic part of Scotland consisting of small villages following the River Clyde on its route from the hills in the south through Glasgow before joining the sea on the west coast. They found a place close enough to Hamilton for my mum to work (remember this was in the days when you could call the doctor at any time of day or night). It was also far out enough in the sticks and away from civilisation for my dad to be able to look at the stars with minimal light pollution. The view of the night sky from the back garden was glorious. On a clear night (alas, not that common in Scotland), the ubiquitous telescope would be out and friends would come over to study the stars and planets. We always had loads of animals, as many as three dogs and lots of cats, as well as assorted rabbits and guinea pigs. I always loved animals.

My parents' life did not revolve around music, although before my sister and I came along they'd been an active part of the local folk scene in the sixties. My dad was a fine singer and had performed with a friend of his, under the frankly tremendous name The Lords of Misrule, but this had waned by the seventies as family and work took over. The only music I remember from my childhood being played at home was the odd snatch of opera or classical music like 'The Hall of the Mountain King', or 'Carmina Burana', or the occasional folk rock record by Steeleye Span or Fairport Convention. I recall one night my dad playing me 'Take Five' by Dave Brubeck, one of his favourite jazz songs. I remember it vividly because it was the same night that Pan Am flight 103 crashed in Lockerbie. While I'm sure my parents were fond of music, it was secondary to literature. The house was packed to the rafters with books. My dad must have had every book ever written by and about James Joyce, T. S. Eliot and Ezra Pound. It wasn't all high culture though; he was fond of pulp novels as well. I remember being shit scared by the covers of the Stephen King and James Herbert books that I saw lying around. I recall staring in terror at the cover of *Carrie*, her face dripping with blood. My dad loved staying up late watching horror films. His sleeping patterns throughout his life were always in flux. He was completely fine grabbing the odd hour or so of sleep here or there. If he had a big telescope order on it would seem as though he barely slept for days.

I owned a few records as a child. One which I loved to bits was the novelty album purportedly made by the weird creatures that starred in the TV show *The Wombles*. The band The Wombles played classic seventies glam rock-style pop. I was besotted with it. But I remember being at a party when I was a child and hearing something that truly did change my life, something that blew the Wombles out of the metaphorical water: David Bowie. It was during a game of pass the parcel that I first heard 'Starman'. There was something about the song that completely transported me. The majesty of the music was beyond anything I'd heard before, the voice completely alluring, the melody so perfect. Perhaps it was the fact I was nuts about *Stars Wars* and UFOs.

For Christmas, when I was four or five, I was given my first ever real record (well, a tape actually); it was a compilation I played to death, a gift from my aunt and uncle from Fife called *Disco 79*, and I loved it. I was particularly taken by 'Le Freak' by Chic. An unarguably perfect song, it was the mysterious glamour of it that really pulled me in. I was in freezing cold Scotland, surrounded by cows, and this could not have felt more escapist. It was the first time I'd owned any music and I played that tape over and over and over. 'Knock On Wood', 'We Are Family' – it was perfection.

I had a wonderful childhood and was incredibly lucky to have the experiences I did, but it was these tiny glimpses into the world of music that really captured me. I also had a handful of music VHS tapes which I'd adopted from my sister that I'd watch on repeat. One was Hendrix's incendiary performance at Monterey. I'd watch him play explosively yet nonchalantly up to the finale where he set his guitar on fire. It was amazing.

There was something unspeakably weird and psychedelic about my childhood. Aside from the almost supernatural memory of flying through glass, I had a few other experiences that seem strange in retrospect. One of them that makes perfect sense now occurred while I was having a routine operation to remove my adenoids. I was sedated for the procedure and, as the gas was administered, I remember seeing fractal kaleidoscopic shapes spreading outwards from my field of vision while my mind played the theme song from *Doctor Who*, the acid squelch bassline pounding through my tiny mind. It felt like a primitive calling. I didn't know it at the time but it was my first psychedelic experience.

The year before I departed for secondary school, age eleven, I was given a guitar. It was a nylon string acoustic, not remotely rock and roll, but I adored it all the same. Seeing how taken me and my sister were with it, my parents arranged for us to have guitar lessons. Our teacher was a guy called Harry who lived above an Indian restaurant near Peacock Cross in Hamilton. Harry was a lovely guy who, as well as showing me the basics of playing guitar (chords, scales and the like), also fulfilled the role of navigator in the world of music. As all good teachers should, Harry started me off by teaching me songs that were simple to play, usually with a maximum of three chords, but sometimes two. It was during one of these exercises that Harry took the what, in retrospect, seems rather an odd decision of teaching a prepubescent child how to play 'Heroin' by The Velvet Underground. Hearing that song was a defining moment in my life. I had no idea what drugs were. It was just a word that people on TV said, something you should say no to (look what happened to Zammo!). The subject of the song didn't matter a jot to me though. I was overwhelmed by the power and raw emotion of the song. The sound was like a wave washing over me. At the time I presumed that The Velvet Underground were all Black. Their music is totally indebted to Black blues so I suppose it makes sense. Little did I know that the bass player was from Wales. I asked what the screeching sound was. It sounded like someone's soul being torn to pieces. Harry answered that it was called feedback. It was what happened when you leant your electric guitar against an amp. I recognised the sound from a band that Victoria had started listening to, The Jesus and Mary Chain. I loved the sound. I wanted to make a sound like that. I wanted an electric guitar.

My dad loved to go to the Barras Market every Sunday, located in the East End of Glasgow a few miles from Celtic Park and directly underneath the ballroom-cum-gig venue named the Barrowlands, two places I would become increasingly familiar with in years to come. He was primarily interested in books, antique trinkets and any scientific equipment he could use to build or repair telescopes – by this point that was his full-time business. I'd often pal along with him, looking for computer games or *Star Wars* toys but mostly just enjoying the adventure of going to the city and all of the weirdness and excitement that it brought. It felt a million miles away from where we stayed in the country, even though it was only twenty miles. The Barras back then was insanely busy and full of the most vivid characters you could ever wish (or not wish) to meet. You'd find people selling everything from rare books and random remote controls to detached hoods from jackets and illicit meat. It was on one of these Sunday excursions that my dad made the purchase that was to change my life: my first electric guitar. My dad was the most generous person I've ever known, and on meeting someone's kid who showed a passing interest in astronomy, he would often send them on their way with pockets full of astronomical paraphernalia to ignite their interest even further. He was similarly generous with me and well aware that I'd taken to playing guitar and was keen on upgrading my nylon strung acoustic to something more . . . rock and roll. The electric guitar that took my eye in between the random artefacts was a shiny, black Japanese copy of a Gibson Les Paul for the princely sum of fifty pounds. I adored it. I would literally play it until my fingers bled. At this time my parents must have been grateful that my bedroom was at the far end of the house and they wouldn't have to suffer my fumbling steps into music at close quarters.

Owning my first electric guitar really accelerated my journey into music. I would tape albums from my sister's LP collection and listen to them endlessly in my room. My sister was a goth at this point so a lot of her music taste was fairly petula-tinged.

9

Bauhaus, The Sisters of Mercy and suchlike. She was also a huge fan of the 4AD record label, with bands like Pixies, Cocteau Twins and, in particular, the New York shoegaze band, Ultra Vivid Scene. I remember one time she went with her friend Nicola to Newcastle to see them play, while telling each other's parents that they were staying the night at each other's houses, which was quite a bold move considering they were both sixteen and had no guarantee of getting into the gig and nowhere to stay. They ended up sleeping at the bus station. As far as I was concerned, Ultra Vivid Scene was one of the biggest bands on the planet.

Of all the bands my sister loved, the one that really got under my skin was The Cure. I had taped every single one of their albums and played them so many times that I knew every word, every note and every nuance off by heart. I'd started with the singles compilation *Standing On a Beach* and had progressed through all of them, from the scratchy punk of *Three Imaginary Boys* to the recently released *Kiss Me Kiss Me Kiss Me*. I loved them all. There was something universally romantic and escapist about their music that really touched me.

By this point I was twelve years old and about to make the jump from primary to secondary school. I went to primary school in the nearby village of Ashgill. I'd had quite a good time there, earning the nickname 'Professor' because I wore glasses and read the odd book. I had quite a few run-ins with the teachers though, mostly over quite bizarre things like how to draw a tree (my teacher said it should look like a triangle whereas mine had more of a round shape; it clearly hadn't occurred to her that trees don't all look the same). My parents weren't keen on me going to the closest secondary school to us because it didn't have a great reputation, and instead sent me and my sister to one a few miles away in a small town called Strathaven. Going to a different school to all of my friends at primary school was daunting but I don't think I actually thought about it too much. As committed socialists there was never any question of us going to private school (like a lot of the other doctors' kids). Having grown up Catholic, a lot of my dad's friends' kids went to Catholic school. Religion was another no-go with my folks, so I wouldn't be following them there. Capitalism and religion made up two of the holy trinity of evils in our household, along with the Tories. Any mention of them would be quickly followed by the word 'bastards'. Not uncommon in Scottish households. As far as not knowing anyone at my new school? My sister was there so at least I'd have one person to speak to.

Before the summer holidays all the Primary 7 kids were shown around the high schools they would be attending. On my trip to visit the school I wore my favourite item of clothing: The Cure T-shirt I'd begged my mum to buy me from the local market. It was a bootleg affair and fairly shoddy in retrospect, but I loved it dearly. While being shown around the unfamiliar classrooms and halls, I heard a shout from one of the other kids: 'Nice Cure shirt, great band.' The other kid was a wee guy with a fuzzy ginger mop of hair. His name was Craig. Craig Wallace. I had a pal. Thank fuck for that.

After the summer I started school, Craig and I became good friends. He lived in the village of Chapelton, about five miles past Strathaven on the way to East Kilbride. The two of us would go to each other's houses and mess around making music. Like me, he had an older, cooler sibling, Mark, whom he could sponge records off. He was also a budding musician. A bass player. Alongside another prepubescent Cure fan called Chris, also from Chapelton, we decided to start a band. Taking our cue from one of our favourite bands whose name had shocked a few dainty relatives and teachers when they'd seen it scrawled on jotters and skateboards and the like – The Jesus and Mary Chain – we went for the name Pregnant Nun. None of us had any idea what being in a band actually entailed. We knew about the *NME* interviews and pop videos but the actual mechanics of being in a band were a complete mystery. The concept of writing songs, for example, never even crossed our minds. We would just endlessly play the simplest riffs we could work out over and over: 'Sidewalking' by the Mary Chain and 'Bela Lugosi's Dead' by Bauhaus were favourites. It was endlessly fun, totally innocent, make-believe teenage nonsense. We weren't making anything new, but just the act of getting together with pals and making a racket was amazing.

In the first year at high school my friends and I had no money but still wanted to hear as much music as possible. We did this by organising a thriving tape community whereby we would give each other blank cassette tapes and copies of whatever records we had, usually belonging to our big brothers and sisters. A few of the bolder kids would steal three packs of blank tapes from the newsagent, which they'd then sell at a reduced rates to the others.

A well as Victoria's record collection, I had a few other windows into the world of music: the weekly music press, (which I was obsessed with), radio and television. Every Wednesday I would religiously buy *New Musical Express*, *Melody Maker* and *Sounds* and devour them. I was fascinated by the characters behind the music. It seemed then that the singers of the bands I loved were even more outrageous than their music. People like Siouxsie Sioux, Robert Smith, Ian McCulloch, Chuck D and Julian Cope never gave dull interviews. Back then, being outrageous was the norm, and barely a week would go by without someone or other threatening or decrying someone else. It was absolutely ridiculous, but I found it mesmerising. I'd study the news sections to see who had a new record coming out or who had left or joined which band. It all seemed endlessly fascinating. So many of the bands were just names on the page unless I heard them on the John Peel radio show or saw them play on a BBC2 TV show which I'd become transfixed by: *Snub TV*, an amazing programme that would showcase and interview a handful of different independent bands or artists each week. Bands like The Cramps, Fugazi, My Bloody Valentine, The Stone Roses and Dinosaur Jr., many giving pretty enigmatic or just plain weird interviews, as well as performing live or showing promo videos made specifically for the show. It was so good to match faces and sounds to the people I'd been reading about in the music papers. The music was strange and the personalities intriguing. I'd never miss an episode. I vividly recall seeing the deadpan, shades-wearing Spacemen 3 ripping through the one-chord, fuzzed-out, anti-authority anthem 'Revolution'. It was exactly what I needed.

Well I'm sick
I'm so sick
Of a lot of people
Who try to tell me
What I can and can't do
With my life

I was a religious listener of John Peel's show on Radio 1. He would have a different band in session every night and his show was anything but predictable. As well as the indie rock that I was mostly tuning in for, he would play a lot of African music, hip-hop and acid house. I remember being captivated by the song 'Voodoo Ray' by A Guy Called Gerald. I was too young to know what a club was, what drugs were, or have any context at all for a record like this, but I adored it all the same. When I think back to this period, I love how wide-eyed I was. Music was such an open book, so exciting. In my mind, all of the people making these records were superstars. The truth was a damn sight less glamorous, but I wasn't to know that.

There was something about the way the music made me feel that completely captivated me.

I'd quickly got to the point where it took up all of my focus and attention, and I wasn't looking back. I was fully on board for the journey.

2.
Fascination Street

By this point The Cure were without doubt my favourite band and I was delirious with excitement when I heard their new single was to get its first airing on the radio, an event that I tuned into with feverish anticipation. 'Lullaby' sounded different from everything they'd done before, but it had a familiarity to it that was unmistakably them. It was wonderful.

'Lullaby' was taken from their new album *Disintegration*. I read how Robert Smith had decided to go towards the darker style of the earlier records like *Faith* and *Pornography*, both of which I adored. I couldn't wait to hear it.

The album was going to be released on 2 May 1989, the week before my thirteenth birthday, and I had to have it the second it came out. It was the first record I'd ever been aware of before its release. My new-found obsession with the music press only added fuel to the fire of my anticipation as they were running weekly previews and interviews with the band in the run-up to the release. It was clear I wasn't alone in my fervour.

In the weeks to come I was to find out something else that was to take my level of excitement to another level entirely. Not only were The Cure touring, but the Prayer Tour (as it was called) was coming to Glasgow. I absolutely *had* to go. My sister had been going to gigs for a while now and, as I knew she'd want to go and see The Cure, I hoped my parents would allow me to tag along with her. My folks' parenting style could be loosely described as 'free range'. They were never too strict with my sister or me, and in all honesty, they were too busy to be overly fussing with their kids. I mean, what kind of trouble could we get into living in the middle of nowhere anyway? (Plenty would be the answer, but more of that later.)

Thankfully my parents allowed me to go. They knew how much it meant to me. More importantly than that, Victoria agreed to take me. It was very kind of her. Not a lot of sixteen-year-olds would be so accommodating of their barely thirteen-year-old wee brother.

My parents bought the ticket as part of my upcoming birthday. I'd never been so excited about anything before in my entire life. I was also counting down the days until the release of *Disintegration*. I remember that in the weeks leading up to it, I had a dream about what it would sound like, its release taking on the role of some kind of magical event. When I woke up I tried to recall what it had sounded like, but like most dreams it disappeared as soon as lucidity took hold. It felt like I'd experienced a clairvoyant event, such was the level of anticipation. I'd listen to their previous album *Kiss Me Kiss Me Kiss Me* over and over, wondering which direction the band would take. *Kiss Me* was such an odd album, a record of extremes. Some songs were ludicrously pop, sandwiched between dark, psychedelic wig-outs. The only song I'd heard from *Disintegration*, 'Lullaby', didn't give much away either.

Hamilton was the town I spent most time in as a teenager. Grey, post-industrial and fifteen miles south of Glasgow, it was where my mum practised as a GP. I'd get the half-hour bus journey there after school and wait for my mum to finish work, before getting a lift home with her. I'd spend hours perusing its small town centre, going from shop to shop and starting all over again, looking through the magazines in John Menzies the newsagent and scrutinising the records in Woolworths, Our Price and the independent shop Impulse. It was in Our Price that I pre-ordered *Disintegration*.

Finally, the day came. Knowing that after school on 1 May I would be going to pick up *Disintegration*, I was even more distracted than usual from my lessons. Not that I wasn't often distracted – I'd gone from being one of the best pupils at my primary school to suddenly being far less interested in schoolwork, preferring instead to have a laugh with my new pals and gabbing non-stop about music. I had already made my choice. If the choice was between education and rock and roll, then education was going to lose.

After a day of fidgetiness, non-attentiveness and staring at clocks, I left school and got on the bus to Hamilton. It was a slow bus anyway, but on this particular day it seemed to stop at every supposed village, some of which comprised of two houses. Clutching my precious ten-pound note, I speed-walked through the precinct to get to Our Price. I was a mess of excitement, but I didn't want to betray my feelings to the staff of the shop because, in my eyes, they were the coolest people on the planet. I handed over my money and received the LP that I'd had reserved for weeks. Getting it in my hands gave me a feeling of total elation. I had no bloody idea what it sounded like. I raced up to my mum's surgery where I could examine it more closely and hopefully decipher some secrets as to its musical contents. I remember pulling the inner sleeve out from within the main cover and thinking that there weren't a lot of lyrics on the album. I'd seen some of my sister's records with separate lyric books that were pages and pages long and *Disintegration* had them all printed on one side of the inner sleeve. I now realise there are loads of lyrics but they are in really small print. Alas, those powers of deduction weren't available to me as a thirteen-year-old boy.

The start of the album was beyond enigmatic. The tinkling of the bells promising so much but barely giving anything away before being washed away by the utter grandeur and weighty sound that is the start of 'Plainsong', the music growing and swelling like a storm in the middle of the sea for what felt like an eternity before the vocals arrived. Having read the lyrics several times in the staffroom of my mum's surgery, I'd already imagined how the line 'I think it's dark and it looks like rain, you said' would be delivered, but I hadn't imagined it to be how it actually was – seemingly overcome with emotion and delivered with a weary sense of beauty. So poignant, delicate and raw. It was perfect, and what followed was just as astounding. The record wasn't all reflected in the ambient grandeur of 'Plainsong'. There were pop highlights like 'Pictures Of You' and 'Lovesong', which struck a huge chord with my blossoming teenage romanticism. I loved everything about the record and my fondness for it only grew the more I listened to it. The fact that it was my own record, not one of my sister's or a taped copy, meant so much to me. I pored over every detail of it as I listened intently. On every level it felt like *my* album.

I was now counting down the days until I got to hear the songs live. In two months I was going to my first live concert. There was a burgeoning group of music fans at our school and it wasn't just my sister and me who were anticipating The Cure coming to Glasgow. Alan McGregor, a gregarious, tall music-obsessive in my sister's year who went by an abbreviated version of his surname, 'Mog', was similarly excited. He'd organised a minibus going from Strathaven to Glasgow for the New Order concert back in March and had plans to do the same for The Cure. In my year, Craig, who had befriended me because of my Cure T-shirt, was going with his big brother, Mark. Coming too was my sister's friend Nicola, a gangly ginger girl who also lived on our street. Mog hired the same minibus that he'd used to go to the New Order gig but, as word got out and the numbers swelled, he had to hire a bigger bus. It ended up being a coach, more than four times the size of the original minibus. Along for the ride with Mog was his friend Kevin McCrorie, a year older than Victoria and quite the character. Kevin was a brilliant, permanently flustered chap with an unparalleled obsession with music.

Kevin could wax lyrical about records, bands and songs for hours on end.

The gig fell in the middle of the school holidays, my first since going to high school in Strathaven. My holiday so far had been spent listening to *Disintegration* and skateboarding. I'd received my first real skateboard, a Powell Peralta Lance Mountain, the Christmas before and had taken to the new form of skateboarding, 'street skating'. It basically entailed hanging around car parks and jumping up and down stairs until police or security guards intervened. I loved it.

Waiting for the gig had only been a few months but it felt like an eternity. Finally, the day of the concert arrived. My dad drove Victoria and me to Strathaven to get the bus to the gig. When we arrived at the bus I couldn't believe how amazing everyone looked. I didn't know most of the people and I was blown away by the efforts everyone had gone to. It was the late eighties and goth fashion was at its peak. Hair was either backcombed up, ála Robert Smith, or crimped. Gallons of hairspray and eyeliner must have been used in preparation. Almost everyone was wearing make-up, both boys and girls. God knows what my dad was thinking when he dropped us off at what must have looked like a travelling freak show. The Cure were flagbearers for our counterculture, and as part of that tribe it was our absolute duty to make sure everyone knew about it. And here they were, looking like they were trying out for a high school performance of *Interview with the Vampire*. Everyone except Mog, that is. He was wearing a Spider-Man mask, presumably in tribute to The Cure song 'Lullaby', which mentioned a 'Spider-Man'. I'm fairly sure it wasn't the Peter Parker type of Spider-Man being sung about, but there you go. He was also, for some mysterious reason, carrying an acoustic guitar. My hair was back-combed and spiky. Craig's was too. With his bouffant ginger hair and my black fuzzy mop, we looked for all the world like a *Bugsy Malone* version of Jim and William Reid from the Mary Chain.

Of all the people on the bus, Craig and I were by far the youngest. Aside from music, our interests were skateboards and video consoles, whereas everyone else had rather more developed leisure pursuits. As the bus departed for the (to us) epic half-hour journey from Strathaven to Glasgow, the mystery unfolded as to why Mog had brought a guitar. As soon as we started moving, the (stringless) guitar's purpose was revealed. From within the hollow body of the guitar Mog magically procured cans of beer. Before I'd even arrived at my first concert I was being exposed to the murky, alluring world of teenage drinking. Unfortunately for Mog the driver of the bus did not share his enthusiasm and promptly pulled the bus over and made him throw away all the beer. Me and Craig were not ready for this level of drama and were frankly terrified that this was going to somehow stop us from getting to see The Cure. Our fears were, however, thankfully unfounded. The disgruntled driver was presumably more than used to the travails of driving miscreant teens and continued on his journey after swiftly putting a halt to Mog's nonsense.

Having survived the scare of beer-gate we arrived at the venue. The SEC is a huge conference centre on the banks of the River Clyde in the centre of Glasgow. Essentially a huge steel barn, it isn't what you would normally think of as the natural home for melancholic rock music. When we entered the venue I was astonished by the sheer number of people, surely in the tens of thousands. I was also incredibly surprised to see rows and rows of seats. I'd expected the gig to be a standing affair like the videos I'd seen of The Cure, like *The Cure in Orange* video when they played a huge Roman amphitheatre in France. But the synth pop band Pet Shop Boys had played the night before and so the venue was all seated. We went to our seats in time to see the opening band – folk rock outfit Shelleyan Orphan. Such was my excitement about seeing The Cure that their set pretty much passed me by. It's a hard truth for support bands that capturing the attention of an audience who are there to see a highly anticipated headliner can be nigh on impossible (a lesson I'd be on the other end of many times in later life).

The time between the opening band and The Cure felt like forever. I watched the hubbub of roadies and stage technicians pottering away like doozers from *Fraggle Rock* with amazed excitement. I'd never been around so many people in my life and hadn't realised just how many people there might be that, like me, loved The Cure. I'd been absolutely obsessed with *Disintegration* all summer long and the moment was almost here. I was a bag of nervous joy, all goosebumps and neck hairs on end. Then. Finally. The lights dropped.

I was struck by two sensations at once: the utter thrill of hearing the chiming bells that signified the start of 'Plainsong', the album opener, and also a curious frenzy that seemed to be going on all around me. It would seem that Cure fans are a different breed to Pet Shop Boys fans as no one seemed remotely happy about sitting in their allocated seating, or sitting down at all for that matter. Someone had the smart idea of ripping out the chair they were sitting on and rushing towards the stage. This spread like a virus and in no time at all no one was sitting down. The chairs had been wrecked and the gig had instantly become way more akin to what I'd imagined a rock concert to be: messy, full of joy and ever so slightly dangerous.

As the band emerged the stage became an absolute carnival of lights, like nothing I'd ever seen before. Lasers and dry ice filled the stage, all built atop industrial structures that looked like something from a sci-fi film. It was wondrous. The sound was no less spectacular. I'd never heard anything so loud in my life, but it wasn't just volume, there was a clarity to it as well. The band played the intro for what felt like an age before Robert appeared, wandering onto the stage looking simultaneously like the shyest man on earth and someone who was born to be there. The first line – 'I think it's dark and it looks like rain, you said' – cut through the music like a ship through ice. Listening to my favourite music in a hectic throng of thousands of people I truly felt at home.

After 'Plainsong' came the second song from *Disintegration*, 'Pictures Of You'. Despite being only a few months old it was already apparent that this song was a classic. It was utter perfection. This was also the first song that Robert picked up a guitar for, playing the main melody on his baritone Fender 6. I was completely entranced. After some more songs from *Disintegration* they played some of the live favourites from *Head on the Door*. I'd pretty much worn out my VHS of *The Cure in Orange* so to be in the room while they played it in person was something else. I was in heaven. Throughout the set they played more songs from *Disintegration* as well as favourites from their early records like 'A Forest' and 'Charlotte Sometimes'. The main set ended with an incendiary performance of 'Disintegration', the title track. It was absolutely spellbinding.

As the band disappeared into the dark I was in shock at what I'd just witnessed and heard. From the live recordings and videos I'd seen of The Cure I knew that they played long concerts and numerous encores. At age thirteen I didn't realise how unusual it was for a band to play such epic sets and I was eager for more. I wasn't disappointed.

The first song of the encore was 'Lullaby', the first single from *Disintegration*. I thought back to when I first heard it on the radio only a few months earlier but what felt like a lifetime ago. Those few short months had changed everything for me, from backseat music fan to record buyer and concert attendee. After 'Lullaby' they played three more singles: 'Close To Me' and 'Let's Go To Bed', which I knew inside out from the *Standing on a Beach* compilation, and then 'Why Can't I Be You?', the weird, funky single from *Kiss Me Kiss Me Kiss Me*. The place had broken into a dance party before they disappeared again into the dark. I thought that was the end of the gig but I was wrong. The band reappeared for a second time, seemingly even more invigorated. This time they went back to their origins by playing some of their very early singles. Starting with the starkly brutal 'Three Imaginary Boys' followed by the perfect pop song 'Boy's Don't Cry'. The final two songs were '10:15 Saturday Night' and their very first single, 'Killing An Arab'. It was in stark contrast to the epic grandeur of their newest material but worked perfectly as an ending.

I was completely overcome by the end of it. It had exceeded even my fairly lofty expectations. I felt transformed.

I was in a bit of a daze on the bus back to Strathaven. Clutching the 'Lullaby' T-shirt I'd bought with my birthday money, I chatted away to Craig and Victoria about how wonderful the gig was, but in all honesty I was in a slight state of shock. The whole experience had been overwhelming. I knew then that it would be the first of many, many experiences like it.

Departing the bus, bedraggled from the night's events, we managed to find our dad who cheerfully drove us back home.

Back in the warm, isolated haven of our house in the country I excitedly regaled my mum about the evening's excitement. I was giddy and she humoured me in her uniquely dry yet endearing manner. Afterwards I went to my room, still high with adrenaline, surrounded by my posters and burgeoning collection of music-related paraphernalia, and I listened to The Cure and reminisced about the night that had just passed.

Life would never be the same.

3.

They Came from East Kilbride

When I went back to school in the autumn of 1989, the memory of The Cure gig was still fresh. I had a spring in my step and the world seemed like a blank page, full of opportunities and fun. None of this, however, had anything to do with the upcoming year of education. I'd already relegated learning to the back of my mind, if in my mind at all. School was a distraction from my principal interests: music and skateboarding. The one element of school I did warm to was the social side of learning, in particular my religious education class. Having been brought up in a militantly atheist household, I had no interest in Jesus or Allah, but instead was more interested in creating perpetual nonsense and havoc with the kid sat next to me, a permanently grinning ginger guy by the name of Neale Smith.

Neale and I shared a similar view on authority (fucking hated it) and music (fucking loved it), as well as a burgeoning interest in teenage hedonism. The poor woman teaching the class really did get the short straw having to put up with us. We were a fucking nightmare. We had zero interest, bordering on contempt, for the subject and were eager to outdo each other in terms of idiotic behaviour. As for the actual schoolwork at hand? That was simply another exercise in displaying how little we gave a fuck. One assignment consisted of celebrating the birth of Our Lord and Saviour, Jesus Christ, by designing a Christmas card. Having observed the commercialisation of Christmas as a holiday, I took the opportunity to indulge in some highly sophisticated teenage satire, blending God's only son with the latest comic and toy craze, thereby creating 'Teenage Mutant Ninja Jesus'. I artfully drew Mr Christ mid-flying kick, alongside the slogan 'Hero in a halo'. That predictably went down like an inappropriate joke at a funeral.

Another task we were set was to write an essay about a lesson that we'd learnt. I'm sure the angle was for us to exude about how the Bible taught kindness, or some other worthy piffle. I, however, had other ideas. My angle was inspired by the music of my psychedelic heroes Spacemen 3, particularly songs such as 'Losing Touch With My Mind' and the (somewhat tenuously) religiously themed 'Walking With Jesus': that you should take as many drugs as possible. This took even more explaining than the Christmas card. They almost chucked me out of school. The only reason I wasn't expelled was because my mum was the teacher's doctor. An early introduction to the concept of privilege.

Outside of school, Neale and I became inseparable. We'd make the absolute most of our weekends, staying over at each other's houses and going on near-religious trips into Glasgow every Saturday. If Neale stayed at mine, we'd stay up till all hours listening to music and endlessly watching movies, mostly trashy eighties video nasties, which we'd rent from the local video shop three at a time. We'd scare ourselves witless watching the likes of *Demons*, *Poltergeist*, and the film that made its mark probably more than any other, *Hellraiser*. Clive Barker's subversive homage to BDSM made a huge mark on my young mind and led me to his books, which were another level of weird and dark.

I was enthralled by it all. Like music, weird films and literature felt like a portal to another world far removed from my country-side existence. Ghosts and demons coming out of TVs and walls captivated me. I always had a pretty vivid imagination and I'd get myself so scared I was too terrified to go to the toilet on my own. My first venture into thrill-seeking wasn't to be the last.

When Neale wasn't staying at my folks', I would stay at his, always bringing a Pot Noodle for nourishment. This amused Neale's mum endlessly. She would have fed me, I'm sure, but I didn't want to be presumptuous. Neale's parents were lovely people and his dad was a huge music fan. He'd wander in fairly merry from the golf club of an evening and play us Neil Young records, telling us in a very good-natured way that what we were listening to was a load of rubbish. Having a music fan as a dad meant Neale inherited a lot of old stereo equipment, amassing a rather tremendous hand-me-down hi-fi system. I'd hear details on records I knew inside out that I'd never noticed before.

It was on those weekends in Strathaven that we took our first steps – or more accurately leaps – into the world of hedonism. We were the youngest out of all the kids we hung around with, and it seemed at the time that everyone else was already getting pissed at weekends. Our big sisters certainly were (Neale's was also called Victoria). As well as our older siblings and pals, our cultural role models at that time were The Jesus and Mary Chain and Lou Reed. Not exactly great examples. Drinking was pretty much a national pastime in Scotland, and it's little wonder that we threw ourselves into it with abandon. In fact, it was almost inevitable.

As well as being extremely young, both Neale and I were (and still are) really small guys. You would think we might realise how little it would take to get us drunk. You would be sadly wrong. Despite each weighing about seven stone, we decided we needed super-strength booze to get us drunk. We'd get our sisters or an older pal to purchase Red Label Thunderbird wine, which is 18 per cent proof and tastes like paint stripper. We'd get a bottle each. Funds for this were procured by being extremely frugal with our lunch money and pocketing enough during the week to have a fiver by Friday to buy the wine. We were both failing maths but at least we could count when it mattered.

Unsurprisingly, the consequences of drinking this vile concoction were almost always disastrous. We had a little crew of like-minded teenage miscreants that we'd hang out with, usually in Strathaven Park. Someone would have a ghetto blaster and play music while we tried our best to drink ourselves into oblivion. The soundtrack of choice for these soirées was usually punk and heavy metal. Sex Pistols, Metallica and Slayer went well with our burgeoning nihilism. Neale and I had more esoteric music tastes, but it was a bit of a hard sell with the others. Being the size of a child, drinking enough to floor a grown adult inevitably led to one of us passing out and needing assistance to make it up the road. Quite often this was in the midst of a bout of projectile vomiting that wouldn't have looked out of place in *The Exorcist*. The next trick was to hide this whole mess from Neale's parents. I suspect they could tell but were just laughing at our sheer stupidity.

Our other weekly ritual was a trip into the big city every Saturday. We'd get the half-hour bus from either mine or Neale's into Hamilton, then take the half-hour train into Glasgow Central station, which felt like a bit of an adventure in itself.

By this point, both Neale and I looked pretty different from most teenagers our age, which brought its challenges. Scotland was a lot more violent back then than it is now, and it was fairly normal for someone to proudly proclaim they were going to kick your head in for such rational reasons as looking at them the wrong way or being from the wrong town/village/street (delete as applicable). Going out of your way to look different from everyone else was a magnet for the wrong kind of attention. In our get-up, which consisted of a random assortment of ex-army clothes, tie dye and black, we stood out a mile from all the other teens in shell suits and football tops.

Having people want to beat the crap out of you was something we grew to see as absolutely normal. It was fortunate we were young and relatively fit, because we were often chased by Neds (a Scottish term for non-educated delinquents). My skateboarding exploits meant I was fairly used to getting chased, albeit by the police. Neds were way scarier. The police might arrest you and phone your parents, whereas Neds would kick the shit out of you or stab you.

Danger apart, these trips were the highlight of the week. We'd alight at Glasgow Central and our first port of call would be Missing Records on Oswald Street. Missing had a massive second-hand section and buying second-hand was the best way to amass records frugally. We'd scour the shelves looking for bargains by the bands we'd grown to love through mixtapes and albums taped from our big sisters – The Cure, Loop, Fields of the Nephilim and Silverfish to name a few. While perusing and making the occasional purchase we'd also get to know the people who worked in the shop. They were extremely patient and would chat to us about the records we were buying or listening to and make suggestions about other records and bands we might like. The people working in record shops had an encyclopaedic knowledge about music and were more than happy to humour us.

After a few months we'd exhausted the city centre of places that piqued our interest, so we started to get the subway train to the city's West End to see what it had to offer. Based around Glasgow University, the West End was a hive of activity. On Byres Road alone there were five record shops. We'd get off the train at Hillhead and emerge into what was the most bohemian part of the city at that time. Amid record shops like Lost Chord, Echo and Fopp, Byres Road also had a bookshop – John Smiths – with great vinyl. The guy behind the counter was Stephen, the singer from The Pastels, a legendary Glasgow band, which added to the mystique. Stephen was super friendly and always happy to chat about music. He was also very patient, especially as we rarely bought anything there. When we did it was a bit of an event. The West End had a load of burrow-like arcades off the main street with shops selling all kinds of bric-a-brac and trinkets. Travelling into town became a ritual for us and was so important for meeting like-minded people.

School became mostly about socialising and very little about learning. I'd managed to find all the fellow weirdos there, and we lived for the weekends and all the nonsense and hi-jinx it brought. Things on the gig front had gone a bit cold though. Most of the bands we liked were playing venues with a strict over-eighteen policy and we were nowhere near that age. Compounding the issue, I was five-foot-nothing and had a particularly babyish face.

My sister Victoria provided a solution to my predicament. She pointed out that even though I didn't look like an adult male by any stretch, I could quite easily pass for an eighteen-year-old girl. By this point I'd abandoned my backcombed fuzzy hair and had grown it pretty long. I was also dying it black, which in retrospect seems slightly odd as my hair is almost black anyway. It was around this time too that I responded to puberty's onslaught of body hair by shaving my legs and chest. I'm not sure if this was in case bouncers asked to look at my legs, or some kind of personal protest against the approach of adulthood, but I think I knew this was not a normal thing to do and I wanted to be as far away from normal as possible.

Another essential tool in the mission to get into over-eighteen gigs was the legendary fake ID. Neale was (and still is) way more arty and proficient than me so he took it upon himself to procure us such an item. He fashioned IDs based on those issued by the local college in Hamilton, Bell College; the thinking being that fewer people would have seen these than the equivalents from more famous institutions in Glasgow. He photocopied the logo, typed out our names and 'new' birthdays, and then had them laminated at a local stationery shop. I'm sure the staff there had a laugh while aiding this act of low-level criminal deception. To our young eyes, the end results were pretty convincing. My ID used my real name, so I'm not sure how that squared with the whole 'pretend to be a girl' plan, but you can't cover everything.

With my fake ID, I was all set. There was one venue that I was determined to visit: the venue so many bands that we adored had played, the place everyone older than us spoke of in hushed, reverent tones – the Barrowland Ballroom. It drove me mad that I hadn't been able to go. The Buzzcocks, The Fall and Sonic Youth had all played there, and I'd missed them all. Reading the music papers one week I saw a gig that I simply couldn't miss – The Jesus and Mary Chain. They were one of my favourite bands. I'd even learnt their songs – three-chord 'Taste Of Cindy' and one-riff 'Sidewalking', which we'd joyously murdered with Pregnant Nun. I had to go.

Incredibly, my parents were totally fine with me going so long as my sister looked after me. I say incredibly, as not only was I fourteen but the venue is in one of the roughest parts of the city. The nearby pubs were notoriously edgy, and during the six-ties the ballroom itself was known as the hunting ground of the Glasgow serial killer Bible John. My folks weren't big worriers though, and their idea of a pop concert was probably a bit more Abba than the Mary Chain. Victoria, having the patience of a saint, had agreed for me to tag along with her and her pals. If the bouncers hadn't let me in, she would have had to go home too. Leaving me on my own in the East End of Glasgow for four hours wouldn't have been an option. I'm eternally grateful to her for taking me.

The Mary Chain were an enigma to me. In their leather trou-sers, leather jackets and shades, they looked like they had come from another planet. The hard truth of the matter was, however, that they came from East Kilbride, twenty miles from where I lived, just a few miles past Strathaven where I went to school. That fact alone, rather than providing some kind of local insight into them and their music, made these impossibly cool rock gods seem even more mythical. How the fuck could this music come from somewhere so bloody normal? East Kilbride is a town known for its abundance of roundabouts and its shopping centre with an ice rink, not as the epicentre of alt rock cool. As I got older I'd realise that the more normal somewhere seems to be, the more eccentric people have to be to put up with it.

The Mary Chain's music had been a constant for me since my obsession started. Their debut album, *Psychocandy*, was ever-present on my stereo. Its lyrics were plain weird: 'How could something crawl within/My rubber holy baked bean tin?' Despite the songs being pretty much perfect pop, the entire record was swathed with layer upon layer of screeching guitar feedback. To my teenage mind, besieged by a repetitive news diet of imminent nuclear threats and IRA bombings, this was the ideal combination, the music oozing drama and the noise making perfect sense in a world that seemed stranger by the day.

My sister also had a VHS of the band's videos, and I was infatuated with them. In 'You Trip Me Up' they wandered around a Spanish beach dressed head to toe in leather with a guitar planted in the sand like some kind of pirate flag. Other videos, like 'Kill Surf City', consisted of cut-ups from sixties B-movies spliced with religious iconography. To me, they epitomised cool. I'd become obsessed with the film *Easy Rider* and this seemed to mesh with its anti-authoritarian counterculture message.

The ending of *Easy Rider*, where the hippy heroes are gunned down by rednecks, was huge for us. It solidified our anti-squares worldview. In our minds we were living the battle, fighting against normal society by being weird and refusing to conform.

In the five years since *Psychocandy*, a lot had changed for the Mary Chain. They'd gone from being the riot-inducing *enfants terribles* of the burgeoning 'indie scene' to being regarded as bystanders. The music press was addicted to hype, and for the Mary Chain this had peaked five years previously. The weekly papers were brutal in their assessment of anyone not considered 'cool' and dished out some savage treatment at times. It'd be fair to say that by this point the Mary Chain weren't particularly hip. In comparison to the classic *Psychocandy*, their most recent album, *Automatic*, had met with a fairly lukewarm reception. This meant nothing to me. I loved it. My dedication was only further fuelled when, on holiday to the Isle of Lewis, my grandad's extremely religious home help lady found my tape of the album and almost had a fit upon reading the lyrics. My parents were nigh on impossible to shock, so I lapped up this rare slice of rock and roll outrage.

To my mind the Mary Chain were the coolest band on the planet and I didn't care if the music establishment no longer thought the same. When something became too popular I tended to go off it anyway. I enjoyed feeling that the music I liked was special and that me and my friends were privy to some cool underground secret that hardly anyone 'got'.

As the gig approached, my main focus was on making sure I actually got in. With my trusty fake ID I felt I had the ammunition if the worst happened and the bouncers asked me what age I was. But hopefully it wouldn't even get to that point. The plan was to not look like a very young boy but instead a young woman. My hair was quite long and tended to cover my face, with just my nose sticking out from the black curtains. Thankfully for me, indie fashion at the time was fairly androgynous, and the clothes I wore (long embroidered shirt, tight jeans and an army surplus jacket) could quite easily have been worn by a girl.

I was all set to try to get into my first ever over-eighteens gig. What was the worst that could happen? Get turned away and see hardly any live music for four years? Actually, that would be really fucking bad . . .

Finally, the night came. The gig fell on a Thursday, a school night, and I was even more preoccupied than normal. I whiled away the day with my usual mixture of apathy and mischief-making, eager for the bell to ring so I could go home. I needed to get ready for the big night, my first gig at the Barrowlands.

My sister and her best friend Nicola had both been accepted to study at university. Nicola was in Glasgow doing law and Victoria in Dundee studying architecture. As Dundee was a few hours away, my sister had moved out of our family home and now lived in halls of residence. She was coming back specially to go to the gig, making the journey in her car, a spectacularly idiosyncratic vehicle – a green Morris Traveller – which looked like a cross between a military jeep and a garden shed with its wooden panelling at the back.

In my eyes my sister and her pals were the height of bohemian chic, and I was more than content to join their gang, which consisted of Victoria, Nicola, and her friend Jennifer, a glamorous goth with long blonde hair. They took great amusement in getting me dressed up, the aim being to make me look as much like one of them as possible. They stopped short of putting make-up on me, an invitation which I bashfully resisted.

Their gig-going ritual started in Hamilton, where my dad was kind enough to drop us off, picking up a carry-out and drinking it on the half-hour train journey to Glasgow Argyle Street station. This was followed by the ten-minute walk east to the Barrowlands. As an apprentice hedonist and eager to fit in, I was completely on board with the plan, frenzied with excitement not only at the prospect of going to my first over-eighteens gig but also seeing my heroes, the Mary Chain. I wanted to get there early to make sure I got in, but also for the support band, The Telescopes. As well as having an immensely apt name (me being the son of a telescope maker and all), I'd heard them on John Peel and was psyched to see them.

After exiting the train in Glasgow we wandered up the Gallowgate glowing with teenage exuberance and buzzing from our rapidly consumed illicit beverages. I was as much scared as excited. My biggest fear was that the doormen at the gig would take one look at me and send me on my bike. I was only fourteen, and not a particularly old-looking fourteen-year-old at that. Approaching the venue, what stood out was the famous sign. I'd seen it a hundred times when I'd visited the market with my dad but never lit up before. It was like something from a fairground, huge and multi-coloured. A mesmerising, truly magical sight. As we joined the queue I made sure to hide my face behind my dyed black curtain of hair. We got to the front of the queue and I was completely shitting myself . . . and then we waltzed in without anyone saying a word to us.

Walking up the stairs from the street level, I felt a feeling of elation unlike anything I'd known before; like I'd got away with something and won a prize all at once, like I'd unlocked a level of life itself. After passing through the foyer with its pungent smell of boiled hot dogs and burgers, we quickly bought drinks at the bottom bar. We all had pints of snakebite and blackcurrant (or snakey black as it was called): a lethal half-lager, half-cider combo with a splash of blackcurrant cordial. It tasted like Ribena and got you wrecked if you drank enough of it.

With our quota of teenage goth booze, we made our way up the farther flight of stairs towards the main hall. The walls were all covered in posters for previous and upcoming gigs, though the venue itself still exuded an air of the faded glamour of its previous life as a ballroom. The room itself was majestic, with an arched roof covered in stars. We found ourselves a spot and eagerly waited for the first band. I recognised the music playing over the PA as the sixties psych band The 13th Floor Elevators, whose music I adored. Being somewhat tipsy and feeling extremely at ease with the world, I started singing along with the Elevators song 'Fire Engine', a psych rock classic with the timeless refrain, 'Let me take you to the empty place in my Fire Engine'. Amazing. A pretty girl with brown hair standing next to us asked me what I was singing along to. I told her it was the Elevators and we started chatting. It turned out she knew some of my friends as she went to school in Hamilton. Her name was Adele. We talked for a bit and I said I would see her around Hamilton because I was there a lot waiting for my mum to finish work.

Finally, the lights went down and the first band appeared. The Telescopes looked fantastic – all tight jeans, stripy shirts and floppy fringes – and sounded brilliant. I remember the wall of noise that came from the guitars like it was yesterday. I had their single, 'Precious Little', and it was the highlight of the set, with its towering repetitive riffs and amazing hook: 'I would be precious little without you.' The set was short and mighty, but I was there for the Mary Chain. We got some more drinks. I was merrily drunk by this point and eagerly awaiting for my mind to be melted.

When the Mary Chain came onstage the entire energy in the room shifted. To an almighty sound from the crowd, four shadowy figures appeared on the stage, which was lit by a back-projected film: flashing images of neon signs, propaganda, B-movies. With the crowd noise intensifying and the projected images burnt into my mind, the band started up with 'Fall' from *Darklands*, two minutes of punk frenzy with lines like, 'Choked up on the dust, hand held holy lust' and 'Everybody's falling on me, I'm as dead as a Christmas tree.' The whole room had transformed into a melee of limbs. There was a huge rush forward and my feet left the ground, carried along by the crowd, and the malevolent nihilism in the air fuelled by the music. It felt like the band weren't just playing but performing a rite of catharsis that we were witnesses to.

The band's anti-star persona extended to the setlist. Most bands who'd made a genre-defining record like *Psychocandy* would be milking it for years, but the Mary Chain only played one song from it, the beautiful 'Just Like Honey'. I couldn't care less though. The fact they played more unreleased songs than they did from their debut was a bonus in my eyes. They had never been crowd-pleasers, pandering to the mainstream. The eighties were a day-glo nightmare, all white suits with shoulder pads, cheesy smiles and blinding white teeth, and the Mary Chain were the antithesis of all this. The second song they played, 'Everything's Alright When You're Down', was an anthem for this outlook: 'As strange as it can seem, like living in a scream, everything is alright when you're down.' It perfectly encapsulated their fuck-the-world attitude, and live it was mesmerising, a completely physical experience. The sound of the bass and the drums was huge in the confined space of the Barrowlands and the atmosphere was unlike anything I'd ever experienced. The contrast with The Cure show the previous summer was marked. This was grimy, and sweaty, and loud as hell. As wonderful as The Cure had been, it had felt very safe and organised. This was anything but. Though the Mary Chain had moved on from their early habit of playing for only twenty minutes, it still wasn't a long gig by any measure. They played just eleven songs and were onstage for less than an hour. The highlight of the gig was 'Nine Million Rainy Days', a stereotypically gloomy song of lost love and longing. As an apprentice in teen angst, the line 'I have ached for you, I have nothing left to give for you to take' struck a chord.

As well as their own songs, the Mary Chain played two cover versions, 'Tower Of Song' by Leonard Cohen and 'Who Do You Love?' by Bo Diddley. I didn't know either song or artist at the time but I'm eternally grateful for the Mary Chain for introducing them to me. The sheer sass and bravado of lines like 'I wear a cobra snake for a necktie' in 'Who Do You Love?' blew my mind, and the weary poetic elegance of the opening line of 'Tower Of Song', 'Well my friends are gone, my hair is grey, I ache in the places that I used to play', were a glimpse into how rock music could be literary as well as primal. Learning about music from musicians being honest about their influences and covering songs they loved was huge. Bands like Spacemen 3 covering The 13th Floor Elevators and Red Krayola opened a door for me into psychedelic music made before I was born. I'm always suspicious of musicians who aren't completely open about their influences. What are they trying to hide?

As the band left the stage, the feedback still ringing out after their final song 'Gimme Hell', I located Victoria and her friends. Descending the long stairway at the back of the hall, the cold air shocked my sweaty body while my ears rang from the cacophony. We made our way back to town down a noisy Gallowgate to get the train back to Hamilton, giddy from the music, the occasion and buzzing from the booze. I was tired but felt I'd entered another world.

That night was a defining moment. Seeing one of my favourite bands for the first time was huge, but just being *there*, a place that I legally had no right to be, was equally important. It was my first taste of the Barrowland Ballroom. A place that was to have a massive part to play in my life. A spiritual home. The very epicentre of everything I was falling in love with, a magical place, both utterly majestic and gloriously shabby. I'd fallen head over heels in love.

4.

Druggy, Dumb and Completely Primal

Seeing the Mary Chain had a catalytic effect. My obsession was snowballing. After my first foray to the Barrowlands I didn't have to wait too long to make my return, going to two more gigs there in the autumn of 1990. The first was to see pop-goths The Mission with my sister and her friends. It was a lot of fun, though profoundly silly, with half the audience covered in flour and wearing sunglasses inside. I loved a lot of goth music but wasn't quite at the flour stage myself.

The other gig I attended was in the company of a new friend I'd made, the girl I'd spoken to at the Mary Chain gig – Adele Bethel. We'd bumped into each other wandering around Hamilton town centre and realised that we pretty much had the exact same interests: indie music, teen and horror films, and getting drunk with our friends. Adele loved John Hughes movies like *The Breakfast Club*, which I dug too, though I was always slightly perturbed that the characters were having more fun than I was.

Adele was obsessed with The Smiths and, like me, The Cure. Being a year older she'd already been to loads of gigs. Adele went to school in Hamilton and was always around when I'd get there to wait for my mum. We got on well, and as two avid gig-goers were happy to have someone to go and see bands with, especially those our pals weren't that fussed about attending. Adele loved The Wedding Present and asked if I wanted to go with her.

I'd heard them on John Peel and liked it but wasn't that familiar with them. The ticket was super cheap and the chance to hang out with my new pal without the somewhat dull concrete confines of Hamilton's town centre was another motivation. The Wedding Present gig was very different from the other shows I'd been to. It was great, but completely without frills. There was no dry ice or strobes and the band pointedly refused to do an encore. The lack of showbiz elements didn't detract from the performance though. They played fast and loud and we had a brilliant time. It would be the first of many gigs we'd go to together as our friendship blossomed.

As I perused the upcoming gigs, there was one that I could not miss under any circumstance. The king of punk – Iggy Pop. Hearing Iggy's first band The Stooges had been a life-changing moment for me. Their self-titled album was pretty much my bible. It was druggy, dumb and completely primal. I'd never heard anything quite like it and even though that band had pretty much fallen apart by the time I was born, I grew to love the three Stooges (ha!) albums as much as any music I'd ever heard. It was actually my guitar teacher Harry that played them to me first. He played *Raw Power* and it just floored me. 'Raw Power has a healing hand; Raw Power can destroy a man!' I hadn't the faintest idea what this Raw Power was (and still don't) but I loved the sound of it and knew I required as much of it as possible in my life. Iggy was the living embodiment of that complete don't-give-a-fuck attitude. The wailing guitars and primal rhythms made so much sense to me. I was enraptured by its intensity and ferocity. It was perfect.

I had a VHS video of Iggy playing live and I watched it over and over. His performance was unlike anything or anyone I'd seen before. He was like a man possessed, doing the weirdest dancing imaginable, getting naked and scratching himself until he bled. The spectacle was great but it was his voice and songs that really captured me. Songs like 'China Girl' were gloriously romantic and railed against the injustices of the world. Iggy was so clearly lost in the performance. I had another video that featured Iggy, a compilation of performances from Factory Records boss Tony Wilson's *What Goes On* show. The performance from Iggy on this was even more mesmerising. It was live footage from the Manchester Apollo where he played 'The Passenger'. It was completely visceral. One moment that really caught me was when he broke it down halfway through into a semi-confessional speech, almost a sermon, and spoke about a girl he met who'd explained that possessions were immaterial and that everything belonged to everyone. I was starting to form a view of how I saw the world and hearing this message really struck a chord with my burgeoning anti-authoritarianism. It was perfect. A pristine mix of the absurd and the profound. I also found out it was at this gig in Manchester in 1977 that the members of Joy Division actually met each other. That only added to the romance and mythology. Iggy and Joy Division were absolutely totemic to me. I adored the music so much that it was hard to believe it had been made by humans, never mind humans that were still alive.

As 1990 bled into 1991, there were a few changes in the world, and for me. Firstly, Neale and I had taken our hedonistic tendencies to another level. I can't recall which one of us realised that Tippex Thinner, used to eke out the famous white correction liquid, had another, far less wholesome application. If you dropped some on your sleeve (or a sock) and inhaled it, you got a bit high. If you did it a few times, you got extremely high. The music we were listening to was very druggy, and this new activity went hand in hand with it, creating an undulating, throbbing sense of psychedelia. Music like Loop, Spacemen 3 and The 13th Floor Elevators transported me to a spiritual place that felt like a high. Now I really was. It brought me back to that experience in the hospital as a child seeing fractal patterns while my mind blasted Delia Derbyshire's acid-squelched *Doctor Who* theme into my brain. The short-term downside was that it gave you a bastard of a headache. There was also the small fact that you were pretty much an apprentice glue sniffer and well on your way to being a total degenerate, but that didn't concern us. We had our little tribe and weren't paying any mind to what the rest of the world thought.

As little as we considered what the rest of the world might be thinking of us, the outside world itself was getting weirder and a lot darker. In early August 1990 Iraqi president Saddam Hussein had invaded Kuwait, causing disquiet among the neighbouring countries and their allies in the West. US president George Bush was making noises about intervening and the UK, as ever, were close behind. I wasn't overly interested in the news but I'd got a portable TV in my bedroom for Christmas and the BBC had started showing news all night. There was a sense of impending doom emanating from unfolding events. I'd stay up pretty late and, when the normal TV shows or whatever weird film on Channel 4 ended, watch the now endless rolling news, feeling that something dark and unspeakably ominous was around the corner.

Having shown his parents that I'd been to a gig at the Barrowlands and returned home alive, Neale got their permission to go to the Iggy concert. This was a big deal: the first time Neale had been to a show, and what a debut! In the months leading up to it, we were immersed in all things Iggy. The Stooges records soundtracked our weekends and we couldn't wait to see the man himself. We had got increasingly into the wave of rock bands coming out of Seattle, largely on the Sub Pop label. Bands like Mudhoney, Hole and most significantly, Nirvana. Neale had the debut Nirvana record, *Bleach*, and we'd played it to death. Iggy seemed like an elder statesman to those bands. The Stooges were Year Zero for the music we loved. Getting to see such a legend was a massive fucking deal.

We studiously prepared for the big night by making sure we had funds for our standard bottle of Red Label Thunderbird wine each. A Real Cool Time indeed. After school, Neale came to mine and we got a lift from my ever-patient dad to Hamilton for the train with Victoria, who I'm sure was delighted at having now doubled her quota of daft fifteen-year-old boys to look after.

We were on a mission. Our pilgrimage to see the living embodiment of punk rock had to be as debauched as possible. Well, as debauched as you can get at fifteen years old. We tanned our bottles on the train. Utterly buzzing on the wine and the night ahead, we met our pal Kevin McCrorie in the queue. He was as giddy as us at the prospect of seeing Iggy. The usual anxiety about the bouncers proved unfounded and we breezed in unchallenged. We missed the opening band, too busy in the downstairs bar catching up with pals and getting as 'moroculous' (a word I think we'd invented for getting fucked up) as possible. It felt like every weirdo in Glasgow was there that night. Punks and goths as well as a lot of older folk who'd grown up with Iggy's music. There was a real feeling of community, a summoning of Scotland's misfits.

In a state of heightened, inebriated excitement we ascended the final set of stairs to the venue. Being five-foot-fuck-all we got as near to the front as possible so that we could actually see the stage. The lights went down and Iggy came on, spinning like a Tasmanian devil and flailing like he was suppressing a seizure. He screamed at the audience before ripping into 'Raw Power', one of my favourite Stooges tracks. When he sang the line 'Can you feel it?', he had the look and sound of someone expressing something incredibly sincere. It was a blistering start, and it didn't calm down. 'Five Foot One' from his *New Values* solo record followed, then 'Loose' and 'Dirt', two songs from *Funhouse*. 'Dirt' in particular was incredible. The drums playing at a quarter of the pace of the punchier songs and Iggy wailing, 'I'm dirt and I don't care!', a mantra for everyone who'd ever felt like a loser or felt looked down upon.

Iggy's band were a bunch of rock dudes who wouldn't have

looked out of place in Guns N' Roses. The record he was promoting – *Brick by Brick* – even featured Slash. They were shred-
ding over all the songs but it didn't matter. We were there to see
Iggy. It was on a song from that record, 'Neon Forest', that he
altered a lyric to sing, 'SCOTLAND TAKES DRUGS IN PSYCHIC
DEFENCE', and the whole place went mental. After a decade of
Thatcher's rule, Scotland definitely felt ignored at best, but was
in actuality persecuted. We had Iggy on our side. One of us. A
soldier in the fight against the system designed to grind us down.

The main set ended with '1969', a proto-slacker anthem from
the first Stooges album that I adored. 'Last year I was 21, I didn't
have a lot of fun, now I'm going to be 22, I say, oh my and a boo
hoo.' As he left the stage the noise from the crowd was intense,
rising to cacophonous levels as people demanded more.

When he came back on to play 'I Wanna Be Your Dog' the
place went ballistic. I think it's the perfect song. Simple, hypnotic,
dumb and beautiful. By this point Iggy was practically naked and
in a frenzy. He addressed the crowd and dedicated 'No Fun' to
Saddam Hussein. The rumbling of impending war had got louder
over the weeks and Iggy knew what was coming down the road
would not be fun by any measure.

Iggy saved the best for last. 'Search And Destroy' was incredible. With its blistering riff and war-themed lyrics, it felt like being
blasted by a jet engine. Iggy, a whirlwind of chaos energy, and the
crowd going apeshit. It was an epic finale. I'd seen some great
bands but this felt like my first true rock and roll show. A unique
frontman laying everything on the stage, performing like it was
his last night on earth.

As we left the Barrowlands, Iggy's booming voice still rang
in my ears. It felt like a baptism of sorts. Iggy was the oldest per-
former I'd seen (though actually the same age as I am writing
this) but he had more energy than anyone I'd ever seen, or have
seen since. He was the glue that ran from the sixties, when John
Cale from The Velvet Underground recorded the first Stooges

record, to the present day, when every exciting rock band around hailed him as an influence.

I got home still buzzing with punk rock spirit and went to my room, which by now had become a shrine to rock and roll and teenage rebellion. On the walls I'd painted song lyrics and covered the rest in the most random paraphernalia I could find. The mess was so all-encompassing that it was rare you could see the floor. It was a fucking riot. I climbed into my pit of a bed, turned on the portable TV, grabbed a sock and the jar of thinner and proceeded to get utterly wasted. High from the intensity of the night and the solvents, I felt elevated. I felt outside of my body, like I was looking down at myself in bed. In my haze, I heard something that brought me back down to earth with a thump. From the TV the newswoman said that the forces of the United States and their allies had started military action against Saddam Hussein's Iraq. The news carried live images of the bombing. Night vision-style shots of what looked like fireworks flying through the air only to explode, turning buildings and vehicle convoys to dust. This carnage masquerading as news was all announced in an excitable manner by the BBC anchors sitting in the safety of their London studios. No Fun indeed. No fun at all.

After Iggy, 1991 rolled along swimmingly. Neale and I continued our weekend adventures in Glasgow, treating school like a minor nuisance we had to endure from Monday to Thursday. I saw a few more gigs, most notably Jane's Addiction. Their Barrowlands gig was a quasi-religious experience for me. Performing in front of the sculpture from their *Ritual de lo Habitual* album, they were simply incredible. From our record shopping we discovered Black Flag, who fitted right into our anti-authoritarian worldview. As well as bands from the past (Black Flag had split up the previous decade), we were also getting into a lot of other bands from the US underground through a variety of means: skateboard videos, John Peel, *Snub TV* and the music papers. Reading the music papers, I found out about an event that really piqued my interest. The Reading Festival taking place that August had an incredible line-up. Iggy was headlining the Friday night and The Sisters of Mercy on the Sunday. Bands playing during the day included Sonic Youth, Dinosaur Jr., The Fall, and the band Neale and I had become besotted with, Nirvana. On top of all this, compering the event was the one and only John Peel. His radio show was the very reason I'd discovered so much of the music that I was now willing to travel to the other end of the island to see.

Travelling to the south of England was an altogether different proposal to going to a gig in Glasgow half an hour away, and I was nervous about persuading my folks to let me go. Thankfully Victoria had been the previous year and returned unscathed. Vic was up for going and even offered to drive in her borderline antique Morris Traveller. Mercifully my folks were receptive to me attending, as long as my sister looked after me.

My parents were kind enough to buy a ticket for the festival for my birthday. I eagerly awaited the trip for the whole summer.

Music wasn't the only thing occupying my time in 1991. It was also the year when I met my first girlfriend, Cher Anderson. Cher was in my year at school. She was into heavy metal and part of the crew of misfit kids Neale and I would spend time with at weekends. Cher was great company and we'd spend a lot of time together, mostly listening to music, but I'm not sure she was particularly into the psychedelic indie music I was into and I was always a bit sceptical of heavy metal, though I did eventually grow to love some of it. Slayer and Metallica in particular. I was still learning guitar and was amazed that anyone could play so fast. But I couldn't deal with a lot of the bands' macho posturing.

The highlight of the summer of 91 was probably the fortnight when my parents went on holiday. My sister was still away in Dundee at this point and they asked a family friend to look after me while they were gone. Getting someone at short notice to look after your teenage son can't be the easiest of tasks, and I'm willing to cut my folks some slack as the list of candidates can't have been too stellar. I won't shame the guy by name, but it'd be fair to say he dropped the ball somewhat. After a few days I asked him for some money for food as my parents had said they'd left some with him. He was very honest in his reply.

'I've spent it all on cocaine,' he said.

I was pretty shocked but knew I could turn this unexpected turn of events to my advantage. My parents' miscreant friend agreed that in exchange for me not telling my parents he'd blown the food money on drugs he would leave me alone to do whatever I wanted for the remainder of time until they returned. In Scotland, getting the house to yourself when you're a teenager is referred to as an 'Empty' and this was the empty to end all empties. Not only did my girlfriend get to stay over (something that would definitely have been frowned upon), but I also got to have all my pals come over, set up amps and drums, make an unholy racket and get drunk whenever we wanted. The parties were pretty biblical. The situation with my parents' friend was also an eye-opener. Until that point I'd always associated hedonism with all things cool in life, and it was clear that what had happened was pretty grubby and a bit of a lesson that getting wasted wasn't always a non-stop party. It would take a while for that lesson to really sink in, but I'd definitely seen where it could take you.

The rest of the summer rolled along in a haze of teenage abandon, but the main event I was waiting for was the trip to my first festival – Reading.

Before the trip I had an inkling that I was in store for some kind of sermon from my parents urging me not to get in any trouble. My parents were lovely people and far from strict, but I thought that this would probably be the moment where I was given some worldly advice. Shortly before we departed, my mum asked if she could have a word with me. I had a brilliant relationship with my mum. She's the sweetest person but has the driest wit imaginable and I wasn't accustomed to being asked for 'a word'. I feared the worst. I thought I was going to get a warning about the dangers of the world at large and a birds and the bees chat all rolled into one. What actually occurred was three words, not one: 'Don't take heroin.' Hebrideans are famously to the point. I dutifully replied: 'I won't.'

The journey itself felt quite daunting. I'd been on long car journeys before because my dad was fundamentally opposed to getting on an aeroplane unless absolutely necessary and insisted on driving wherever we went on holiday. My parents had a real penchant for barely roadworthy cars and that fact, along with destinations as far as Brittany in France and the north coast of Spain, led to some fairly epic driving experiences. What with young children moaning and needing to pee constantly, my dad must have really detested flying.

My sister's car was a thing of endless charm, but I had some reservations as to its ability to successfully take us on the 700-mile round trip from Lanarkshire to Reading. Victoria was more bullish and had no worries that her trusty steed was up to the job. It had, after all, successfully transported her numerous times up to her university in Dundee and back. A few hundred miles would be no bother at all.

We set off on the Thursday determined to get there in time to set up our tent in preparation for the Friday. Friday was the cream of the three days, with Iggy headlining and pretty much every band we wanted to see. We left quite early as Vic's car would make extremely unhappy sounds if asked to drive above fifty miles per hour. We had more than enough C90 mixtapes for the drive, that being my major concern. Food and clothes definitely came way behind music in my priorities. The journey started well enough as we trundled our way down the M74 towards Carlisle. Once we entered England the M74 became the M6 and we started to see road signs for places that were pretty exotic to me. Liverpool made me think of the Bunnymen. Manchester – Joy Division and The Smiths. I saw everything through a music-filtered lens.

We were making decent headway and still hadn't run out of tapes to listen to. We'd probably have had to drive to Moscow and back for that to happen. It was around Birmingham, however, that things started to get a bit sticky. As is normal for that part of the world, we were confronted by a fairly gargantuan traffic jam. Sat in traffic with the car at a standstill, I leant back in my seat and rested my foot on the gear stick. I instantly regretted this when the gear stick became detached. In the days before mobile phones, our options were rather limited. Victoria decided to stick it back in its socket and physically hold it in place for the duration of the trip, all 500 miles of it.

When we eventually got to the festival, we were fairly weary. Victoria had been to Reading the year before and was a keen camper. I was grateful for her know-how as she expertly found us our camping pitch and went about assembling the tent. With her camping nous in full effect, Victoria managed to feed us both. We had a few drinks and settled down for the night. We were both excited about the next day of music, and as we were both shattered from the drive, we got an early night.

Upon waking and having a look around, the first thing that struck me was the sheer number of people. I don't think I'd ever seen such a big crowd – and it was a crowd of people like us. Thousands of people wearing band T-shirts with every kind of non-traditional hairstyle imaginable.

We made our way over to the main stage of the festival to see the first band on our list – Babes in Toyland. They were perennial Peel favourites, an all-female outfit who specialised in heavy riffs and screaming vocals from their enigmatic singer, Kat Bjelland. They were a mighty and brilliant start to the weekend. Next up was Silverfish, a riotous noise band from London fronted by an incredible Scottish singer, Lesley Rankine, who screamed over every song. A review had described her as 'a fat Axl Rose' and they'd used the phrase to name their debut album. They were really great, as were Babes in Toyland. Neither quite prepared me for what was coming next though. A performance that was to change everything for me – Nirvana.

Having listened to *Bleach* and the 'Sliver' single non-stop over the previous year, I was excited about seeing Nirvana, but at this point they were a niche draw. Although people were intrigued, they didn't have the biggest crowd of the weekend. I'd heard they had a new drummer, having kept Dan Peters from Mudhoney for only one single, 'Sliver'. They ambled on-stage, Kurt wearing a white Sounds shirt and a brown leather jacket, Krist the bass player wearing a Dinosaur Jr. cow T-shirt. Dave, the new drummer, looked like a ball of brown hair. As well as the band members, there was a half-naked guy on-stage with 'God is gay' written on his torso. He was introduced as 'Tony the interpretive dancer'. They had a real ease about them, making nonsensical jokes and not seeming particularly perturbed by the size of the crowd, which I'm fairly sure they weren't accustomed to.

The first song they played was 'School', which I knew well from their *Bleach* album. The riff that continues through the entire song and the opening line, 'Won't you believe it's just my luck', set the tone for the whole set, completely primal. Kurt's demeanour when he started playing was completely different from that of the amiable guy who wandered onstage making jokes with his bandmates. It was clear he was channelling something. 'School' was a tour de force. They played another song from *Bleach* next before a run of four new songs. As a general rule, bands try not to play too many new songs consecutively in their sets, but it soon became apparent that this rule did not apply to Nirvana. 'Drain You' started with Kurt singing and playing incredibly melodic guitar before the band kicked in. The song was brilliant. It was obvious something very special was happening. The next song seared into my mind more than any other. With Kurt's choppy riff followed by Dave Grohl's massive drum fill, 'Smells Like Teen Spirit' hit me like a ton of bricks. As a fifteen-year-old kid fully embracing non-mainstream music, it was everything I wanted to

hear. After the first chorus, Kurt wailed along with his guitar –
something the like of which I'd genuinely never heard before. As
the song climaxed with the repeated refrain, 'A denial, a denial, a
denial, a denial', I was in total rapture. The following two songs,
'Come As You Are' and 'Breed', were great too. It was clear their
new record was going to be something special.

After the run of new songs they launched into 'Sliver', a pure
pop song about being a kid at your grandparents and one of my
favourites. Next was a cover of The Vaselines' 'Molly's Lips' that
I'd heard on their Peel Session the year before. A guy with floppy
brown hair and a backpack ran on stage to sing and play some
pretty exuberant air guitar. I didn't know it at the time but this
was Eugene Kelly, The Vaselines' singer. What I also didn't know
was Eugene was a Glaswegian who'd grown up about fifteen
miles from where I lived. The world of international rock and
roll seemed eternally sophisticated to me and I didn't know those
connections existed. It was a great moment, adding to the chaos
and joy emanating from the stage.

During the next song, 'Love Buzz' (another cover, but I wasn't
aware of that), Kurt left the stage with his guitar feeding back
and jumped into the crowd. It was utterly chaotic. People were
into it, but not in any kind of 'rock star touches fans' kind of way.
It felt more like a party that we were all at. With Kurt floating
about on top of the crowd there was literally no barrier between
the band and audience. Even though the crowd was big, it still
felt intimate. After 'Love Buzz' they played two more songs from
Bleach – 'Negative Creep' and 'Blew'. 'Blew' was my favourite
Nirvana song from *Bleach*; it had a vocal line that followed a discordant guitar line, with lyrics that seemed nonsensical but were
delivered with an intensity that suggested something weightier.

For their final number Nirvana played another new, unnamed
song which was as atonal and heavy as anything they'd released
before. It was totally different from the new pop songs they'd
played earlier. 'Endless, Nameless' – as I later discovered it was

called – was monolithically huge with completely indecipherable lyrics. It was a fitting finale. Completely punk. I could see a gaggle of musicians from the other bands watching from stage side. I couldn't even imagine being up there. The whole thing was just so fantastical. As down to earth as the band seemed, the music they were making felt like it came from another world. As the song ground to a halt, Krist threw his bass into the air as high as he could and (mostly) caught it. Kurt looked out towards the cheering crowd and, with a vacant look in his eyes, turned around and launched himself into the drum kit, sending toms and cymbals flying. The rest of the band ambled off the stage as the audience cheered wildly. I'd been looking forward to seeing Nirvana but this exceeded my expectations. It remains one of the best performances I've ever seen. It's no exaggeration to say that seeing Nirvana on that Friday afternoon altered everything.

Incredibly, it was only mid-afternoon and my life had changed irrevocably. The next band I was excited to see was Dinosaur Jr. It was their cover of The Cure song 'Just Like Heaven' that had been the gateway for my love of noisy American underground rock. I'd watched their segment from *Snub TV* on repeat, and to a budding guitarist their frontman J Mascis was someone I adored. I found metal far too macho, and other than Hendrix I didn't like that many guitar players were unafraid to completely let rip. J had a way of playing that seemed instinctive and unique. I also loved the songs because they felt simultaneously romantic and lethargic. Some of my friends complained about his constant guitar solos but I was absolutely there for all of it.

Their show at Reading was everything I hoped it would be. The band absolutely tore it up in front of a massive crowd. When they played 'Freak Scene' everyone went absolutely apeshit. The lines, 'Sometimes I don't thrill you, sometimes I think I'll kill you/Just don't let me fuck up will you, 'cos when I need a friend it's still you', could be heard as loud from the audience as they could from the PA.

After Dinosaur, the next band to play were Pop Will Eat Itself. I'd grown to love the Poppies, as they were affectionally known, from hearing them on various indie compilations. They had started as a straight-up indie band but had adopted hip-hop and sampling into their sound and morphed into something pretty unique. I'd actually seen them play once before, up in Dundee on a visit to stay with my sister at her university digs. They didn't take themselves too seriously and referenced a ton of stuff I was into, like Alan Moore comics and The Stooges. The Poppies' main frontman was a super enigmatic guy called Clint Mansell. With a huge pile of hair on top of his head and a stage presence not unlike Zebedee from *The Magic Roundabout*, it was hard to take your eyes off him. They were great and a huge contrast to all the guitar-heavy music I'd seen so far.

I was absolutely in my element, and I still had Sonic Youth and Iggy to come.

Seeing Sonic Youth was something I'd been excited about for a long time. They'd played Barrowlands just prior to me summoning the courage to go there, though I'd loved their music immediately. *Goo*, which came out the previous year, was on constant rotation in my bedroom and they seemed to be at the epicentre of everything good that was happening in music. A modern-day Velvet Underground, oozing artsy cool. They came onstage looking incredibly at ease and dove straight into the incredible 'Schizophrenia'. The sound was immense. The twin guitars of the dishevelled Lee Ranaldo and the gangly Thurston Moore made a noise unlike anything I'd ever heard before. Kim Gordon, the bass player, was the epitome of nonchalance and Steve Shelley was one of the best drummers I'd ever seen, pounding away on his toms like his life depended on it. It was incredible. Their set was riotous. They absolutely played their hearts out for over an hour, performing a lot of the songs I knew from *Goo* and earlier classics like 'Teen Age Riot'. It was the final song, though, that really blew my mind – 'Expressway To Yr. Skull'. With its constant chiming drone building up to a cacophonous frenzy, the whole band apparently lost in the noise, it was truly inspirational; a noise that I felt pulse through my body like electricity. Sonic Youth engulfed you like a wave. It was absolutely transformative.

To finish off the night was Iggy Pop. My second dose of the year. As we waited on Iggy to bless us with his presence, I looked to the side of the stage and saw Kurt from Nirvana sitting on the stage waiting, like us, to watch Iggy. Sitting next to him and holding his hand was Courtney Love from the band Hole. They looked blissfully happy, contentedly hanging out to see Iggy close the night.

Iggy was astonishing again, playing a similar set to the Barrowlands show with a couple of notable additions: the visceral 'TV Eye' from *Funhouse* and a rousing rendition of 'Louie Louie' by The Kingsmen to close the set. It was another ferocious performance – this time in front of tens of thousands of people – the perfect culmination to an incredible day of music from bands that had taken the punk baton from the likes of The Stooges and The Velvet Underground and reinvented it. So many people viewed punk as a style or a fashion but it's so much more than that. It's a view of life and a philosophy of music as self-expression over virtuosity, of DIY over corporate rock. Little did I know that with the songs Nirvana had played that day, punk was about to give corporate rock a bloody nose and shake things up for generations to come.

After the music ended we headed back to out tent. Our friend Kevin McCrorie was down too, so we hung out with him. There was still loads to come but we'd be hard pushed to beat what we'd seen on that incredible day. We also got chatting to a lot of people whose tents were pitched near ours. Most of them were cool but one bunch of folk were far from it. They were annoyed that the hip-hop band De La Soul were on the weekend's bill, clearly thinking that Black people should not be performing among predominately white rock bands. They proudly declared that they were going to throw bananas at them the next day. I'd been brought up to abhor racism. Our conversation stopped immediately after they came out with that. We had no time for it.

The next day we met up with Mog, who had travelled down with a load of other friends. I told Mog about the racists we'd met the night before. They had gone by this point, presumably to buy bananas in bulk. Mog asked which one their car was, so I pointed it out. They had somewhat unwisely left the sunroof open. Seeing this opportunity, Mog climbed on top and took a shit in their car.

With that bit of anti-racist vigilante justice out of the way we prepared for day two. I was having the time of my life, being away from home and around (mostly) like-minded people. On the music front, things were a lot thinner on the ground. Most of the bands were fairly lightweight, the kind that I'd maybe pick up the odd single by if it was 99p and I'd heard it on the radio. The two bands I was excited about seeing, however, were Mercury Rev and Teenage Fanclub. Mercury Rev were noisy and amazing. The Fanclub were having the times of their lives, clearly on the verge of having a big moment. I watched a few other bands that day – Blur, The Fall and Carter the Unstoppable Sex Machine. They were all fun, but nothing compared with the bands on the Friday. To be fair, little else could.

Sunday was a more exciting prospect. The headliners The Sisters of Mercy were one of my favourite bands and I hadn't had the chance to see them. In fact, they hadn't been playing gigs at all for a long period in between their first and third albums. As well as The Sisters, there were other bands I wanted to see, such as noisy shoegazers Swervedriver and the cartoonish Ned's Atomic Dustbin and Senseless Things. I loved all of them, Swervedriver in particular, whose twin guitar assault was like a cross between Hendrix and My Bloody Valentine. They sounded absolutely huge. Those bands were great, but it was the headliners that I was mostly there for.

I'd been waiting for so long to see The Sisters of Mercy and I could barely wait. You could hardly see the band as they came onstage in an onslaught of dry ice, like silhouettes from John Carpenter's movie *The Fog*. The thunderous sound of their signature drum machine cut through, followed quickly by the instantly recognisable riff from 'First And Last And Always', the title track of their debut album. I liked all of their records but was particularly enamoured with their early singles, EPs and the first album. To my delight, their set leant heavily on that period. Songs like 'Temple Of Love' and 'Alice' sounded immense through the gargantuan festival PA. Andrew Eldritch was a great frontman, looking like he'd just stepped out of a vampire movie and prowling the stage while delivering his trademark baritone vocals. To finish their set, and the whole festival, they played '1969' by The Stooges, shorn of all its original looseness, reborn as a motorik beast with Eldritch channelling Iggy. A generation apart but the themes of teenage rock and roll eclipsing the adult world's pursuit of war and money as pertinent as ever. It was a fitting end to a weekend which was nothing less than an initiation.

As me and Victoria wandered away from the main stage towards our tent, the whole festival had developed a weird atmosphere. The smoke from everyone's campsite fires had met the dry ice from the Sisters' show and the entire area felt like something from *Apocalypse Now*. The haze and orange burn of campfires gave everything an air of eeriness – and the noxious smell of illicit things being burnt heightened the atmosphere. My formative festival experience had been illuminating. I'd discovered these were places where life stands still for a few days and wonderful things can happen onstage – music that can change every person who hears it.

The following morning we trundled back to Scotland, with me dutifully holding the gear stick in place, bedraggled but invigorated. Seeing Nirvana in particular had been unforgettable, and getting away from home and immersing myself in music had felt liberating. My first big musical adventure, but far from the last.

I wasn't to know it then, but the next time I'd be back at Reading I'd be on the other side of the barrier.

5.

Living for Today

In the autumn of 1991, two of the bands I adored made the unlikely journey from obscurity to the charts, and I was swept along
with them.

After returning from Reading somehow intact, I resumed my
normal life, going to school and hanging out with pals. I'm sure
my mum was relieved that I returned without a heroin addiction,
but I was still buzzing from the experience. It felt like the start of
something, having seen how music connected people on a massive level.

Going back to school after an amazing summer was a drag,
but on the music front there was loads for me to look forward to.
Tribalism was everything back then. People could tell everything
about you just by looking at you. Clothes. Hair. Even badges were
a signifier as to what type of person you were, where you would
hang out and what music you liked. A lot of people didn't like the
music me and my friends were into. Most were into chart music
like Phil Collins or Simply Red. Real bland Patrick Bateman crap.
That or hair metal. We liked music which was much more under
the radar. But the underground status of a couple of bands we
liked was about to be transformed.

As a keen John Peel listener, I was excited when he said that
he had the first radio play of the new Nirvana single, 'Smells Like
Teen Spirit', the weekend after I got back from Reading. Nirvana
had blown my tiny mind the previous weekend, so I made sure to
listen. Peel's show was the usual incredibly eclectic mix of genres

and styles, swinging from traditional African music to uber-fast Belgian techno. After his usual journey around the world via the medium of music, finally he got round to playing the new Nirvana song. The opening riff was instantly recognisable. The guitar bend after the chorus left such an impression on me at the festival that it felt like I'd already heard it a million times. At this point Nirvana were just a cool little secret that my friends and I knew about, but that was about to change. Peel had been a longstanding fan of the band, having had them record two sessions already. I think he had an inkling they were on a steep upward trajectory and he even made a little joke about them now being on Geffen Records. As well as playing 'Smells Like Teen Spirit' that night, John also played a song by Hole called 'Teenage Whore' and mentioned that he'd met Courtney Love the previous weekend. There was great excitement about the new Nirvana album, *Nevermind*, which was due out soon.

Primal Scream were another band that I adored. They had made their own unexpected raid on the mainstream the year before with the song 'Loaded' – a remixed version of 'I'm Losing More Than I'll Ever Have' by journalist-turned-acid house DJ Andrew Weatherall. I'd loved Primal Scream since the moment I first heard them. I was initially drawn to them because Bobby Gillespie, their singer, had been the drummer in The Jesus and Mary Chain. They had two albums out: the jangly Byrds-esque *Sonic Flower Groove* and a way more rock and roll self-titled second album. I loved both and listened to them all the time. Their re-invention as a dance-orientated band had caused consternation among some purists who saw it as selling out. I didn't see it that way at all though. Living in the countryside and still being a kid, I had no idea of club culture but just accepted it as great music. A rock band getting excited by dance music and wanting to incorporate it into their sound seemed like the most natural thing in the world.

Spaceships Over Glasgow

In June 1991, Primal Scream released 'Higher Than The Sun', a collaboration with the psychedelic-ambient group The Orb, an astonishing record which resonated with me completely. The Orb's debut album, *Adventures Beyond the Ultraworld*, came out earlier that summer, coinciding with the release of the video game *Sonic the Hedgehog*. I'd get lost in the ambient world they created while frittering away hours and days at a time playing the frenzied platform game on my SEGA Mega Drive. I knew the album inside out, and the game so well I could complete it easily. Once I finished, I'd go back to the start and do it again. Increasingly into The Orb's towering, spacey weirdness and already a huge fan of Primal Scream, 'Higher Than The Sun' was the perfect record for me. The lyrics, 'I wasn't born to follow, I live just for today, don't care about tomorrow/What I've got in my head you can't buy, steal or borrow' echoed The Byrds' classic 'Wasn't Born To Follow' that I loved from the *Easy Rider* soundtrack, and its anti-establishment vibe resonated with me completely. The music was immense and the sound unique. The Scream were one of my favourite bands and the journey they were on fascinated me; at this point it was only the musical side, but the chemical side wasn't too far off in the future. After playing 'Higher Than The Sun' and 'Loaded' to death, I couldn't wait to hear their new album, *Screamadelica*, which was coming out on the same day as *Nevermind*. Two bands doing completely different things, but both doing them with total dedication.

I'd tried to see Primal Scream play Glasgow in July at The Plaza, an old ballroom just across the river in Glasgow's Southside. Unfortunately, my lucky streak of successfully gaining entry to gigs while underage ran out and the bouncers wouldn't let me in. The fact that I was leglessly drunk may well have been a factor. As a general rule you could probably get into gigs either drunk *or* a few years underage. Sadly for me, the combination of both was too much for the doorman that night. I wasn't to be deterred though. Primal Scream announced another Glasgow show for a few months later, at the famous Barrowlands, and there was no way that I was going to miss this one.

In the second week of September, Nirvana released 'Smells Like Teen Spirit' as a single. As well as the title track, which was becoming weirdly omnipresent, the single had two great B-sides. One of them in particular, 'Aneurysm', was one of the best Nirvana songs I'd ever heard, starting with a wailing drone, almost like an elongated version of the guitar bend/vocal wail on 'Teen Spirit', before slowing down to a grinding sludging riff followed by a cacophonous crescendo. The lyrics were hard to decipher but somehow held massive meaning for me. The delivery was so physical and personal that it just carried you along. As weeks went by it was clear something was happening with them, from only being played on Peel to airing across many different radio shows, even during the day. Music I liked was *never* played during the day on the radio. They went from having small interviews in the music papers to starring on covers. The band seemed to be relishing it, even using this new platform to promote more obscure bands and rallying against sexism, homophobia and racism. It felt like a real moment. So much mainstream rock until that point had felt contrived, pretty backwards-looking and unattainable. Having a popular band whose songs you could play without practising for ten hours a day, whose views chimed with ours, was amazing. It felt like a full-on assault against the mainstream. This was our punk rock.

Alongside the single, they announced a tour with two shows in Scotland. One in Glasgow at the QMU, a student union in the West End, and one in Edinburgh at a venue called Calton Studios. The single even had the tour dates printed on the back. Having been too young to see them when they'd played Scotland the previous year, and after being blown away by their Reading performance, I had to go. Neale wanted to go too. That is, if his mum would let him – she'd been disgruntled when he came home from one of our Saturday outings to Glasgow with a Nirvana

'Fudge Packin Crack Smokin Satan Worshippin Mother Fucker' T-shirt and made him take it back. Thankfully she had forgotten about the T-shirt debacle and said that Neale could go. I can't recall if it was because of funds or simply because Glasgow sold out quickly, but Neale only got a ticket for Edinburgh while I managed to get a ticket for both.

Screamadelica and *Nevermind* came out at the end of September. *Nevermind* was a pure blast of melodic punk rock. I remembered loads of the songs from the Reading performance; the lyrics printed on the inside sleeve were weird, enigmatic and mysterious, and the music was visceral. *Screamadelica* was fantastic too. Their version of The 13th Floor Elevators' 'Slip Inside This House' was mind-bending (it seemed that the music of the Elevators was a constant thread through my musical discovery), and the rest of *Screamadelica* was similarly psychedelic, swinging from full-on techno to spaced-out ambient jams. I adored it.

I'd been spending a bit more time with Mog and Kevin outside of school. Being a few years older, they had great record collections and were totally fine with Neale and me tagging along. They were going to the Primal Scream gig and offered to take me. They had a deal with each other to share driving duties, and as Mog had done the Plaza gig, it was Kevin's turn to take the wheel for the Barras gig. By this point in Scotland there was no tolerance for drink driving, so Kevin would be on the Irn-Bru. Mog most certainly would not. With DJs instead of a support band, the gig was a lot later than most, finishing at 2 a.m. rather than the usual 11 p.m.

The timings and lack of support band apart, I wasn't thinking of the gig as any different from those I usually went to. Come the night itself, I engaged with the normal plan and got a bottle of wine to drink before the show. In the car, as all the non-drivers got wired into our carry-outs, Mog asked me if I wanted to take acid with him. Being pretty obsessed with all things psychedelic, I didn't take much persuading. Most of the music I loved felt like it came from people mind-altered in some way, and though I knew drugs were dangerous I refused to see the downside in almost any situation. I was many things as a teenager, but risk-averse was not one of them. Reassuringly, Mog said he'd look after me, and being a bit older than me that was good enough. He told me that it took about an hour to kick in, so with that in mind we both took the little paper squares with a strawberry printed on them and washed them down with our sugary, caffeinated Buckfast tonic wine. All three of us were buzzing about the gig. Mog and Kevin said the Plaza show I hadn't got into was great but the Barrowlands would be even better. Glaswegians love it when their own do well and it was clear that the Primals were on the verge of something special. We got in, no bother. By now I'd kind of given up worrying about that. I reckon body language is 95 per cent how people judge these things, and if you don't look worried no one ever stops you. These days when I go in and out of venues we're playing, I'm hardly ever asked for a pass and it's certainly not because I'm so well known. It's just that when you look like you belong somewhere no one feels the need to question you.

Safely inside the Barras it became pretty obvious that this wasn't just another gig. People were different. For one thing, the music had started already. The DJs' music was as loud as any band I'd seen. As I got used to what was happening, I started to feel different. My legs felt like rubber and I had a feeling like I was constantly bursting with excitement. Like constant elation. The lights in the room seemed brighter and the music completely vivid. The stars on the Barrowland ceiling were hypnotising me as we danced. The DJs were Glasgow's Slam and the by-now somewhat legendary Andrew Weatherall. The music was all encompassing, euphoric and hypnotic; it felt like part of my body. One track just kept building, and building, and building. The bass in the song sounded like the end of the world. Like the whole building was shaking. I'd never heard anything like it. We later found out it was 'Digeridoo' by Aphex Twin, and it was incredible. It was as if I was in a trance. I was so swept away with the energy of the night that I had pretty much forgotten about the acid. I was too busy having the best night of my life. Time as a concept became redundant as the music kept playing and the atmosphere built and built, as if the whole room was one. The music and the people had become one entity. The vibrations of the music seemed to be doing something to my mind. I felt simultaneously focused and distracted. Glowing with euphoria.

And then it went dark.

The first thing I remember hearing was the opening bars of 'Slip Inside This House'. I remember the bass shuddering through my body. Bobby bounced onto the stage, his shiny gold shirt sparkling in the lights, looking like the happiest man on the planet, with a smile as wide as the Clyde. The music the DJs had been playing had seemed loud but it was nothing compared to the sound now the band had started. I was enveloped by the bass, and the energy coming from the stage was as intense and euphoric as that coming from the audience. The crowd were going for it and the Scream were having the time of their lives. As the effect of the acid took hold, the songs started to melt into each other. The night went from being a linear event to one where time folds in on itself. All I knew was that there was nowhere else on earth I'd rather be at that time. It was as if my brain was only now just being turned on. Higher than the sun and completely immersed, I was deep in an experience of oneness and communion with the music.

When the band finished, the DJs kept the music playing. Everyone kept dancing until the lights went up and the music stopped. We floated out of the Barrowlands into the cold of the street. Me and Mog were on another planet, completely in awe of the whole night. Kevin had loved the show, although doubtless slightly envious of his wasted pals.

As we made our way down the M74 from Glasgow to Lanarkshire, it occurred to me that in my altered state I might not be in the best shape to be talking to my parents. They were open-minded but totally anti-drugs. With that in mind, I asked Kevin to drop me at the end of the road to give me ten minutes or so to get myself together and reassimilate to some kind of normality. We lived on a long country road with six houses on it, but it's mostly just fields with some trees at one end. I got out of the car and was immediately overwhelmed by everything I could hear. Normally I would have described it as silence, being in the middle of nowhere at 3 a.m, but what I was hearing was anything but silence. I could hear every bird and animal. It seemed really loud, which was especially odd as only half an hour earlier I'd been assaulted by deafening music. The experience was mesmerising. It was then that I looked up. The sky was a million shades of blue and the shadows of the trees against the sky were making the most incredible shapes and patterns. When I closed my eyes I could see the blood vessels behind them, which melded into the shapes of the trees. I could see that every living thing on earth was connected. Me. The trees. The sky. Everything. Music was the glue that held it all together. I felt completely transformed. As I ambled along the road to get home, I reflected on what had been an incredible gig and experience.

When I got in my dad was up. He kept weird hours and it wasn't unusual for him to be up reading in the middle of the night. He was a voracious reader, consuming several books a day most days. He'd taught himself to skip extraneous words, meaning he could read way more than anyone I've ever known. As a scientist and astronomer my dad was constantly fascinated by something new. He'd often tell me all about new discoveries he'd stumbled upon. It wasn't too long since he'd been on the TV show *Tomorrow's World* talking about his invention of a flexible mirror for large telescopes and satellites. I can't recall exactly what that night's conversation was about – truth be told, quite often they would go over my decidedly unscientific head – but I do remember sitting, having a cup of tea with him, trying not to get too distracted by the walls and his beard flashing while he exuberantly regaled me about science, religion or politics. One thing about my dad was that he'd found a place of contentment, managed to build a life where he could spend his time working and learning about things that he loved. Even though our interests were worlds apart, it was great hanging out and chatting. A lovely way to end my first psychedelic experience.

After the Primal Scream gig, it took me a few days to come back down to earth. I told my brother-in-hedonism Neale all about my LSD experience and we agreed this was an avenue we had to explore further. As well as the mind expansion and reset worldview, another benefit of acid was that it was cheap. One hit of LSD was less than a bottle of Buckfast and we were always on the lookout for ways to get wasted that wouldn't overly impinge on our record buying funds. We'd spend many hours furthering our psychedelic experiences, listening to far out music and occupying ourselves by staring at my parents' bathroom floor, the paisley pattern design of which would become an impromptu kaleidoscope while tripping.

The autumn of 1991 was an amazing time, going to see as many bands as I possibly could. Things had fizzled out with Cher and I was spending more time with Adele. I went with her to see the brilliant shoegaze band, Slowdive. I'd never heard guitars that sounded so unlike guitars. The predominant style at this point was mostly grunge, with everything cranked up to eleven to sound like a chainsaw. The guitars in Slowdive were totally different to my young ears, sounding like a bank of synthesisers. It was really beautiful and definitely made a huge impression. Adele was fun and I discovered loads of new music, films and books from her.

The other big event that autumn was the two Nirvana shows. Their assault on the mainstream was going full steam ahead. In November, John Peel broadcast a new Nirvana session that had been recorded when they were over for Reading. By now they were everywhere. The week after being on Peel they were on the Channel 4 show *The Word* playing 'Smells Like Teen Spirit'. *The Word* was a really popular show, with a weird mix of music, guests and gross challenges. I recall one episode where a guy snogged an old lady for some reason. Nirvana's performance on *The Word* was incredible. Before they played a note, Kurt announced that 'Courtney Love from the band Hole is the greatest fuck in the world.' This was memorable for a bunch of reasons. Firstly, swearing on TV was still extremely taboo, and secondarily it was quite a random piece of information to be sharing so publicly. After this pronouncement the band tore through the song. The crowd of *Face*-reading fashion wannabes didn't quite know how to dance to this kind of music, but the band absolutely grasped the moment and from then on became megastars. People that we considered 'normal' getting into music we liked was an odd experience, however. Earlier that year the single 'To Here Knows When' by My Bloody Valentine had managed to creep into the Top 40 singles chart and a girl who sat next to me in biology brought it up. 'I heard that band you like on the charts last night,' she said. 'Cool,' I replied, but she followed it up by saying that the radio was broken and she couldn't hear the song properly.

With Nirvana the band of the moment, our plans to see them later in the month at relatively intimate venues seemed all the more exciting. Every time you turned on the radio you heard them; every magazine seemed to have them on the cover. It felt like a real cultural shift. Only a few months earlier bands like Nirvana and Sonic Youth had been the property of the weirdos and misfits, but not now. People were describing jeans and flannel shirts as 'a look' rather than just what skateboarders and people in indie bands wore. Having music you loved partly because it had nothing to do with fashion become suddenly fashionable was a really weird experience. I loved the music so much, though, that I was all in for the ride.

My sister had a ticket for the Glasgow gig but not Edinburgh, so me and Neale had to figure out a way to get over there. Mog and Kevin were both going, and Mog kindly agreed to drive. A friend of theirs, Wendy, was going too. A few years older than me and Neale, Wendy was the older sister of Jill, a girl in my class I was friends with. I got dropped off at school about an hour early every day and would amuse myself by perusing the music papers until the bell went at 9. I think Jill was in the same boat – her dad was a dentist – and we'd hang around together in the mornings. I was developing a huge crush on Jill but didn't see it ever going anywhere. Jill and her friends were all pretty respectable, going round to each other's houses to study, whereas Neale and I were more likely to be passing out drunk in parks. I couldn't see her ever going out with someone like me, so I never told anyone about it.

Seeing Nirvana together was a real event for me and Neale because, at this point, there was a direct parallel between how excited we were and how drunk we intended to get. Teenage logic at its absolute finest. We were extremely excited about seeing Nirvana; this meant we were going to get extremely drunk. We utilised our finely honed tactic of saving lunch money to make sure we had the requisite funds to get our bottle of Blue Label Thunderbird wine for the gig. We were prepared. We could hardly wait.

Finally, the night came. We were absolutely up to high doh at the prospect. Going to Edinburgh for a gig always felt like an adventure in itself. It took over an hour to get there and, while only thirty-five miles from Glasgow, felt a lot further away because the cities are so different. We all squeezed into Mog's far from spacious Ford Fiesta and headed off from Lanarkshire towards Edinburgh, me and Neale gleefully drinking our wine. By the time we arrived we were both wrecked. Me especially. I was mortal. There was a feeling that this wasn't just a normal gig. Two nights previously they'd been on *Top of the Pops*, Kurt infamously singing like Andrew Eldritch from The Sisters of Mercy while making a mockery of the enforced miming on the show by playing his guitar backwards. *Top of the Pops* bands didn't normally play venues this small. Calton Studios only held 300 to 400 people, a grimy sweatbox about as far from the world of *Top of the Pops* as you can get. There were huge crowds hanging around the venue, with a gaggle of ticketless people hoping to somehow get inside.

We got in just in time to see the first band, Glasgow's Captain America. Kurt had worn their T-shirt on the cover of the *NME* and had covered Eugene's old band, The Vaselines, several times. It seemed Kurt had a thing for Scottish indie. Captain America were great, as were the other support band Shonen Knife, the all-female Japanese trio. I was in a state of heightened excitement. There was only one problem though: I was way, way too drunk. I'd had a few more drinks when I got into the venue, which on top of the bottle of 18 per cent Thunderbird had got me absolutely hammered. It was a lot to drink, especially for someone as small and young as me. Neale was fairly wrecked too but not quite in the same league. I had that weird swimming sensation where you feel like you're on a ferry in choppy water.

Finally, the band came on. From the first note it was abundantly clear that this Nirvana show was not going to be anything like the one I'd seen them play at Reading. In only a few months, everything had changed for them. Back then they were fully underground. Now to all intents and purposes they were rock stars. Kurt didn't seem like the type of person to embrace that though. Moments before they came on stage, Neale had seen him at the bar, queuing alongside everyone else. They opened the show with another Vaselines song, 'Jesus Doesn't Want Me For A Sunbeam'. It was more of a ballad than the others they'd covered, with a hymn-like quality. Really beautiful but way more subdued. There had been some rumours that Kurt was struggling with his voice, and that might explain the unusual start. They followed with 'Aneurysm', the incredible song on the B-side to

'Teen Spirit'. As the instantly recognisable ascending, wailing guitars and pounding drums began, the sense of occasion in tandem with my extreme inebriation transported me to some other place; it's difficult to put into words, but it felt like some kind of epiphany. Seeing the best band in the world with my best friend on the week they'd raided the charts was a real moment.

The rest of the show went by in a bit of blur. I remember they played a cover of The Velvet Underground song, 'Here She Comes Now'. It was one of my favourites Velvet's songs and Nirvana's version was brilliant. It seemed that Lou Reed and The Velvet Underground were never far away. For a band that had broken up before I was born, their influence was everywhere. The gig went by really quickly and before we knew it, they'd finished.

Back in the car everyone was buzzing. I was the only one who had a ticket for the next night in Glasgow, but Kevin and Mog immediately began scheming to get in. With an hour's journey ahead, Wendy took the opportunity to go to sleep. Me and Neale, still giddy from the wine and excitement, occupied ourselves by chatting drunken nonsense with Kevin and the sober man out, Mog. With Wendy safely asleep and my inhibitions lowered, I confided in Neale about my crush on Wendy's sister, Jill. Neale wasn't particularly surprised. I'm sure it was pretty obvious. Having all had far too much to drink, we asked Mog to find somewhere we could go to the toilet. He pulled in at the service station. Before all running in to use the loo, we discussed whether we should wake Wendy to see if she needed to go too. Amid our deliberation, she piped up: 'I'm not asleep.' The revelation that Wendy hadn't been asleep at all hit me like a ton of bricks. I couldn't believe I'd divulged my feelings for Wendy's sister within earshot of the very-much-awake Wendy. I spent the rest of the journey squirming with embarrassment.

Still, the embarrassment was some respite from the other issue preoccupying me – how the hell was I going to hide my drunken state from my parents? Tolerant they may have been, but coming in legless would not have gone down well at all. The previous month I'd managed to hold a conversation with my dad while tripping after the Primal Scream gig, but this was another set of circumstances altogether. I could barely walk and my conversational skills were suitable only for other drunken teens. I had a hard enough time focusing on conversations with my dad at the best of times, but in this state? No chance. The plan I formulated was to get in the house as quickly as possible and go straight to bed. But my parents knew that I'd been really excited about going to the gig so might find it odd that I sneaked off to bed without saying anything.

I was the first to be dropped off. Mog drove up the windy country road and I exited the car as quietly as possible. The living room lights were on, indicating that my dad was still up. I opened the front door as quietly as I could and meekly shouted, 'Goodnight' in the general direction of the living room before scuttling off towards my bedroom. In my mind I was stealth-like, a tipsy ninja sneakily hiding my toxic state from my parents. In reality, I was a baby elephant high on glue who smelt like the floor of a pub at midnight. Unsurprisingly, my plan did not work.

'ARE YOU DRUNK?' my father asked me as he pulled the duvet away from my pretending-to-sleep face. 'I only had one beer,' I replied, a lie that would make Boris Johnson blush. 'We can talk about this with your mother in the morning,' my dad said, before emphasising the fact that I was in deep shit with the words, 'and you're grounded.' My mind was doing somersaults. Not only had I stupidly divulged my secret about Jill to her big sister, but I had also ruined my chances of seeing Nirvana again the next night.

I'd fucked it.

I woke the next morning hungover as hell, with added knots in my stomach, an anxious consequence of the impending trouble with my folks. It was a sensation I wasn't used to. There wasn't much that could piss my parents off, such was their easy-going nature. I had managed it though. They were furious. I was summoned in the morning to speak to them both and they were more disappointed than angry (always a good tactic). I was told I had to stay in and study, that I couldn't go to any gigs or hang around with my friends. In a pre-internet age, being confined to your bedroom really was a punishment. It was boring as fuck. Having been read what passed as the riot act from my exceedingly reasonable and lovely parents, I knew this was my moment. It was now or never. I plucked up all the courage I had and just blurted it out.

'Can I wait till tomorrow to be grounded? I really want to go and see Nirvana again tonight.' I followed this quickly with a potted history of the cultural significance of the band at that moment in time, how sorry I was for being so stupid and that I would never do it again. A lie so heinous it would shame Pinocchio. Whether it was my sheer chutzpah or I'd just made a great case, or – most likely – that my parents were just really nice people, they said yes. My grounding would commence in twenty-four hours. I'd somehow talked my way out of missing Nirvana in Glasgow.

It was a Saturday so I didn't even get to go to school to escape from my parents' disapproval. I spent the day sheepishly skulking about and eagerly doing the kind of tasks that I would normally mump and moan about. I knew I'd dodged a bullet. Victoria had come home from Dundee to go to the gig, and I think the fact that she was taking me was one of the reasons my parents were letting me go. There was no way I could possibly get into any trouble under her watch . . .

The Queen Margaret Union was a student union in the West End of Glasgow. It was about half the size of the Barrowlands. Back in August I'd seen an amazing grunge double bill there with Mudhoney supported by Hole. It was a great venue and I knew that seeing Nirvana there would be something special.

In their pursuit of tickets, Mog and Kevin had taken matters into their own hands, heading into Glasgow as soon as they woke up to hang about outside the gig in the hope of bumping into any of the bands and blagging the guest list. Bands are allowed a certain amount of free tickets for every show, and especially if a band is from out of town and feeling charitable, sometimes they'll help out fans who plead poverty. Their plan succeeded. In fact, it succeeded so well that they were on three different guest lists. The venue's, Nirvana's and Captain America's. Good to have some insurance, I suppose. I'd arranged to meet them around doors opening time.

After dinner, Vic and I headed into town for the gig. As the day went on I think my parents' attitude to me softened. They seemed more amused at how sick and hungover I was than they were angry with me for getting so drunk in the first place. I was eternally grateful for them letting me go.

Arriving at the QM, we saw Mog and Kevin. They were already pretty drunk, with Mog definitely making up for the enforced sobriety of the previous night.

I eschewed my now almost traditional bottle of uber-strength wine for the night. Even if I'd wanted to, I don't think I could have managed it. I had the worst hangover of my young life and the last thing I wanted was to get into even more trouble with my folks. This was probably the first show I'd been to totally sober since The Cure two years earlier.

Even though I was subdued, this gig was anything but. People in Edinburgh had been excited about seeing Nirvana but the crowd in Glasgow was something else entirely. There was stage diving and a mosh pit even for the support bands. Nirvana had missed out Glasgow when they came to Scotland the previous year and the anticipation was electric. Still feeling tender, I decided to watch from the balcony instead of being in the crowd. Looking down at the stage before the band came on, I noticed that Kurt's mic was placed really high and pointed down, like Lemmy's from Motörhead. It's a bit of cliché how Glasgow crowds are much more lively than Edinburgh ones – my dad used to say you'd have more fun at a Glasgow stabbing than an Edinburgh wedding – but these two shows went some way to proving the cliché true. When Nirvana came on everyone went fucking nuts. The show was way more full-on. Kurt's voice having a bit of a night off had clearly paid dividends. The set was longer in Glasgow too, including most of *Nevermind* as well as a clutch of new songs, like 'Rape Me' and 'All Apologies'. They played with a focus and ferocity befitting their new status as one of the world's biggest and best bands. They would never sell out. They flew the flag for the underground forever.

It had been a truly triumphant show. In just a few months I'd gone from watching Nirvana at a lunchtime festival slot in between Chapterhouse and Silverfish to seeing them play sold-out shows and raiding the charts.

Sadly, it would be the last time I saw Nirvana. Shortly before they were due to play Glasgow in 1994 in support of their third and best album, *In Utero*, Kurt took his own life. I had tickets but alas never got the chance to see them again. As for Primal Scream, I'd see them dozens more times, our paths intertwining as musicians years later. We would even share stages. Back then I had no clue of what lay ahead, though the wonder of that autumn of 1991 would stay with me forever.

6.

Rollercoaster

I've always thought of music as being romantic. It can take you from wherever you are to somewhere else in an instant. When I was a teenager, in particular, I romanticised about music and musicians endlessly. I'd daydream about how records were made and what the lives of those making them were like. The music itself would set fires in my imagination. In the days before social media, you really had no clue about the personalities behind the music you loved. There were interviews, but on reflection those were mostly just attention-grabbing exercises. In my younger days I wouldn't associate normal problems with music people. I thought they lived some kind of mythical existence completely different to the world the rest of us lived in.

In autumn 1991, I'd find romance in real life as well as in music.

After going to see Slowdive in Glasgow, I spent more time with Adele. It had started with chats about music, then proceeded to us becoming inseparable. We both liked the sitcom *Kate & Allie* and would watch it at my house every week. My dad would drive Adele the fifteen minutes from the Clyde Valley to her house in Bothwell. It wasn't long before we were boyfriend and girlfriend.

The main thing we had in common was music. We were both obsessed, though not always with the same bands. I was fond of The Smiths, whereas Adele was a devotee and would go to club nights where they played nothing but The Smiths and Morrissey. I was a Cure fan and back then it felt like you had to pick a side, and I was on Robert's. Adele introduced me to a lot of great music though, like Bikini Kill and PJ Harvey. Most of the bands we loved equally – the Mary Chain, Buzzcocks. If there weren't any good gigs on, we'd go to the video shop. We both loved horror films, Clive Barker in particular: we watched *Hellraiser* and *Nightbreed* endlessly. I still know them pretty much off by heart. It was a really nice time, free from the pressures of life, just hanging out and having fun. We could spend hours pontificating which was the best of the *Nightmare on Elm Street* sequels (for the record, it's *3: Dream Warriors*).

But music was our main passion, and 1991 was shaping up to be one of the best years ever.

Since hearing the cacophonous 'Feed Me With Your Kiss' on a mixtape, I'd been fixated on My Bloody Valentine. Their music was simultaneously frail and huge. They seemed to bridge a gap between the Mary Chain and American bands like Dinosaur Jr. and Sonic Youth. I adored their first album, *Isn't Anything*, and the *You Made Me Realise* EP was one of my favourite records, mixing incredible harmonies with brutal noise. By autumn 1991 they'd released two singles from their upcoming second album and both were brilliant. There were murmurings in the music papers about the album costing a lot of money, but I had no idea what that meant. I had zero clue how an album was even made, never mind how much it cost. *Loveless* was due out at the start of November. Not only that but they were playing the Barrowlands and there was no way we could miss it. The night was made even more enticing by the inclusion of My Bloody Valentine's Glaswegian labelmates Teenage Fanclub on the bill.

Loveless arrived the month before the gig. I'd never known a record come out with such a fanfare. The prose thrown around in pre-release reviews in the music press was so ridiculously hyperbolic that it only added to the excitement I already felt.

When I finally got to listen to the album, I understood why. It genuinely sounded unlike anything else. I knew that the music was coming from guitars because I'd seen pictures of the band play, but they didn't sound like any guitars I'd ever heard. The first song, 'Only Shallow', started like a jet plane taking off, with a huge swooping alien riff. So much of the album was made up of perfect songs but interspersed with weird experimental segments. For once, the hype was completely justified. From the moment it came out it was our soundtrack, a permanent fixture on my turntable.

In between the release of *Loveless* and the Barrowlands, something happened that the people of Scotland had been waiting a very long time for: Margaret Thatcher resigned. Thatcher had shown real disdain for Scotland during the entirety of her decade-long reign and had taken brutal steps to decimate Scotland's industry. Lanarkshire, where I lived, consisted of mining communities, and after the pit closures that followed the Miners' Strike in the mid-eighties, the effects on people's lives were horrendous. When the news arrived that she was finally resigning there were literally people dancing in the street. I've seldom seen my father so happy. He fucking despised her. To this day her name is dirt in Scotland. Her disappearance from public life felt like a huge cloud lifting, kind of like when *The Wizard of Oz* goes Technicolor. Ding dong indeed.

After a long wait, the Barrowlands show arrived. It was a typically cold, dark Scottish December night. There's something evocative about that time of year in Glasgow. A certain romance about the early nights that I always associate with going to the Barrowlands. Glasgow has an aura in winter unlike anywhere else.

It must have been a special night for Teenage Fanclub, who were enjoying a brilliant moment themselves. Their second album, *Bandwagonesque*, had come out to an amazing reception and, like Nirvana, had benefited from an invitation to play on the trashy TV show *The Word*. They'd been championed by the big hitters of the US underground like Sonic Youth and Nirvana and seemed to be enjoying every second of it. Even though they were ostensibly the support band, the hometown element and the trajectory they were on made it feel like they were co-headliners. The Fanclub's music was wonderfully catchy and they had an engaging, friendly stage presence, helped no end by their hilariously eccentric drummer Brendan O'Hare who cracked jokes in between every song and spoke more than the other guys in the band who all sang the songs. I was a fan, particularly of their first single, 'Everything Flows', which is pretty much a perfect record. Playing Barrowlands was clearly a huge deal for the Fannies – and this would be the last time they played there as a support act.

Before My Bloody Valentine came on, we got as near to the front as possible. Neither Adele nor I are the tallest so we had to make sure we didn't spend the entire gig looking at some big guy's back. I'm not sure if we were worried about not being able to hear them properly, but there would prove to be no worries on that front. The lights went down and without any 'hello' or other pleasantries the band started playing 'Glider'.

It was without doubt the loudest sound I'd ever heard. The bass felt like it was rearranging my organs and it was nigh on impossible to tell which instrument was making what sound. The way the music slid in and out of tune only added to the sense of otherworldliness. I truly felt like I was leaving my body: not unlike seeing Primal Scream, but this time I couldn't blame the drugs.

The next two songs, 'When You Sleep' and 'Only Shallow', with their huge riffs, were mind-blowing. The guitar melodies, augmented by a flute player, managed to cut through the noise. It was an utterly psychedelic experience. As the show went on, the sound seemed to get even louder. They ended with two of my favourite songs: 'Feed Me With Your Kiss' and 'You Made Me Realise'. 'Feed Me With Your Kiss' was the song that had made me fall in love with noise in music, and hearing it played live was exhilarating. I felt like my whole body was being shaken.

I was in ecstasy, but still unprepared for what was to come. On the recorded version, 'You Made Me Realise' breaks down to guitar noise for a few seconds towards the end of the song. Live, the noise section just . . . didn't . . . stop. It just built and built until it was impossible to hear anything. The sound collapsed in on itself, bringing about a kind of trance-like state. I'd never experienced anything like it. I was swaying from back to front, losing myself in the cacophony, forgetting where I was and then remembering. At one point I looked down and could see my trousers flapping like I was standing on top of a windy mountain. After what felt like an age, the end section of the song kicked back in even louder than the noise. It was the best thing I'd ever heard.

When the band left the stage, the lights went up. We were in a happy daze. On the way out, Adele went to buy a shirt featuring the cover of the *Glider* EP. She changed her mind when I pointed out that it was a picture of people snogging. She shouldn't have listened to me.

Our ears rang for days after seeing MBV. We didn't care.

When not going to gigs, Adele and I would spend almost all our time together. Whether at my place or hers, we were pretty much inseparable. We'd listen to music and watch movies, and when we were away from our parents' gaze we'd get drunk and occasionally take LSD. We both had a fairly abysmal attitude to school. The only class I cared about was music because my teacher, Mr Mackay, was a real music fan. One day he played us the Sex Pistols and he would become animated talking about Stockhausen, who he'd studied for his PhD. Another time when talking about boogie woogie piano, he went full-on Jerry Lee Lewis while playing us an example – kicking his stool away in the throes of musical joy. He had a four-track and made a tape of school bands that he recorded. Me and Neale cobbled something together to get on the tape but never took the band much further. Other than music, I had little time for school at all. It didn't help that I was falling foul of the strict dress code on a regular basis.

I would wear black clothes all the time when I was supposed to wear brown or grey, which led to me getting regular lectures. I can't really remember anything much about school other than dreadfully boring old men. I ignored them. I had a zero-tolerance policy towards authority. Fuck them all.

In early 1992 a gig was announced that we were all incredibly up for. The Rollercoaster tour was the brainchild of The Jesus and Mary Chain: a touring four-band bill headlined by them, with a revolving support cast of My Bloody Valentine, Dinosaur Jr. and Blur. The Glasgow date was to take place at the SEC where I'd seen The Cure four years earlier.

On top of the tour, the Mary Chain had a new album coming out – *Honey's Dead*. The first single from it, 'Reverence', was one of their best songs in years, with swathes of feedback and the most nihilistic lyrics imaginable: 'I wanna die just like Jesus Christ, I wanna die on a bed of spikes.' With its dance-looped drum machine and Stooges riff, I was completely sold. They played it on *The Word* and it was clear they were on brilliant form.

Me and Adele were so excited about the Rollercoaster tour. After all, we'd first met at the Mary Chain gig two years earlier. The gig fell on a school night, so we met up in Hamilton and took the first train we could into Glasgow. Safely inside we made our way as close to the stage as we could.

The first band were Blur. I had one of their singles and quite liked it, though they couldn't seem to decide whether they wanted to be baggy or shoegaze. Hedging their bets, I suppose. Their set wasn't particularly inspiring. They seemed to be mucking about and had a projection behind them of some backwards footage of someone taking a shit. It was the other bands that we were really there for. My Bloody Valentine were next and thankfully this time we were prepared for what was to come. The same couldn't be said for a lot of the audience though, and the noise section in 'You Made Me Realise' managed to thin the crowd out considerably. Then came Dinosaur Jr. I had tremendous memories of seeing them play at Reading the previous year, but this show was curtailed by malfunctioning amps. The short time they did play was brilliant. J Mascis, Poison Ivy and Robert Smith were my guitar heroes.

When the Mary Chain came on, the place was bedlam. *Honey's Dead* had been a big success. This was their biggest ever home-town gig and, as a spectacle, it was dazzling. The projections and lights were outrageous, and it felt like a real moment for the band.

Seeing those bands together that night seemed like an incredibly special time. Over the years ahead I'd meet so many people who were also there and had similarly profound experiences. I've no doubt this tour played a pivotal role in inspiring music fans and musicians wherever it went.

Another band making a comeback in 1992 were The Cure. The follow-up to *Disintegration* was called *Wish* and it seemed like they could do no wrong. To launch the album they did a tour of 'small' venues to mark its release and I was delighted to find out that two of them were in Scotland: the Caird Hall in Dundee, and the Barrowlands. I was determined to see both. I knew tickets would be hard to get, so I begged my parents to let me take the day off school to try to get them. Amazingly, they did. Me and Victoria got up at the crack of dawn and queued outside the Virgin Megastore in Glasgow's Union Street. After a long wait we got the tickets. Then we had to drive two hours to Dundee in the hope there would still be some left by the time we got there. Luck was on our side again.

The run-up to the release of *Wish* was surreal. *Disintegration* had been a huge hit and the band were definitely present in places that I wasn't used to them being. Their tour began in America and the band were travelling on the *QE2* ocean liner and doing a daily broadcast on the breakfast television programme *Good Morning Britain*. It's an incredibly cheesy show and seeing my black-clad heroes being interviewed by Lorraine Kelly felt extremely odd. I'd loved 'High', the first single from *Wish*, despite it being a good bit poppier than most of *Disintegration*. The drive into Glasgow to pick up *Wish* was soundtracked by the godawful Freddie Mercury tribute concert on the radio. I wasn't particularly a fan of Queen (to say the least), but no one deserved their back catalogue to be mutilated like that. I got home with my copy of *Wish* and fell in love – more varied than *Disintegration*, mixing lighter and darker songs, akin to *Kiss Me Kiss Me Kiss Me* or *The Head on the Door*. I was enthralled and couldn't wait to see them in relatively small surroundings.

I'd been to Dundee quite a few times to stay with Victoria. By this point she'd decided she didn't want to be an architect and had returned back to our folks, though she was my wingman at the gig. The Caird Hall is a grand ornate building at the centre of Dundee City Square. I remember The Cure show vividly. I wasn't surprised to see them start their main set with the song 'Open' and to close it with the song 'End', both from *Wish*. They also played 'In Your House', which was a favourite of mine from their minimalist classic *Seventeen Seconds*. Seeing them again was a different experience from the first time three years earlier. Shorn of the bright-eyed wonderment of seeing live music for the first time, I could better appreciate what an amazing band they were and the effort they put in. No other band played for so long or played so many songs. The sheer range of emotions took you on a journey, from despair to unbridled joy and back again. As a teenager you feel everything so deeply. All your feelings are new and to have that reflected back to you is such a powerful thing.

Victoria came again the next night in Glasgow. Adele was there too. She was a huge Cure fan but had never seen them play before. My friend Jill from school also went with her big sister Wendy, my relationship with Adele having relegated last year's crush to platonic friendship. We got drunk before the show, demolishing bottles of wine on the train to Glasgow, holding it together enough to convince the bouncers we were sober adults rather than drunken teens.

We knew every song and sang along like it was the end of the world. The Cure are the perfect teenage band and these were perfect teenage times, completely careless and living each day like it was our last.

Even though I now had a serious girlfriend (well, I was serious about having a girlfriend; Adele thankfully wasn't particularly serious at all), my taste for hedonism hadn't abated. After my first LSD experience at the Primal Scream show, Neale got on board and we started to trip regularly. My parents were out of town quite often and Neale would decamp to mine, where we'd take acid and get up to all kinds of nonsense. Running about the woods behind my parents' house, scaring ourselves witless and testing the limits of what taking more and more LSD would do. We'd listen to music and watch stupid trippy videos like *The Magic Roundabout*. My parents had loads of cats. I hallucinated that they were multiplying and the house had turned into a cat jungle. Another good pal from school, Simon Johnstone, got so high that he spent an entire night phoning every shopping arcade in Scotland to find out when they were getting the game *Mortal Kombat*. Unsurprisingly, they were all shut. One time we phoned a local chip shop to deliver us food but forgot to eat it. Neale decided to heat it in the oven, paper wrapper and all. The next day we found it in the oven, a solid lump of carbon. It was a miracle we hadn't burnt the house down.

Adele would take LSD sometimes, though not as exuberantly as us. Me and Adele would spend days on end playing *Sonic the Hedgehog*, taking acid and listening to *Adventures Beyond the Ultraworld* by The Orb – its sound weirdly mirrored the sounds you'd hear on acid, and the songs felt like mini trips themselves. We whiled away that summer getting as wasted as often as possible, tripping, drinking wine and hanging out. It was glorious.

With The Orb featuring prominently as the soundtrack to our new-found psychedelic pastime, we were delighted to learn that they were about to go on tour and come to Glasgow to the famous Barrowlands. They transformed the old ballroom into a weird hallucinogenic wonderland, erecting a giant sofa in the middle of the dancefloor and placing two massive inflatable orbs at both ends of the room. Neale, Adele and I all took our tabs of acid on the way into Glasgow, so by the time we made our way into the venue our legs were feeling tingly and we were starting to come up. The DJs were playing pounding techno and the whole place felt like something from *Alice in Wonderland*. As we all started tripping, Adele pointed out that one of the giant orbs had Freddy Krueger from *Nightmare on Elm Street* projected onto it. She definitely got a wee fright.

Like Primal Scream, the pre-show DJs were as much a part of the show as the bands themselves. In fact, it was thanks only to our forensic obsession with their music that we recognised The Orb were onstage at all. Hearing those songs so loud and in that setting was incredible. In our heightened state, it wasn't just the music that was interesting, however. The men's toilets in the Barras are huge and I met so many utterly fried people in there that night. One guy whose nose was bleeding uncontrollably told me he was freaking out on E and needed to take two tabs of acid to take the edge off. Even in my somewhat spangled state I knew that this wasn't a wise course of action. Drifting out of the venue that night, it would take a few days to come down.

By autumn 1992, my lack of effort at school was starting to catch up with me. Whereas before I'd managed to get by on the bare minimum, it had now got to the point where that obviously wasn't going to cut it any longer. I'd always been pegged as quite a smart kid but the path I was on wasn't suited in any way to academia. I liked reading, but horror novels or books on Hendrix and The Velvet Underground sadly weren't on the curriculum. Quite a few of my friends were going to try to go to university but that wasn't looking too likely for me. As soon as it became clear that actual effort and studying was needed, I was in deep trouble. The only class I was remotely interested in was music and that was only because I was often left alone to sit and play guitar. I'd get two tape recorders and record myself playing something, then play it back on the other deck and record myself playing along. I'd keep going until I had layers and layers of guitar parts. Mr Mackay saw how enthusiastic I was and suggested I should study music and sound recording at college. He knew someone running a course that he thought was really good and suggested I apply. The only issue was that the college – Jewel and Esk – was on the other side of Edinburgh. Never one to be daunted, I applied. At this point I was working part-time in my mum's surgery as a receptionist, and although I quite liked it, the idea of getting to play the guitar all day seemed a lot more fun. Living away from home was appealing too; not that my folks were strict, but the thought of doing whatever I wanted without any supervision was attractive.

I was invited to audition to get into college; I just needed to work out what to play. Most of the music I played was beyond simple and unlikely to impress any academic musos. I certainly wasn't going to get away with playing a one-chord Spacemen 3 song for half an hour, as much as I'd enjoy that. I settled on The Only Ones' 'Another Girl, Another Planet', which as well as being a great punk-pop song also featured some relatively dextrous lead guitar. I went about learning it and got to a point where I could play it from start to finish without fluffing any notes. I headed through to Edinburgh for the audition feeling pretty prepared. I could play the song and had always been good at talking my way through situations.

The guy doing the audition was called Dougie, and he had a huge bouffant mullet. He was clearly into hair metal and would most definitely not have been charmed by Spacemen 3. Dougie asked me a bit about music, which went fine, and then invited me to play my song. I played it without making a mistake and thought I'd definitely done enough. 'Just one more thing,' Dougie said. 'Do you know any scales?' I knew three: major, minor and blues, which I proudly played. He then asked if I knew any more. Sensing that saying, 'No' would not look good, I panicked and said, 'Yes.' 'What is it?' asked Dougie, to which I replied without thinking, 'Jazz scale.' I had really dug myself into a bit of a hole, as I wouldn't know a jazz scale if it slapped me on the arse. I went from the low strings, guessing which frets had anything jazzy about them and traversed the guitar using a similarly demented logic until I got to the high strings. I did the same thing on the way back down, almost certainly playing different notes than on the way up. 'Thank you,' said Dougie. He must have thought I was such a wee chancer, but it can't have mattered too much because they let me in.

Adele wasn't particularly happy about me going to college in Edinburgh. She didn't drive and was going to college in Hamilton, near our folks. We were still close though, and I wasn't worried about it being too much of an issue.

In early 1993 there was an announcement that blew all of our minds. After years of animosity and estrangement, The Velvet Underground had decided to reform for a tour. Since first hearing them, I'd been fanatical about their music. It was The Velvets that had shown me how magical music could be. Even though Lou Reed had a reputation as a total curmudgeon, I'd had a lucid dream years before that he'd given me a fiver so I loved him. The other exciting thing was that the whole tour would kick off in Edinburgh, at the Playhouse: a huge old theatre and the perfect place for their first shows in decades.

As grand as The Velvet Underground's music is, it felt odd seeing them somewhere so highbrow. I imagined them belonging to the grimy streets of sixties New York – somewhere I'd never been, but felt I knew so well from the music of Sonic Youth, Television, Dylan and The Velvets. On the night, they walked on stage holding each other's hands. They sounded brilliant, John Cale in particular, who filled in on vocals for the sadly departed Nico. Lou was changing the way he sang a lot of the songs. It was a bit weird but he had good grace in the bank for that fiver he gave me in a dream. 'Heroin', 'I Heard Her Call My Name' and 'The Gift' were all incredible. It was spellbinding to see a band that had been so criminally under-appreciated play to thousands of people and receive the acclaim they deserved.

A week later I saw more legends play, this time in less salubrious surroundings. The Buzzcocks had always been one of my favourite punk bands. They'd recently reformed and were visiting the west coast seaside town of Ayr. Me and Adele would get the train from Glasgow down to Ayr quite often and just potter about the beach. We both adored the Buzzcocks: in many ways they're the perfect teenage band, with songs full of unrequited and forbidden love and other famously teenage pursuits, such as onanism. The train from Lanarkshire to Ayr takes a while, with a change in Glasgow. We decided to make a day of it, getting pretty drunk on the journey down. It was a beautiful day and after a saunter up and down the beach we made our way to the venue, a dingy nightclub called Powerhouse. We plonked ourselves down outside and nursed the remains of our carry-out. The band's van was parked nearby and out came Steve Diggle, one of my favourite guitarists. We were about to approach him to say hi and get our tickets signed when we realised that he was holding a bucket. Not only was he holding it, but he was about to puke into it. We decided not to get our tickets signed.

The gig itself was spectacular. Buzzcocks' stage show was pretty extraordinary, consisting of a bunch of old TV sets scattered around playing porn films. The band themselves were on fire. Clearly an afternoon chunder wasn't enough to throw Steve Diggle off his stride. He was immense. Pete Shelley was on fire as well. They played all the songs we wanted to hear. It had been the perfect day, the only problem being that we'd completely lost track of time. By the time the band finished it became apparent we had missed the last train. We'd never really factored in how we were going to get back to Lanarkshire. In those circumstances

I did what I always did: phoned my dad, who would cheerfully drop whatever he was doing and come and get me from wherever I was. Ayr is an hour away from my house though, so this was going above and beyond. He didn't mind. He was always there for me; an Olympic conversationalist, blethering on endlessly while traversing the backroads and motorways of Scotland.

Come the end of July, I left school. I was going to go to college but in truth I was leaving school no matter what. I'd been told I wasn't welcome back for a sixth and final year. My school was one of those that did well in the league tables of results for state schools, and I suppose with my attitude I was just going to drag down the figures. Other than having a laugh and learning about Stockhausen and punk from Mr Mackay, I'd not bothered too much with it. I'd chosen the path of rock and roll.

We spent the summer hanging out, getting drunk and generally doing as little as possible. Adele wasn't particularly happy about me going but knew this was what I wanted to do and respected that.

The night before I went to college we went to see the Smashing Pumpkins play the Barrowlands. I'd been a fan since their first album and they were getting really big now. I enjoyed the show but felt sad that I was saying goodbye to Glasgow. The Barrowlands had become my home away from home, and I knew that I'd be seeing less of it. Two years is a long time when you're seventeen.

My life was about to change – but I was ready for it.

Part Two
Teenage Riot

7.

Lord of the Flies

1995 was the year everything shifted for me.

I'd had an inspiring two years studying music at Jewel and Esk Valley College, near Edinburgh, despite making no effort to learn anything at all. I'd spent the first year in halls of residence before moving into a grotty flat with some college pals in Polwarth, which was so close to Hearts' ground, Tynecastle, that you could hear the roar when a goal went in on a Saturday.

We weren't interested in football though. Our passions were equally divided between obsessing over music and getting fucked up, with the emphasis probably on the latter. We'd spend every penny we had on cheap booze, real tramp-fuel like Blue Label Thunderbird and MD2020. If the opportunity arose, we'd take acid. Someone had mentioned what a terrible idea it would be to watch *The Shining* while you were tripping. So we went right ahead and did just that. I can confirm that it was indeed a truly awful thing: my mind turned itself inside out in slow motion while the blood flew out of the elevators. I'd taken to collecting any abandoned television set I found in the street and piling them on top of each other in my bedroom so it resembled some kind of Warholian squat. The flat itself was fucking freezing because the only heater was in the tiny kitchen. One night during a particularly cold spell I went to bed after having a shower and woke up to find my hair had frozen solid. When not drunk, high or freezing to death, we'd spend our time discussing records: *Hunky Dory*, *Lust for Life* and *Marquee Moon* being favourites in the flat.

College wasn't particularly exciting for me from an educational standpoint, but I was having a lot of fun playing in the band I'd formed there: Deadcat Motorbike.

On bass was my friend and flatmate, 'Wee' David Robertson. (There were two Davids in our friendship group, David Jack and David Robertson. This being Scotland and David Robertson being slightly shorter, he was automatically 'Wee' David.) David was a diminutive and sharp-witted Highlander who played a fretless bass, a super-intelligent guy with an encyclopaedic knowledge of almost everything. On drums was an affable, mop-topped stoner called Ally Anderson. I sang and played guitar, the latter with more success (but not much more). In a nod to the Ramones we all used the word 'Motorbike' as our surnames. Stuart Motorbike. Ally Motorbike. You get the picture. In my mind we sounded like a cross between The Cure and The Stooges, but in reality it was probably closer to a hybrid of The Mission and the Smashing Pumpkins. Our songs had titles like 'Emu Bucket' and 'Strawberry'. Random nonsensical words that had little to do with the painfully angst-ridden music. We also had a penchant for ridiculous cover versions, such as the theme from *Happy Days* and Beethoven's 'Ode To Joy'.

In time we might have improved but, alas, DCM's time would be short, due to Ally's imminent emigration to Australia. David had his own band going (Chapter 24, later to become Magic Drive) and, as brilliant a musician as he was, we weren't totally on the same page musically. He was getting heavily into Britpop, whereas I was becoming more and more enamoured with noisier music like The God Machine and a lot of the shoegaze and grunge bands that had already become utterly unfashionable by the mid-nineties, when cheeky chappies with faux-Cockney accents doing Kinks' pastiches had become the be-all and end-all for rock music. The *NME* had just run a piece about Sonic Youth with the headline: 'Old and Indie Way'. Seriously.

*

The previous year, Deadcat Motorbike had played a gig forty miles along the M8, at The 13th Note in Glasgow, a show that was to prove a lot more significant than it felt at the time. Located on Glassford Street amid a cluster of gay bars and nightclubs in Glasgow's city centre, The 13th Note was fast becoming the focal point for an increasingly exciting Glasgow music scene. Bands would play upstairs or downstairs, and people would often congregate on the stairs between the levels, like they do in the kitchens at parties. The 13th Note had a vegan cafe too, a concept that the teenage me hadn't quite grasped yet, often bringing my sausage and haggis suppers into soundchecks to disapproving sighs and tuts. Deadcat Motorbike had played there alongside The Blisters, Alex Huntley's band. Alex was extremely dapper, always wearing great suits and no stranger to tweed, which was quite a shock to me in my manky cardigans and T-shirts. He was the booker of The 13th Note. The Blisters were quite an unusual group compared to most of the bands around then, in that they could actually play their instruments really well. They traded in super-tight, slightly jazzy, quick-witted songs. We all thought they were going to be famous, something that didn't come to pass until Alex's next band, by which time he was Alex Kapranos and his band was called Franz Ferdinand. He'd been really supportive of Deadcat Motorbike, as he was with anyone making music that wasn't trying to fit in. (Years later, Alex told me he was massively prejudiced against anyone over twenty-five; people were so snotty about young musicians that he wanted to do everything he could to promote them.)

Another band on the bill that night were called Bullwinkle. While it was safe to say they didn't have the same promise as The Blisters, they did, however, have a tall, gangly bass-player. Dominic Aitchison.

Dominic really stood out: with a huge mop of curly hair and his six-foot frame, he was one of the few folk I'd seen who actually looked cool with a bass. More importantly, he played with a really powerful, muscular style. It turned out that we'd actually met briefly years earlier, at a Ned's Atomic Dustbin gig at the Barrowlands. The connection back then was his friend Colin Kearney. Colin's big brother Paul was dating my sister Victoria's best friend Nicola. Our older siblings had actually planned to keep us apart as me and my friends were a good bit wilder than Colin's group. Any plans to stop me becoming a wayward influence on Dominic and Colin, however, would be short-lived.

With my college course about to finish, I had to come up with some kind of plan. I wasn't particularly inclined to continue with education, because I wasn't even sure I'd get my diploma at that point (I did in the end – just). As for getting a job . . . the truth was that I'd got so used to my lifestyle of drinking with my pals whenever I liked and listening to (and playing) psychedelic rock music, that that's all I was interested in, so I needed to find a way to continue doing it. By the spring of 1995, I wanted to start a new band, playing the kind of intense, shoegazing music I'd got into. It never crossed my mind that it would be anything other than a three-piece. To me the perfect band was (and still is) The Jimi Hendrix Experience. Not to mention Nirvana and Motör-head. Dominic hadn't given the impression that he was heavily invested in Bullwinkle, so I got his number and rang him to ask if he wanted to start a band. I even had the name, which I'd nicked from the Steven Spielberg movie *Gremlins* . . . Mogwai. Little did I know that it was also a Chinese word for demon – something that sounded infinitely more sophisticated than admitting it was taken from a 1980s kids' film.

The first time me and Dominic played music together was at his parents' house in leafy Bearsden, in the western suburbs of Glasgow. Dominic picked me up from the train station. He sniffed the air in the car and asked me what the weird smell was. The smell, friends, was me. More specifically, my feet.

Since moving out of my parents' house, every penny I had was spent on records and alcohol. New shoes were an expense that would never even have occurred to me, so I had been wearing my old school shoes for the last three years. I had also pretty much given up on wearing socks because finding clean ones was just a hassle I simply didn't need. My staple outfit at the time was the Ramones T-shirt I'd bought in Poundstretcher, velvet leggings and a velvet jacket (I dug the velvet jacket because Hendrix wore one and you could find them for next to nothing in charity shops), with three-year-old shoes moulded to my black, sockless feet. Also, I still had hair at this point, which I had cut myself in a deranged attempt at recreating Ozzy Osbourne's hairstyle from a 1970s TV performance of 'Paranoid'. That's right – I was an utter fucking disgrace.

Thankfully, Dominic somehow managed to see past all of this.

That first day we both messed about with loose ideas we had for songs. It became instantly clear that we had a musical connection way beyond anyone else I'd played with before. When Dominic came up with a bassline, it seemed obvious to me what would sound good with it. I know that this must seem apparent but it's not always the case. It felt like we had a genuine understanding and that we could do something with the music we were working on.

We always had an extremely serious attitude to music. It was an obsession for both of us. Dominic is probably the most passionate music fan I know, and this was clear right from the start.

To help get the ball rolling we made each other mixtapes, and looking back it's instructive how much of my musical education came from those. Remarkably, given that we were the same age and grew up twenty miles apart, we had very different music tastes. There were a few bands we were both huge fans of – Sonic Youth and My Bloody Valentine – but other than that we were listening to very different music. Dominic's tape had mostly American contemporary music like Fugazi, Palace Brothers and Minutemen. All fantastic, but the band I didn't know that blew me away more than anything else was Slint. Dominic put the song 'Washer' on the tape and I had never heard anything quite like it. The complexity of the song, without ever descending into gratuitous virtuosity, as well as the restraint and truly vulnerable vocals, created something incredibly powerful. They would go on to be a huge influence on Mogwai and my life in general. On my tape for Dominic I included a lot of sixties psychedelic music as well as Spacemen 3 and Loop, bands with a huge monolithic sound, something that I wanted to create with Mogwai.

Over the next few months we got together as often as we could to work on music. With enough songs under our belt, the next step was to get them recorded, so I decided to take advantage of the free recording time available at my college, inviting Dominic to come to Edinburgh. We were going to record a demo. Being a two-piece band at this point, I recruited Wee David to step in on drums. David also fulfilled the role of recording engineer. As summer approached, I was living in a rented room in Polwarth across the road from the place I'd shared with my pals. We'd had to move out of that one as one of the flatmates had stopped paying rent.

I was a lot less content with the new flat. And my flatmates. One in particular. I had cultivated a serious disdain for a French guy who lived in one of the other rooms. A proper loathing. It had got to the point where I was reluctant to leave my room for any reason whatsoever. He was a total nag and used to incessantly moan about weird crap, like people using the shower because he had his showers at the local swimming pool. A profoundly unreasonable stance. An unfortunate by-product of this was that to avoid going to the toilet and encountering him, I had taken to peeing in empty Irn-Bru bottles. Not only that, but I'd taken to storing them in a drawer next to my bed. The night before we recorded, Dominic stayed in my room and I slept on David Jack's couch at the flat across the road. As Dominic and I shared a love of comics (*Sandman, From Hell, Moonshadow* – it was truly a golden age), I mentioned to him that I had some good comics in my room. In an unusually wise move we opted to have an early night because we were recording the next day. In my room Dominic had a wee search for some comics to read. He peered into the drawer next to my bed and was, I'm sure, unpleasantly surprised to find no comics but instead a plethora of Irn-Bru bottles filled with piss.

Lovely. Fucking lovely.

The next morning as we waited for the bus to get to my college to record, Dominic enquired as to what we would have for breakfast. 'Crisps,' I cheerfully replied and went into a corner shop to procure our breakfast of fried potatoes from a bag. Dominic looked somewhat dazed as he consumed his. He confided that until that moment he'd never eaten crisps for breakfast. Dominic still stayed with his folks and wasn't au fait with the semi-feral ways that we had developed as teenagers staying away from home. Conversely, one night at Dominic's his mum made us scallops for dinner. I'd never tasted seafood in my life, and only ate them because I had no idea what they were. I think I thought it was pasta. With the bottles of piss and crisps for breakfast, it's a miracle that Dominic didn't get on the first bus back to Glasgow.

There were three songs on the demo: 'Summer', which was largely instrumental, and two more straightforward affairs. One was an indie pop song called 'Citrus', featuring a lamentable amount of bird noise samples (it's good to get the terrible ideas out of your system as soon as humanly possible). The other was quite a long song with a dramatic ending, simply called 'D'. Not the first and certainly not the last song I'd write and be too lazy to give a name to. The demo was a patchy affair but there were enough ideas to at least get us a gig, and more importantly a full-time drummer.

Upon leaving college I officially became unemployed. When my first giro cheque arrived I went straight out and bought a silver RAK delay guitar effects pedal. This would become absolutely integral to the music I'd be making in the years (and decades) to come. It essentially echoes every note that you play, allowing you to build and build your part to a cacophonous crescendo. A fantastic example of government spending done well. I also said goodbye to Edinburgh and moved back to Lanarkshire to stay with my parents. After two years of living a *Lord of the Flies* existence, it was really nice to have somewhere warm to stay where there would always be food to eat. In all honesty, I also missed my parents and being close to my girlfriend Adele.

The next step was to find someone to play drums for our newly born two-thirds of a power trio. We did what every aspiring musician seeking a bandmate did in the pre-internet age – we placed an ad in the *NME*. This proved extremely unsuccessful, as we only had one enquiry. I'm guessing that joining a band influenced by The Cure, My Bloody Valentine and Slint wasn't that appealing a prospect in 1995. The one person who did reply asked what the monthly wage would be upon joining the band. You might as well have been asking us what the water tastes like on Mars. We were so far removed from the concept of making money from music that this notion seemed ridiculous. His question clearly indicated that he wasn't our guy.

Around this time I had an idea for someone who might fit the bill. A few years previously at high school in Strathaven, I had met a wee ginger guy called Martin Bulloch. He lived in the nearby village of Chapelton and was friends with some of my school pals. I'd had a faint recollection of Martin saying he was a drummer. The last time I'd met Martin had been at a party in Rutherglen where we all took acid and had a jam session playing Cure covers in someone's bedroom. Martin was a really sound guy. Bespectacled with bright red hair, and though he was no taller than me, he gave off the energy of someone not to be trifled with. Martin had grown up in East Kilbride, which isn't the friendliest place in the world. I'm sure he had to have his wits about him as a kid. Martin was super dependable and being in a band with good people was at the absolute top of my list of requirements. He'd also had a heart pacemaker since he was a kid. The youngest person in the UK ever to receive one apparently. I remember bonding with Martin over our shared love of David Bowie and The God Machine. Martin had even seen the latter live – something I'm eternally jealous of as they'd disbanded in 1994, just as their second album was released, due to the death of their bass player, Jimmy. Martin had heard from his pals that I was a really good guitar player. A rumour that was probably started by me . . .

I called Martin to ask if he'd be interested in joining the band, but unfortunately he wasn't home. He was actually at Glastonbury. His mum passed on my message when he returned and he called me straight back. We arranged to have a rehearsal the following day. Not many people just back from an 800-mile round trip would be so keen. I was impressed by his enthusiasm.

We met up to play at my parents' house. The place was always full of telescopes and sometimes clearing a space big enough to practise could be tricky. My folks' house was always lively, with three dogs and the constant flow of my dad's eccentric pals, who were always swinging by to chat for hours on end about every subject imaginable. It was never a dull place, and having a rock band practising in the hall was par for the course. It was also far enough into the countryside that no one would complain about us making a racket.

When Martin turned up he was fairly chipper, if a little bedraggled from his Glastonbury trip. He'd been playing in a punk band called The Divers and – not being particularly into fast songs and shouting – wanted to do something different. Dominic told me a while later that he was quite taken aback by the Oasis sticker on the bass drum of Martin's red Pearl drum kit. At this point he was a lot more into mainstream indie than me or Dominic, but I knew that Martin was into good music and, way more importantly, a decent, reliable person.

Thankfully when we played, it sounded good, in that we could play our instruments just about to the point where it could be described as music. I'd never had any interest in virtuosity. All of my favourite bands, such as The Velvet Underground, The Jesus and Mary Chain and Joy Division, learnt to play the music they wanted and needed to make as opposed to playing music to show off how well they could play. We already had a handful of songs and Martin slotted in perfectly. He wasn't a pro by any means, but his economic style really fitted the music and having him join the band was a no-brainer.

With Martin on board we jumped headfirst into rehearsing as often as we could. Martin's incredibly accommodating parents, Cecilia and Graham, drew the short straw as we ended up rehearsing mostly in Martin's bedroom at their house in Blantyre. This was good, too, because Blantyre is conveniently located roughly halfway between Bearsden, where Dominic lived, and the Clyde Valley where I was staying at my folks. I should mention at this juncture that from day one it was absolutely imperative that we played as loud as possible. At all times. Always. Deafening. One of my most vivid memories of this time was finishing our song 'Lower' in a cacophony of feedback and watching a jar of coins on Martin's bedroom floor glide across the room, magically floating from the ferocity of the vibrations. We'd play so loud that my head would feel weird for hours afterwards. His parents were incredibly accommodating.

When it came to organising our debut gig, the first person we spoke to was Alex Huntley. He'd been so supportive of Deadcat Motorbike. He even invited us to play a show when he heard John Peel would be there (to watch Urusei Yatsura). I gave Peel a tape that night and even though he didn't play it, we kept in touch.

As well as the connection with Alex, The 13th Note was the place that all of our friends played. They didn't charge you to play so it was possible to play there over and over again. It's how bands improved. It also took away any financial risk of putting on a gig. Towards the end of my time in Edinburgh I'd taken to coming to Glasgow to see as many bands at The 13th Note as possible, getting the bus or driving my barely roadworthy brown Vauxhall Chevette the hour-long journey along the M8. I'd go and see bands like Bis, Pink Kross, The Blisters and the like as often as I could. It was such an exciting time. It's incredible how many talented musicians came through this venue and went on to make glorious music.

Tuesdays were The Kazoo Club and entry was free. Thursday was the 99p Club, with 99p being the entry cost, unsurprisingly. Alex was kind enough to offer us a slot at The Kazoo Club, playing with a band he suggested and that I adored, Trout. It's quite hard to describe Trout because they genuinely were the most incredibly weird, hilarious and genius bands of all time, but I'm going to try. William Rogan, the singer, had a very unusual stage look. His hair was like a cross between Shaggy from *Scooby Doo* and Joey Ramone. He painted around his eyes in the style of a superhero. Or a panda. The bass player, Steenson, and the drummer, Kenny, both looked really normal. Looks can, they say, be deceptive. Neither of them was remotely normal. They were (and are) eccentric, funny, talented guys. They had songs like 'Skunk Rap' (CHICKEN CHICKEN CHICKEN CHICKEN, MONKEY MONKEY MONKEY MONKEY) and 'Living In An Oven'. They were unique. Coming from Glasgow's East End, their humour was born from being the only weirdos in a fairly rough area. They remain to this day one of the best bands I've ever seen. We were all excited to be sharing the stage with them.

With the gig booked (less than two months after our first full band rehearsal) we stepped up our practice schedule. We practised as often as we could, often for hours at a time. If we could only manage one hour then we'd do that. We were incredibly dedicated, and although Martin had a job working in a Chinese restaurant in East Kilbride, me and Dominic had plenty of free time.

We'd written a few more songs to go with the three we'd re-corded on the Edinburgh demo, as well as a few covers: 'New Dawn Fades' by Joy Division and 'It's All Over' by The God Ma-chine. Our newest songs, 'Tuner' and 'Lower', seemed a bit of a step up from the songs we'd demoed. 'Tuner' was a Pavement-esque ballad and 'Lower' was a lot thrashier, somewhere between Swervedriver and Sonic Youth. Our final rehearsal was back at my parents' house – in the hall this time, because my dad needed the living room for something telescope related. We'd got into decent shape and were ready for the gig.

We made the decision not to play 'Citrus' the next night. We all decided it was shite. A fairly ruthless attitude to what is or isn't good enough has always been an important part of what we've done. Another memory from the final rehearsal before the show was Dominic and Martin having a car race around Strathclyde Park. I can't recall who won, but it captures the way we've always managed to have fun and not take anything too seriously. Apart from the music. We always took that seriously. From the first day we had an almost religious drive to make something really special – music with permanence. We'd grown up with music that meant so much to us and wanted to do something that stood in comparison with it.

On the day of the gig itself, Martin came straight from work to my parents' to pick up his drums and drive us all to The 13th Note. Despite months of intense, studious preparation for our first ever gig, me and Dominic decided the best plan for the evening was to get a bottle of Lambrini (extremely cheap fizzy white wine) each and drink them both in the car on the way to the sound-check. It might have been nerves but more than likely the actual reason was traditional adolescent idiocy. We were obviously seri-ous art rockers, but still simultaneously fulfilling the role of daft teenage boys. The soundcheck was a doddle. Our set-up at this point consisted of three pedals: one distortion for Dominic, one distortion for me, and my trusty government-sponsored delay pedal. Alex Huntley was doing our sound that night. As charming as Alex could be, he was also someone not to be messed with. I'd seen him fell someone – a particularly obnoxious singer from a Manic Street Preachers copycat band called The Cyanide Dolls – with one punch for messing with the mics at The 13th Note, so I already knew not to mistake politeness for softness. I'd get to know the two Cyanide Dolls who didn't get punched years later when they became Arab Strap's rhythm section.

After the soundcheck we hung out at the venue waiting for the friends and family that we'd invited. Adele, Victoria and her boyfriend Jared were there, as well as my pal Keiron Mellote from Edinburgh. Martin had a bunch of his pals there, plus a smattering of folks from other bands: Eska (with whom I was now playing drums) and members of The Yummy Fur.

As well as Trout there was another band on the bill called The Forensics. With an average age of fifteen, it's a miracle they were allowed into the venue never mind onto the stage. They played a youthful, noisy, lo-fi inspired set. Then it was Trout's turn.

Trout were on imperious form as always. William sang like a man possessed on 'Owl In A Tree' (a song about an owl asking what time it was) and 'UFO' (an improvised song about aliens that had a fantastic Glitter Band stomp to it). They were amazing.

When it was our turn to play we scooped our pedals out of carrier bags and plugged them in on the ominously dark stage. We had written an instrumental intro which had a Mary Chain-like swing to it and played that before segueing into our new thrashy song, 'Lower'. There was an intensity way beyond anything I'd experienced in my previous bands. We were raw but managed to create something more than the sum of its parts. When we played 'Summer', now a fully formed instrumental shorn of the random screaming vocals of the demo, it all seemed to click. Something about the guitar line over Dominic's picked bass and Martin's long drum roll leading the crescendo just worked. In that song we had found a voice for ourselves. As well as the handful of our own songs, we also played a cover version of 'New Dawn Fades' by Joy Division. With a repeated four-chord sequence, it reflected a lot of what we were trying to do. Covering a song from one of the greatest debut albums by one of the greatest rock bands of all time was quite a ballsy move, but we were so high on youthful exuberance that that consideration wouldn't have even crossed our minds. It was just a good song by a band we liked. When you're a teenager you live in the moment and do whatever seems like a good idea.

We ended the set with our song 'D' and its jammed-out epic ending, me and Dominic bashing away at our pedals and strings like maniacs while Martin leathered seven shades of shit out of his cymbals. It felt cathartic in a way that sometimes comes from knowing you haven't played as well as you wanted. But we were exactly where we wanted to be and the noise we were making was something real. Undefinable, as the best music always is, but definitely tangible.

After we played we hung out with our friends and the other bands at the Note. When the pub shut and everyone was given their marching orders, Dominic, Adele and I, accompanied by William, Steenson and Kenny from Trout, headed up to Victoria's flat in Glasgow's West End. It was a big flat that she shared with Jared and her friend, Louise. I'd go up there a lot after gigs in Glasgow and it was a good feeling to be going there after one I'd played. I was no stranger to their couch and they were gracious hosts. Everyone had a good time drinking, staying up late and reflecting on the night.

It had been a whirlwind couple of months – from having no band and nothing to do, to having a sense of purpose for the first time in my life. We were blissfully unaware that tonight's gig would be the first of thousands we would play together for decades to come. At the time it felt exciting and no end of fun, but I had no idea how far the racket me, Dominic and Martin had managed to conjure would take us. No idea at all.

8.

Rock Action

After our first gig at the Note, we never looked back.

Alex got in touch soon afterwards and asked us to play again. He was always supportive of young bands that kicked against the mainstream and we definitely benefited from his pro-youth agenda. We continued to rehearse as often as we could and started writing more and more music. As happy as we were with our first few shows, we felt we had a long way to go and could get much better.

I'd go to Dominic's house as often as possible and we'd work on music whenever we could. Even though Dominic's subdued and outwardly serious demeanour seemed the polar opposite to my gregarious nature, we got on very well and it was the start of a great friendship. We'd stay up till absurd hours writing tunes and listening to records. The Sonic Youth album *Washing Machine* had just been released and we were completely besotted with it, the song 'The Diamond Sea' in particular. At twenty minutes long it was an epic, with huge swathes of droning guitars that built to a crescendo then seamlessly collapsed back into the main part of the song. Dominic figured out that his dad's turntable would play backwards if you just spun the deck in the opposite direction. We'd play it backwards and then forwards and then backwards again, while inflicting as much damage on his parents' wine collection as we could. Their house was pretty cavernous, and with Dominic's dad working away most of the time, his mum would just let us get on with it. We'd also endlessly watch the Sonic

Youth tour film *The Year Punk Broke*, which documented their festival run four years earlier in 1991 – the year I'd seen them play
Reading with Nirvana. There was actual footage of that day in the
film. It was our dream to go out on a festival tour, playing with
bands we loved every day, though at this point it was nothing
more than drunken teenage chat. For that to actually happen
seemed the stuff of fantasy.

I'd moved back in with my folks when I finished college but that
wasn't to last too long. With the band getting a bit more serious
I wanted to be in the city. As well as keeping myself super busy
doing Mogwai with Martin and Dominic, I'd also volunteered
to step in on drums for another of my pals' bands – Eska. Their
drummer Martin Donnelly had had enough and they needed a
replacement. I gleefully announced that I could play drums. In
retrospect, I was somewhat overstating my abilities. I had barely
played since school and, even then, hardly at all since a friend of
a friend had borrowed my kit, never to be seen again. Thankfully
such minor details didn't get in the way of me becoming their
drummer.

Eska had been going since the guys in the band had been at
school, and they were pretty established in the Glasgow scene.
They'd even made a single. I joined the band just before the single
came out and I played at the launch gig. Back then the norm was
for bands to have single launch gigs where the entry fee would
include a copy of the record. This worked out well as the money
from the gig would help with the manufacturing costs and the
chance of getting left with a pile of unsold records was greatly
diminished. Eska's single wasn't on their own label, however – it
was on a label started by another Glasgow band, Urusei Yatsura,
called Modern Independent. As well as the label, Urusei also
ran a fanzine called *Kitten Frenzy*. With their name taken from
a Japanese Manga comic and their sound heavily influenced
by American indie rock like Pavement and Sonic Youth, they
were starting to get known outside of Glasgow too, having even

recorded a session for John Peel. It was through Eska that I'd get to know them.

The guys in Eska were all really sound. I'd known Colin for as long as I'd known Dominic, whereas Chris, the other singer and guitar player, and Kenny, the bass player, were relatively new pals. We all got on really well and I enjoyed playing with them, though I'm not sure I took it as seriously as I should have. I'd sometimes pretend that the drumsticks were devil horns and I had a tendency to jump a few feet off the stool when I hit the cymbals. I like to think that what I lacked in technical proficiency I made up for in entertainment value.

After playing in Eska for a few months, Kenny and I hatched a plan to get a flat together in Glasgow. Kenny was staying with his parents in the southside but wanted to get somewhere a bit closer to town. Kenny's girlfriend Vic played in a great all-female punk band called Pink Kross, and she told us that Geraldine, their bass player, was also looking for flatmates. The three of us found a flat to rent in Finnieston. Back then, Finnieston was a touch edgy. The local kids used to come down and smash all the windows in the corner shop every Friday night. The actual flat itself left a bit to be desired too. There was a hole in the living room floor where you could actually peer down into the flat below. There was also a problem with the heating. It was actually more than a problem: there was no heating. But being a veteran of Baltic flats from my Edinburgh experience, I was fine with that.

Issues aside, we had a great time there. Geraldine was a lovely person and, being a few years older than me and Kenny, probably got endless amusement from our perpetual teenage dysfunction. As squalid as our flat was, none of our pals seemed to mind. It became the place where everyone would end up whenever we all got chucked out of wherever we were hanging out. It wasn't unusual for hordes of people from Nice N Sleazy, The 13th Note or the Art School Union to pile back to ours to stay up late drinking till all hours. Geraldine was also seemingly the only person in

the entire scene who owned a bass amp and as she was a generous person, folk would borrow it all the time. The flat was always
a hive of social activity.

On the band front, we were making decent strides. We'd written a few more songs, alongside the ones we'd played at The 13th
Note, so musically things were starting to take shape. Unfortunately the only recording of the band was the demo made at my
college with Wee David on drums. We'd changed a lot since then
and no longer played any of his songs except 'Summer', and even
that had developed quite a bit from the loose jammy version we'd
done in Edinburgh. We wanted to record properly. Yet having
now left college, I no longer had access to free studio time. Studios cost money and we didn't have any.

Only Martin had a job. He was a chef at a Chinese restaurant
in East Kilbride – but he'd just bought a brand-new drum kit and
didn't have any spare cash. We were still rehearsing in Martin's
bedroom at his folks' house in Blantyre. Not only were his parents extremely accommodating putting up with the noise, but
they also offered to help us out with our recording conundrum.
Martin's twenty-first birthday was coming up and Graeme and
Cecilia offered to pay for our first recording as his present. We
found a studio in the city that we could afford called the Brill
Building. We booked one day with the engineer, Larry Primrose,
to record and mix three songs: 'Tuner', 'Lower' and the song we
played as our closer, 'D'. As the date approached we realised that
it coincided with Dominic's first day at college. He'd bombed out
the previous year but had promised his folks that he'd put more
effort in this year. That was a promise soon to be broken.

When we arrived at the Brill Building, we found Larry the
engineer to be a bit of a curmudgeon. For all our youthful enthusiasm he was the diametric opposite. He could barely muster
anything positive to say at all, spending most of the session complaining about other bands and life in general. Studio engineers
don't see a lot of the sun and that tends to make them a bit weird.

He was capable enough, though, and we managed to scramble through the three tracks quickly. Dominic couldn't stay around for the mixing because he had to head home and pretend that he'd been to college. It would seem that on day one, the battle between education and rock and roll had already been won by the latter.

With the three tracks recorded we had to decide what to do with them. Our ambition was to get played on John Peel. Our only other ambition was to play the Barrowlands. Not necessarily headline, just play there. Peel didn't play demos on the radio so we needed to make a record. Having had Martin's folks help out with the money for the recording, we couldn't ask them again. We worked out that we needed about £600 to make a seven-inch. We didn't have anywhere near that, but helpfully my sister's boyfriend Jared had just left his job and been given some money. He bought himself a new motorbike and then generously offered to lend us the leftover cash to make the record. We were sorted! We were going to make a record. We needed a name for the record label though. I suggested we use the nickname for Scott Asheton, the drummer from The Stooges – Rock Action.

We'd managed to record the songs and procure the funds to make a record. That seemed like the hard part taken care of, but there were other sides to being in a band, a lot of which we didn't have a clue about. Thankfully, soon all that stuff wouldn't be up to us because after our second gig we were approached by a tall, cumbersome chap called Colin and he offered to be our manager. He'd played in a band himself called Big Burd and also managed a highly entertaining band called the Johnny Seven, who played lounge covers in a shambolic fashion and wore matching comedy moustaches, the kind that someone would wear for a racially insensitive Halloween outfit as a Mexican bandit. I guess you had to be there . . .

Colin was an ambitious guy and said we had potential. To be honest, all we wanted to do was write music, put out records and play gigs. All the other stuff wasn't of any interest to us. Colin said that he had everything else covered, and that was good enough for us. He was hired.

Our biggest challenge was how to replicate live the sound of the music we'd recorded. On both the demo and the recording that was going to be our first single, I'd recorded a few guitar parts. Clearly, being in possession of only two hands, I couldn't manage to do it all live. The obvious solution to that predicament was to find someone else to play guitar. John Cummings had been at our first handful of gigs; he was a 13th Note regular and a fan of the incredible Trout, who had played at most of them. John was easily recognisable there, with his shocking mop of bleached blonde hair and tendency to wear a kilt, which wasn't (and still isn't) particularly normal attire even in Glasgow. John was not the most proficient player but had a guitar and was into a lot of the same music as us. It seemed like a good fit. At the University of Glasgow studying physics, his attitude to education wasn't too dissimilar to that of Dominic. Although extremely bright academically, John was way more interested in music than studying.

Missing the first day of college set the tone for Dominic's second attempt at his graphic design course. To say that his heart wasn't in it would be an understatement. In fact, after a few weeks he'd abandoned going in altogether. When he went into town, supposedly to attend college, he'd entertain himself by going ten pin bowling on his own or pottering around the record shops. When me and Kenny got our flat he'd come up and hang out. One day though, having seen neither hide nor hair of Dominic, the college called his house to ask why he hadn't attended for months. This was of course news to his mum, and she took it upon herself to investigate where he'd been going every day instead of college.

Me and Dominic weren't actually at home when his mum came round to find him. It was just Kenny. At this point Kenny had long blue hair and weighed about six stone. He wasn't exactly a picture of health. Our flat was also far from homely. It had definite squat vibes. It was a shithole. When his mum eventually caught up with him, as well as being extremely disappointed that Dominic hadn't been to college, she was also seriously unimpressed with the environment his friends were living in. It would be fair to say that Dominic's mum wasn't overly keen on him hanging around with us. She wanted him to continue with his education and I think she saw us as a barrier to that happening. In fairness, Dominic wasn't interested in college at all and wouldn't be going whatever the alternatives were.

Despite my ropey drumming, things were looking up for Eska. After the single on Urusei's label, another label got in touch with the band to see if they could release something. Love Train was run by a gregarious, bespectacled American woman with bright red hair called Lisa Paulon. Lisa's incredibly well-connected boyfriend Simon Williams wrote for the *NME* and had his own label, Fierce Panda. Her day job was running the European operations for Sub Pop. Being teenagers who'd grown up idolising Mudhoney and Nirvana, anyone connected to Sub Pop was clearly a big deal. Despite the corny name, Love Train was a great label. They only released 7s but the bands they'd released to date were special. Broadcast, Hood and Flying Saucer Attack: some of the best bands around. The underground scene then was really strong. Another band that had put music out on Love Train was Bob Tilton, a Nottingham hardcore band named after a US TV preacher. Bob Tilton refused to play on stages and had one of the most intense singers I'd ever seen, truly a force of nature.

Putting a single out on Love Train seemed like a big deal. It was unusual for bands from Glasgow to attract much attention from outside the city. Urusei Yatsura had closed a deal with the London label Che and had a Peel Session, but that seemed like a bit of an outlier. Usually, bands in Glasgow didn't get much attention at all.

Having agreed to record the single, Lisa invited us to play a show she'd arranged at the Dublin Castle in London. The Dublin

Castle was in the (at that time) most happening part of London – Camden. We piled into the back of a transit van to head down south. Not a splitter van with seats and a table. A regular van like 'A Man with a Van' uses to move furniture around. A family friend of Colin's, Eska's singer, filled in as driver at the last minute because our regular driver couldn't make it. He was already quite nervous driving a van, but his nerves were about to get a hell of a lot worse. When we were barely out of Scotland one of the tyres blew, sending the van careering all over the road. The amps were piled up precariously high in the back of the van while we huddled among our bags. The motion of the near-crash sent the bass amp, a heavy-as-fuck Ampeg SVT, off its perch and it landed on Kenny's head. We all thought it had killed him but thankfully it landed at an angle, meaning that Kenny's face was left unscathed. It was a dreadful way to start my first ever trip to London to play music. After a lengthy walk to someone's house to use their phone, we managed to get a mechanic to repair the tyre and soldiered on. The seven-hour drive seemed endless, with everyone still reeling from the trauma of the near-crash.

When we got to London, spirits lifted at the prospect of the gig. I really enjoyed playing the drums and loved the lack of pressure playing in someone else's band. The gig went really well, and it was great to meet Lisa. Confident and funny, she seemed to know absolutely everyone and had an extremely irreverent attitude to pretty much everything. After the gig we met loads of Lisa's pals, many of whom were journalists for *Melody Maker* and *NME*. I wasn't shy in telling everyone I met that I had my own band, Mogwai, and that we had a single coming out soon. I even gave Lisa a tape. We headed home in the van, happy at how our first excursion to London had gone. I'd bent enough people's ears about my 'other' band and I hoped that when Mogwai finally made it down to London I could persuade a few of them to come along.

On the Mogwai front, things were rolling along nicely. Having chosen the two songs for the single – the Pavement-influenced ballad 'Tuner' and the more thrashy 'Lower' – we had to decide what to put on the front cover. Thankfully my partner in teenage delinquency, Neale Smith, provided the answer to that quandary. Neale had left school with one Higher, in art, and had taken to photography with a passion. Neale said he was happy for us to use one of his photos and we chose an enigmatic shot of a barely recognisable man walking through an underpass. I wanted it to look modern, like record sleeves of bands like Codeine and Slint, but I also wanted it to echo the new wave bands that I'd grown up with, like Joy Division and The Sisters of Mercy. I had the photo in the middle of the sleeve, with our name at the top left of the photo and the song names at the bottom right. It would be one colour, which was cheapest to print, with fold-over sleeves which we got printed by an anarchist printer in Glasgow. We found a place in the Czech Republic that pressed vinyl and sent off the DAT of the songs. There was an option to have test pressings made but we didn't have the money for that.

The next issue was finding someone to distribute the record. Some bands would just take copies by hand around all the record shops in Glasgow, but our ambitions were broader than that. This was really the first thing that Colin had to do for the band, as most of his time up to that point had been spent trying to stop us agreeing to every single gig offer we received. Apparently playing every two weeks in your hometown wasn't the 'done thing'. He also encouraged us to take a few months off playing gigs, to rehearse as much as we could so that we were sounding great for when the record came out. Colin sent tape copies of the single around all of the record distributors in the UK. He really struggled though. Apparently our list of influences wasn't that appealing to most. He lost count of the number of times he was told no one wanted another band that sounded like Slint. If only we were actually good enough to sound like Slint! Eventually Colin found a distributor willing to take a chance on us: Southern

Records Distribution. SRD was an institution in indie music, distributing labels like Fugazi's Dischord Records. We were thrilled that they wanted to work with us. Harry, our contact there, was really enthusiastic about us. He was a very tall, rather droll chap with an absolute passion for music. It was a great fit.

Finally, we got the call that our records had arrived and we had to get to Glasgow Airport to collect them. Dominic drove over in his red Polo. We couldn't wait to get a copy and listen to it. The sleeves were already in a pile of boxes at my mum's. After some confusion discovering where we had to go to collect them, we loaded up the car and headed up to Dominic's folks' as fast as we could. It was the first time any of us had had any music we'd made actually pressed onto vinyl. Up at Dom's we stuck the record on and listened. Hearing the needle get in the groove and play back the song we'd written in my parents' front room was an indescribable feeling. Thankfully there was nothing wrong with the pressing, as we didn't have the money to get them re-pressed if there had been. We then got on with the job of folding up the card sleeves, putting them in clear plastic bags and inserting the records. It seemed to take an age but we were so excited about the whole operation that we didn't really mind.

With records assembled, we had to work out what we were going to do with them. The very first thing I wanted to do (obviously) was get one to John Peel. Having a record played on his show had been a dream ever since I was a kid. I'd also met him briefly when Alex had asked Deadcat Motorbike to play at a show the previous year, so I presumed that he would at the very least give it a listen. The other people we sent copies to were two bands that we were really into at the time – The God Machine and Swervedriver. The God Machine were a band that we all loved, particularly an epic B-side of theirs called 'Pictures Of A Bleeding Boy'. We'd sit after rehearsals and listen to it at deafening volumes in total awe of the epic, emotional heaviness of the song. Robin, The God Machine's singer, also had a label called

The Flower Shop. If there was a label we wanted to be on, that was it. We took a handful of copies for friends and family (we definitely needed to make sure Jared got one since he'd donated £400 to its existence), and we sent the rest to SRD. I really hoped they wouldn't be getting sent back to us a few months down the line.

Things with Eska were also progressing. Lisa Paulon invited us back to London to record for Love Train, and we had been asked to do a session for *The Evening Session* of Radio 1. We also had another gig at the Hope and Anchor. For this trip I made sure to bring a bunch of copies of the Mogwai 'Tuner/Lower' single with me. It's all well and good *telling* people about my other band, but having an actual record was a million times more substantial.

Recording the BBC session with Eska was an eye-opener. In the indie scene no one really cared that my drumming was fairly amateurish, but the seasoned engineers at the famous Maida Vale Studios were way less forgiving. I recall the producer stopping us mid-take, coming through to the live room, pointing to the middle of the snare drum and telling me to hit it there. It's a good job I've got thick skin! Also during the London trip we were interviewed for *NME*'s new band section, ON, by a writer called James Oldham. I got on well with James straight away – he was only a few years older than us and had an impish grin and a dark past as a goth, something I could definitely relate to. I made sure to give James a copy of Mogwai's single, and one to Lisa as well of course. I was enjoying playing with Eska but didn't feel that it was something I wanted to do forever. I was taking things with Mogwai really seriously, and truth be told, Eska probably deserved a drummer who was fully dedicated to the band and actually owned some drums. I was really happy with my contribution to the single we recorded, and despite the chastisement I'd experienced during the session recording, I was pleased with how it had turned out. More importantly, I was happy with the experience and the people I was meeting.

Things were starting to get really exciting with Mogwai. We didn't hear anything back from The God Machine or Swervedriver, but we did hear back from John Peel's producer, who told us that he was going to play our single! It's hard to describe how elated I was to hear that news. I'd grown up listening to his show and this was the first time something was happening to us that I could directly equate to the bands I'd grown up with and adored. A single play on Peel had been our main ambition, so to realise that less than a year after forming the band was incredible. We couldn't wait to hear ourselves on the radio. John Peel playing 'Tuner' gave us an amazing confidence boost. We were sure of the music we were making, but this made everything feel slightly more . . . real. Such was the importance of this to me that I took a photograph of BBC Ceefax (an incredibly primitive version of the internet, I suppose) to show that it had actually happened. I started to wonder if one day he might invite us to record a session . . .

As if Peel playing the single wasn't enough excitement, there was more to come. James Oldham, the ex-goth *NME* writer that I'd befriended when playing in London with Eska, had included 'Tuner/Lower' in his singles review column. We were in the *NME*! It was a typically irreverent *NME* review but definitely positive, mentioning great bands like Sonic Youth and Bark Psychosis, and even mentioning the 'long forgotten' band The Telescopes. I loved that especially because they had been the first band I'd seen at the Barrowlands when they opened for the Mary Chain six years earlier.

By the time 1996 rolled around, we'd been playing quite a lot around Glasgow and even occasionally heading through to Edinburgh. We'd made it onto the bill with an incredible band from Dayton, Ohio, called Brainiac. They were hands down the weirdest and most engaging band I'd seen. Their singer, Timmy, was like a spasmodic Iggy Pop and the music was straight-up weird. Super melodic but incredibly obtuse. They were also really sweet people. We were just kids but they were really kind to us. Our paths would cross a lot over the next few years. Our by-now four-piece line-up was getting better all the time. One thing that was changing, however, was the make-up of the type of songs in our set. When we started, about half the songs had singing, but it was now sliding more into the instrumental category. 'Summer' was definitely our best song and we'd written a few more instrumentals that were working way better than those with vocals. Colin was working away in the background trying to make connections and find opportunities for us, and one that seemed to be coming together was with the London indie label Che Records, the label Urusei Yatsura were on. As Colin was good friends with them, he had managed to get our music to the people at Che, who were interested in potentially working with us. Through that connection we got our first ever gig outside Scotland. We were going to play in London at The Monarch, the first band on of three. The other two bands were both on Che: The Bardots and Glasgow's own Urusei Yatsura.

As well as the two songs from our first single, we'd also introduced a few more songs into our live set. 'A70', named after the road between Edinburgh and Lanark where me and Dominic had seen a UFO, and a song that we never got round to naming called 'Dom's Song'. It was clear that our instrumental songs were becoming more prevalent. We'd abandoned our old closer, 'D', and finished the set with another new song called 'Angels Vs Aliens', which was named after a chapter in a great comic that me and Dominic were into called *Seekers into the Mystery*. We had a real obsession with UFOs at that point, particularly after seeing weird lights in the sky on that backroad in Edinburgh. We'd stopped the car when we saw them and stood in awe as the glowing craft silently passed around us before disappearing behind a hill. I'd read that Hendrix used to get people to keep watch while he was playing to see if his music was attracting aliens. I was into this idea but never managed to find anyone willing to take up the duties. I doubt anyone took me seriously. I really was though. There had been a spate of UFO sightings in Scotland around this time, particularly in a town near Falkirk called Bonnybridge. People were so alarmed by the frequency of these sightings that they wanted to know what their local politicians were doing about it. A public meeting was called, so me and Dominic went along. It was a pretty rowdy affair – think pitchfork-wielding villagers demanding to know what the fuck's going on at Frankenstein's castle. It was a genuinely surreal experience made all the more bizarre by a couple of guys our age determined to disrupt proceedings in any way they could by taking the piss and heckling all the politicians. Years later I found out it was Aidan and Malcolm from Arab Strap.

We were all excited about our first venture out of the country, but there were a few issues we had to consider. In theory, I was the only full-time band member. Dominic and John were ostensibly in further education, which they were giving scant regard to. Martin, on the other hand, had actually finished college and was now working in a Chinese restaurant. His bosses weren't particularly accommodating, however, and he needed to be back in East Kilbride the day after the London gig to open up the restaurant. We would need to leave after we played to drive back to Scotland. At least that stopped us worrying about where we were going to stay. Urusei kindly said we could use their drums and amps, meaning that we wouldn't need to hire a van. The plan was set. We would drive down to London, all five of us in my mum's white Vauxhall Astra, and drive home as soon as we finished playing.

The Astra wasn't the biggest car and it was a bit of a tight squeeze getting all five of us in for the drive down. We didn't mind too much because it was such an adventure. It was a beautiful, sunny day and I was psyched at the thought of playing our music in a totally different environment. We hadn't been going that long but it already felt like we'd played most of the places that a band like us could play in Scotland. We'd even been up to the Highlands to play in Inverness, a rather eventful, drunken gig at a working men's club. Playing in London was entirely new and held countless opportunities (and hazards). At this point, Scotland didn't have much of a music industry. There had been flashes here and there, with cool labels like Fast and Postcard, but nothing had much staying power. Back then, if bands were serious they tended to up sticks and head to London. We didn't intend on doing that, but fully realised that to get noticed to the point where people all over the world knew our music, we had to make an impact in London. We didn't want to mess it up. We also didn't want to play to no one. In Glasgow you could always rely on a bunch of your friends to come and see you, especially when you're a teenager. In London, we didn't know anyone and didn't know if getting played on Peel and having a single review in *NME* would be enough to get people to come out to see us.

We left first thing in the morning. Picking everyone up individually, it took ages just to get on our way. With five people and all our guitars, pedals and cymbals, not only were we crammed in like sardines but the car was so overloaded it couldn't go very fast. It was a beautiful day, and even though it took about eight hours we were in pretty good spirits and the time flew by quickly.

We got to London late in the afternoon. The venue was in Camden, which at that point was the epicentre of the music scene. After loading our guitars into the venue we dispersed to have a look around. Camden was chock full of small venues with gigs on every night, and had a ton of cool little record shops and other unusual places. Prince had opened a boutique selling all sorts of insanely expensive stuff with his emblem on it, which intrigued Dominic because he was a huge fan, though everything was well out of our price range. We found a bar with seats outside. Hanging out in the sunshine waiting for soundcheck felt beautiful. It had only been a few short months since me and Dominic had scrabbled together that first demo at my college in Edinburgh, but it felt like so much had happened already. I wasn't totally content though. I believed our music was special and wanted as many people as possible to hear it; that what we were doing had a substance to it that I didn't hear in a lot of other music at the time, particularly in the mainstream. There was a good underground scene and we felt an affinity with bands back in Glasgow, and further afield, in Leeds and Bristol and with bands like Hood, Flying Saucer Attack and Third Eye Foundation. The mainstream, however, was a different story. It was hideous. Britpop was at its peak, the complete antithesis of everything we cared for. It lacked imagination, beauty and scope. It was also completely reliant on the past. I loved music that looked to the future, and seeing people ape The Kinks and Small Faces seemed deathly dull. This felt like an opportunity to demonstrate what we could do. There was a definite snobbery towards Scottish music and this was a chance to show people what was happening.

After our wee adventure around Camden we headed back to the venue for soundcheck. Soundchecks didn't tend to take too long back then because we didn't have that much equipment to check; generally, about 10 per cent of the time was spent checking our instruments and the rest arguing with the sound man about the volume. Since day one we had been very loud. Seeing bands like My Bloody Valentine, Sonic Youth and The Jesus and Mary Chain had been massive for me, and I wanted to have that kind of impact. Music had to be a physical experience. You had to actually feel the music, and for that to happen it needed to be loud. This was rarely a view held by sound guys at venues. To be fair, their priority was protecting the equipment and avoiding a migraine, but that wasn't our problem. We were always insistent. They'd often tell me to turn my distortion pedal down, but I'd just pretend to and eventually they gave up.

After soundcheck we said hello to the other bands. I knew Urusei because Eska had played with them, but it was the first time the others had met. We were grateful to them for lending us their gear, so passed on our thanks. While we chatted and nervously pottered around, Colin sorted out the guest list. He said that quite a few people were coming down, implying that we should try to play to the best of our abilities.

The Monarch is a typical old English pub with the top floor converted into a venue. Essentially a black box of a room with a bar at the back. It felt a bit more fancy than downstairs at The 13th Note, where you played on the floor. We were the first of the three bands to play. Not an ideal slot but, given that we had to drive all the way back to Scotland after the gig, we weren't complaining. As I was helping Colin with the driving, I abstained from drinking, though the rest of the band had a few beers, probably out of nerves more than anything, because we knew it was an important show. When the doors opened, thankfully a few people came in. In the back of my mind I'd considered the doomsday scenario of us driving 400 miles and back to play to no one. It wouldn't be the first time that had happened to a band from Scotland. I recognised a few friendly faces, one of them being Lisa from Love Train. I was super pleased to see her. Not only because she was an incredibly fun person, but also because getting a Mogwai single released on Love Train was something I really wanted to happen. I said hi and continued to mingle with the folk coming in. There wasn't a dressing room. We'd never played anywhere that had one.

After what seemed like an age, it was our turn to play. We opened our set with 'Summer', the first song we'd ever written. Looking out at a crowd featuring barely any familiar faces was an odd feeling. Up until that point, most of our gigs had been full of people we knew. People who would be pretty nice about us even if we didn't play great. Which wasn't so unusual – we were, after all, still finding our feet. But this felt different. We couldn't rely on our friends' kindness, and blowing it at our first gig outside of Scotland wasn't an option. We were confident in the music we were making but had high standards. Standards that we didn't always manage to maintain. 'Summer', with its bursts of noise and huge crescendo, was always a good start. Like a lot of our songs, it starts plaintively and suddenly changes direction. It always got people's attention. It had also come on dramatically since its inception when we made that first demo in Edinburgh.

As well as the two songs from our seven-inch, we played a new Tortoise-esque song, then the imaginatively titled 'Dom's Song' and 'A70', finishing with 'Angels Vs Aliens'. The closer started with an ambient drone before meandering into a two-chord pattern with abstract lyrics and a simple beat. Halfway through it went into a discordant riff reminiscent of the Louisville bands like Slint and Rodan we were getting into, finally descending into a tribal beat and a one-chord drone. I'd leave my guitar feeding back, then get on my knees and beat the hell out of a snare drum. We wouldn't always manage to synchronise the drums and the feedback cacophony, but we were probably the only people who'd notice. On that night we nailed it. The room was far from full, but we'd managed to hold the attention of everyone there.

After the noise died down we gathered our stuff and shuffled off the stage. We were really happy with how it had gone but mindful that we had a long drive ahead of us. Lisa accosted me when we were done and said that she'd loved it. She introduced me to her boyfriend Simon who ran the label Fierce Panda, which, amusingly, scored a big hit with a record of an audio interview with Liam and Noel Gallagher arguing, called *Wibbling Rivalry*. He seemed to have liked the gig too, which boded well. While preparing to go, Colin quickly introduced me to some of the people from Che Records, a big brash chap called Chris and a small Indian woman called Vinita. Chris seemed decent and I really warmed to Vinita. She'd worked with a lot of my favourite bands, like The Telescopes and Loop, and had an infectious smile and a true believer's enthusiasm for music. They enjoyed our gig and seemed keen on working with us. They'd been putting out a lot of split singles featuring the likes of fellow Glasgow bands Bis and The Delgados. It was great to have people interested. I was proud that we'd put out our first single ourselves but wasn't totally sure we could juggle playing in the band and spending all day folding record covers. At that point, my idea of what a record label actually was didn't really go much further than that.

Once we finally got out of the venue we squeezed back into my mum's car and started on the long road back to Scotland. I say long road, because we messed up straight away and drove the much longer route on the M1 towards Newcastle rather than the normal way via Birmingham on the M6. We'd realised the error too late to change to the correct route. By now it was getting really late and me and Colin were getting pretty tired. Not only had we gone the wrong and longer way, but we'd been banking on filling the car up with petrol en route to Birmingham. We were near Newcastle and the petrol light was on, and we had no idea when we'd find a service station open in the middle of the night. Colin was getting fairly delirious with exhaustion and wasn't dealing too well with the situation. He was making monkey noises. We were on the wrong road. It was going to take us hours longer to get home and we might end up stuck in the middle of nowhere having run out of petrol. Definite shades of *American Werewolf in London*.

Like a mirage in the desert, we finally saw a petrol station. Disaster averted. With the sun coming up, we finally reached Scotland just in time to drop Martin at his parents' so he could get out the door to go to work. No sleep till Hamilton. After that we were dropped off one by one. Since it was (kind of) my car, I was the last. I got back to my flat in Finnieston and climbed into bed, beyond shattered but happy that our trip to London had been a success. My gauge for success had been minimal: to get there and back in one piece and not get bottled off.

It was clear in the weeks after the Monarch gig that things were moving for us. Lisa's boyfriend Simon gave the gig a good review in *NME*. Lisa herself enquired if we'd put out our next single on Love Train, and the people from Che asked if we'd want to be part of a series of split singles they'd been putting out. It was an exciting time – and things were about to get even better.

9.

Enter the Capital

By now everything seemed to be clicking into place. New, exciting things were coming up almost every day.

We were going on our first tour, opening for Urusei Yatsura. We had actually also been invited to go to America to support the psychedelic band Ween, but not only did we not all have passports, we had no idea how we could possibly amass the funds to get there. This tour was far more manageable. It was a two-week jaunt around England's so-called toilet venues, the charming name given to places around 200 capacity, some of which had actually been public toilets before holding gigs. Most of these venues have, themselves, disappeared down the proverbial toilet. We shared travel and accommodation with the headliners. All eight band members and Colin squeezed into a minibus owned by a rather eccentric chap called Nick from Brighton. Me and Nick butted heads at every soundcheck because he wanted me to turn my distortion pedal down (an argument that he lost every time; I wasn't for backing down). Most nights we'd stay at the promoter's house or flat. As the support band we always ended up on the floor. Fergus, the singer, and Elaine, the bass player, from Urusei always ended up with the bed because they were a couple. None of us had any money at all so we were reliant on selling copies of 'Tuner' to provide funds for lunch each day. One night in Oxford we sold ten, which was monumental. That night we got one of the best receptions we'd ever had, a guy in the crowd shouting 'Tremendous!' in his big loud posh voice after a pretty underwhelming rendition of 'A70'. We'd reuse the phrase *ad nauseam* for years to come. Still do, in fact. We didn't always go down that well unfortunately. One night in Chelmsford after we played our first song no one clapped at all. At the time I thought they'd hated us but on reflection I think that they thought it was the soundcheck and were confused by the lack of singing. Who knows, it'll remain an eternal mystery. But we were having a blast and settled into the routine of driving to a new place, playing every night and getting drunk like ducks to water.

The final two nights of the tour were back in Glasgow at King Tut's, and in Dundee at a place called Lucifer's Mill. The Glasgow show was great, properly packed. I'd noticed a huge difference in the band just from playing every night. We definitely sounded better than ever before, and I remember a lot of people commenting on how different we sounded before and after the tour. We'd also managed to not wring each other's necks, which was a bonus. Being in close proximity with the same people for weeks at a time can be pretty stressful.

A few weeks after the tour proper ended we went back to London to play with Urusei again, this time at The Garage. The Garage was a different proposition altogether to the tiny venues we'd played so far. It was where a load of the touring bands we loved played when they came to London, and it was HUGE. Not being part of a normal tour, we had to make our own way there, so we took the bus down, travelling overnight and back to Glasgow the next day. I amused myself on the journey by staring out the window trying to spot UFOs. We were staying at Vinita from Che's house alongside another band on Che, Backwater from Belfast. Backwater were a great band and lovely guys too. The gig felt like a real celebration. We'd all bonded over the tour and Vinita was a great host. We partied all night with Backwater and some of the guys from Ash. We were in a sorry state by the time we got the bus back to Glasgow. Around that time I always wore a red Marks & Spencer cardigan that I'd found in a charity shop. Back at Vinita's, she gave me a matching blue one that I wore non-stop from then onwards.

Our bus journey coincided with the England v Scotland football game in the European Championships at Wembley, and no one on the bus knew what the score was. We'd heard a rumour that Scotland had won and witnessing the sea of comatose bodies strewn around the streets of Glasgow when we got back made us think the rumour was true. Sadly, it wasn't the case and England had won 2–0.

Ever since the Monarch gig it had become abundantly clear that Che wanted to sign us. *NME* had invited us to contribute a song to their *C96* compilation CD, a ten-year anniversary nod to their famous *C86* tape which had highlighted bands like Primal Scream, The Pastels and The Wedding Present, among others. Our track for it was to be 'A70' but we didn't have time to go into a studio so we recorded it at a soundcheck on the Urusei tour. When it came out we were disappointed that they'd used the wrong take, where the song comically fell apart at the end. One of our issues was that Dominic didn't actually own a bass, he was borrowing his big brother's. When it came to talking about signing us, this was mentioned to Che and they offered to lend him another bass. We weren't demanding a lot but I think this fell a good bit short of what we were expecting. Another disappointing thing was the split single itself. Che Records had paired us up with a band called Dweeb, whose sole reason for existence seemed to be copying our friends' band Bis, who were doing really well at the time, even getting onto *Top of the Pops*.

Our song for the split single, 'Angels Vs Aliens', turned out really well all the same. We'd recorded it with Paul Savage from The Delgados, who was a friend of Colin's. He worked in a studio in Hamilton just round the corner from where I'd taken my guitar lessons from Harry all those years ago. Harry had died a few years previously, sadly. He'd surely have thought it was cool that I was making a record a stone's throw from where he'd first showed me how to play 'Heroin' by The Velvets.

We were happy with how things had gone with Paul and decided to work with him again on our single for Love Train, which was to be 'Summer', the first song we'd written. For the B-side we recorded a new song, 'Ithica', which me and Dominic had written up at his house on an old acoustic with loads of strings missing. It was in a mad tuning we'd made up and had the biggest noise section we'd done so far. We were really excited about it. Paul was such an easy guy to record with. None of this 'turn your distortion down' whinging that I was getting very tired of hearing from soundmen (they were always men). He was enthusiastic about the music and, being a Lanarkshire native like me, we had a lot in common. By this point we'd really started to click. John had written a great new guitar part for 'Summer' and Martin's drumming was getting better all the time. We decided to use a real glockenspiel as opposed to the keyboard sound from the demo. However, none of us possessed a glockenspiel. I had the bright idea to get in touch with my old school music teacher, Mr Mackay, and ask to borrow one from the school, and thankfully he said yes. I'd been happy with what we'd done before but this really sounded great, closer to what we'd been aiming for. I was so excited for people to hear it.

After the Urusei tour, things calmed down. We continued to write and rehearse in Martin's bedroom in Blantyre all the time, working constantly on new music. Going on tour had been great but we felt like it was just the start and didn't want to stand still. Sometimes we'd write songs and bring them to the rest of the band, but most often songs would just materialise when we'd all be playing together. Back then we'd quite often swap instruments. I'd play bass and Dominic would play guitar for a lot of the time, though being so much shorter than Dominic I'd play sitting down because playing bass standing up was as difficult for me as it was comical to everyone else. It was while doing this that we magicked up something pretty special, the song that would end up as 'Helicon 1'. I was playing a bassline based on the rhythm of the Jane's Addiction song 'Summertime Rolls' but using different chords, Martin providing a swinging beat, totally unlike the strict 4/4 he normally played, with Dominic picking out melodic guitar through a delay pedal. As a band we always laugh at the scene from Oliver Stone's ridiculous movie about The Doors when they magically burst into 'Light My Fire', but this was as close to that as anything I remember. One second we were scratching away at our instruments and then a minute later we were making a glorious sound the likes of which we hadn't known before. There was something so utterly heartbreaking about the way the bass chords and the guitar melody played against each other, and then the sheer bombast of sound when we all came in loud and heavy during the second half of the song. It was really special and it had to be our next single. In the time since 'Tuner' we'd been approached by quite a few labels about releasing singles and the one that we definitely wanted to work with was called Wurlitzer Jukebox. Like Love Train they'd been putting out music by great bands like Pram, Stereolab, Broadcast and a fantastic outfit of fellow Glaswegians, Ganger. Keith, the guy who ran the label, had a day job managing a caravan park. He was as anti-music business as possible. We agreed he should put out our third single, 'New Paths Helicon'. We recorded it in Hamilton again, this time with the other engineer, Andy Miller, because Paul was on tour with The Delgados. It was our best recording to date. We'd really managed to capture something special.

While we waited for the singles to come out, we played whenever we got the chance. One show in particular stood out, opening for the American band, Low. My friend Keiron, who'd previously got us on the bills with The Make Up and Brainiac, asked us if we wanted to do the gig and gave me the band's new single, a cover of the Joy Division track 'Transmission'. As a Joy Division obsessive my interest was immediately piqued, but good as their cover was it was the rest of the EP that really captured me. They played with a restraint that was astounding. I was fan of a lot of minimalist bands like Codeine and Bedhead, who were both wonderful but nowhere near as sparse as Low. Their vocals were perfect too, the harmonies between the two singers Alan and Mimi sounding utterly sublime. Having discovered a new favourite band, I told Keiron we'd do the gig. There was a problem though: I hadn't checked with the rest of my bandmates and unfortunately Martin couldn't get the night off work. Determined to do the gig I decided that we'd play sans drummer, which was a bold move in the extreme. On the bill that night were Eska, who now had a way more capable chap behind the sticks called Willie Moan, and an Edinburgh band called Oilstars featuring a baby-faced guy with floppy brown hair I'd met at The 13th Note called Paul Thomson. Our line-up that night consisted of me and Dominic assisted by my pal and old flatmate David Jack, who attempted to keep us in time by hitting a tambourine. Our music was based so much on velocity and power that playing without a drummer was a truly terrible decision. The reason we were there, though, was to see Low and they didn't disappoint. In the run-up to the gig I'd got hold of the album that Low were touring, *The Curtain Hits the Cast*, and had become obsessed with it. It was a masterpiece in minimalist beauty. I adored it. But live they were on another level. One of the songs 'Do You Know How To Waltz', consisted mostly of Alan the guitarist creating swathes of layers of delayed guitar, not unlike what we were doing with 'Helicon 1', but taking it to the next level. I remember staring at the lights reflected from the mirror ball on the ceiling and getting totally lost in the music, thinking that it really could not get better than this. After the show I went to speak to them to tell them about how amazing the show had been. They were really sweet, lovely people, and even though they were not that much older than us, they seemed so much more adult than we were. Alan and Mimi were Mormons and didn't drink, which seemed really unusual to us miscreant hedonists. I gave them a copy of 'Tuner' and said it'd be great if we could play with them again sometime.

In November, 'Summer' came out. On the cover we used another of Neale's photos, this time of a field in Lanarkshire near where we'd both grown up. It was a completely different proposition to when 'Tuner' came out because 'some' people actually knew who we were by this point.

Towards the end of 1996 we got the call that we had dreamt of since we started the band, an invitation to record a session for John Peel. I was ecstatic when I found out. It felt like I was floating I was so happy. Our name was to join the hallowed list of bands who'd done sessions for him – Joy Division, The Cure, The Banshees, Hendrix. We were to record our session in London at the end of the year. Things were starting to feel very real. Lisa at Love Train was super supportive of us and acted as radio plugger, press officer and pretty much everything else that we needed. We'd had good support in the music press right from the start, but things were starting to really go up a gear. I was still religiously buying all the music papers and it had got quite surreal seeing our name among all the other bands that I considered superstars. The week 'Summer' came out I bought *NME* as usual, and when I got to the single reviews page I couldn't believe what I was seeing: 'Summer' was single of the week! It's hard to explain this feeling in a digital age where *NME* isn't even printed any more, but at the time it was seismic. I'd grown up checking single of the week every week and now it was us! The review mentioned us in the same context as My Bloody Valentine, which I was absolutely fine with.

In the second half of the year we made sporadic trips to London and continued performing in Scotland, but playing in other cities like we had with Urusei was tricky without a booking agent. We'd played a few more gigs down south with our by-now good pals Backwater. One gig has really stuck with me for a few reasons, in Brighton at a tiny venue called the Freebutt. Like most places we played back then there was no dressing room and the toilet at the back of the stage kind of deputised as one. We played our set, which was super intense, and finished the show with a huge thrash out with all of us battering seven shades of hell out of our instruments to create a wonderful cacophonic stramash. We all headed into the loo when we finished and we could hear something going on outside in the room. People were . . . still . . . clapping. I remember it so vividly. One of us said, 'Should we go back on?' We'd never played an encore (we were usually the support band to be fair) but this was something entirely new. Feeling humbled we ambled back onstage and played another song, which felt amazing. At the show that night was Brighton resident journalist Jerry Thackray, who wrote as Everett True. As he loves to tell people, he was instrumental in alerting the world to the wonders of Nirvana and many other great underground bands. He was a big deal in our music world. He'd loved the show and gave us an amazing review in *Melody Maker*, mentioning us alongside our heroes Slint as well as other amazing contemporaries like Flying Saucer Attack and Labradford.

The few attempts we'd made to book tours had proved pretty disastrous due to bad communication and flaky promoters. We needed an agent. Colin had been occupying his time trying to get someone on board with little joy. I suppose that despite some good music press write-ups, being a mostly instrumental band whose primary feature was playing at the volume of a jet plane taking off wasn't that appealing a prospect. Finally, one booking agent did respond and said he'd come along the next time we played in London – Mick Griffiths. Mick also booked My Bloody Valentine. Perfect.

Our next gig in London was booked to coincide with our trip down to record our Peel Session, on an old boat in Battersea called the *Ross Leopard*, and it was going to be our most important trip so far. Not only was this our chance to finally get a booking agent but it was also the recording of our long-awaited session for Peel. Martin was working the night before the gig so we had to leave that morning. We arranged to meet in the West End of Glasgow at Colin's flat at 9 a.m.

When we got to the venue after the early, long drive down south, it wasn't what I expected. It looked like the only thing holding the ship-cum-venue together was rust. It also bizarrely had a log fire in the middle of what I supposed was the dancefloor. It was weird. It might have been nerves or just a reaction to what had been quite a stressful day, but we got stuck into our rider with a bit more enthusiasm than usual. By the time we were due onstage we were fairly drunk. Our nerves weren't helped any by the fact that the crowd might generously be described as sparse. The place was fucking empty. It wasn't the easiest place to find and that was reflected in the lack of bums on metaphorical seats. When we started up it was clear that something wasn't quite right. I could tell by the look on his face that Martin was struggling. He was hitting the drums. His arms were moving but it wasn't quite making sense. There were times when me, Dominic or John would play a bit wonkily if we'd drank too much but it was a different story if it was Martin because he was holding the whole thing together. It can't have helped that we were all pissed too. We muddled through the set as best we could, though I had an uneasy feeling that we'd blown it and that our prospective agent might have left the rusty ship before we'd even finished. We sloped off to further drown our sorrows with booze. After a while Colin shouted me over to meet someone. It was Mick. He'd really loved the show and wanted to work with us. We had an agent. Hallelujah!

That night we were spread out all over London. Although we still didn't have the funds to stay in hotels, we had accrued enough acquaintances for us to find places to stay so none of us had to sleep on floors. The glamour! After an epic, stressful day we went to bed as soon as we could. Tomorrow was a big day. Our first Peel Session.

Maida Vale was shut for renovations so we were recording our session at the Hippodrome instead. I didn't let the change in location dampen my spirits though. This was a real dream come true situation. I was hoping that we wouldn't be recording with the grumpy, mulleted tosser who'd recorded Eska and was relieved when upon our arrival we were greeted by a charming, older Asian chap who went by the name of Miti. He couldn't have been nicer. As far as the actual place went, the Hippodrome was impressive. Usually used to record huge orchestras for Radio 3, the place was vast. The massive recording space was strewn with fantastically grand-looking instruments that we made eager plans to utilise. We didn't get the chance however as we were already pushed for time. Recording and mixing four songs before dinner time was a challenge for the best of bands, but with our songs sometimes twice or even four times as long as most bands it was even trickier. We cracked on though, as we planned to record four brand new songs. One was a reworked version of 'Summer' in a different time signature, the others were three more instrumentals. Miti was impressed by how grand our music sounded and said that it reminded him of Gustav Mahler, which was high praise indeed, and fitting for the setting. We didn't have names for the songs so we named them after each band member: 'Stuart', 'Dominic', 'Martin' and 'John'. The four new songs we'd recorded definitely felt like a progression. There was less bombast and the music felt like it was going somewhere. I'd always dreamt of recording a session for Peel and this truly lived up to my expectations. Every time we'd travelled down to London it felt like something great happened. It constantly felt like a vital new experience was round the corner.

It didn't take Mick long to have an impact. A week after he became our agent he called and said that we'd been invited to play London next month at the Astoria as part of a series of gigs organised by *NME*. We were to play on a bill headlined by Pavement. It was incredible news. We were obsessed with Pavement. Dominic had seen them open for Sonic Youth and put them on the tape he'd made for me when we started the band. Since then I'd been completely immersed in their music. 'Tuner' came about when

I had tried and failed to work out how to play a B-side of theirs, 'Strings Of Nashville'. I absolutely loved Stephen Malkmus's deceptively dextrous spazzy guitar playing and his dry-witted lyrics. They were the exact band we dreamt of playing with. We agreed in a heartbeat. Not only that but the gig was at the Astoria. Compared to the wee places we'd played up to that point it was ENORMOUS. At our first rehearsal after finding out, we watched a VHS Martin had of Radiohead playing there and we marvelled at the sheer size of the place. As far as we were concerned it was like playing Wembley Stadium. Also on the bill were two other great bands, Broadcast and Gorky's Zygotic Mynci. We were on first but it didn't matter a jot. This was HUGE.

The gig was at the end of January so we used that time to practise as much as possible and write as much new music as we could. We'd grasped every opportunity we'd had and this seemed the biggest of them all – to be playing with one of our favourite bands in a prestigious venue.

As it was our first ever gig in a 'proper' venue we were going to do things a bit differently. Up to that point we'd always used the venue sound person or whoever was mixing sound for the head-line band. This was fine because in pretty much every situation the noise coming from our amps would engulf anything coming out of the PA anyway, so it was just a matter of making sure that the drums were audible above the din we created. In a big place like the Astoria, however, that wouldn't be the case, and it was essential that we sounded as good as possible coming out of the PA. With that in mind we hired someone who would only be mixing us. The guy we got was called Jamie Harley, an affable, tall Londoner who had worked with loads of big touring bands and was used to doing sound in those kinds of rooms. He'd heard some of our music and seemed excited by it, throwing around a lot of frilly language to describe it. This was a bit strange because we tried to talk as little about our music as possible but we appreciated the enthusiasm.

Onstage was another place that we needed to upgrade. Normally we'd have a spare guitar and, if a guitar string broke, we'd quickly grab it and keep playing. That's all fine and well in a tiny venue, but on a big stage, the time that would take and the dead air it would bring would be horrendous. We therefore recruited a guy called Ally Christie, whom we knew from Glasgow, to come along as our guitar tech. Ally had been on tour with our friends Bis ever since leaving school and, even though he was a few years younger than us, seemed like a consummate professional. As well as knowing his stuff he was also hilarious and great company. We felt lucky to have him around.

When we got to the Astoria the enormity of the occasion and the venue itself seemed overwhelming. The venue was an old ornate theatre with two seated balconies and held about 2,000 people. The same amount as the fabled Barrowlands back in Glasgow. As the first band on we had to wait until the other three had done their soundchecks. We roughly set our instruments up on the floor in front of the stage and watched the other bands go through the process of checking every instrument and playing a couple of songs to make sure everyone could hear themselves. Watching Pavement soundcheck was great; you could tell what an incredible guitar player Stephen Malkmus was straight away. When all the bands did their check we dragged our stuff onstage. I was struck by the sheer enormity of the room. The tables on the balcony all had lights on them and from the stage they looked miles away and mesmerising. It was a really beautiful sight. After quickly setting up we played a song. It was surreal having to actually rely on the monitors. Normally, if I couldn't hear something onstage I'd just shuffle over to whatever it was I couldn't hear. On a massive stage that wasn't possible. Happy enough with onstage sounds and with Jamie fine out front, we left our guitars onstage and headed backstage. Before heading to our dressing room (OUR DRESSING ROOM, WHAT A NOVELTY!) we passed Pavement HQ and they summoned us in to say hi. The chattiest of them was Bob Nastanovich, the avuncular percussionist-cum-hype man, a big guy who was always up for having a good time and seemed charmed by our enthusiasm. Stephen was lovely too, and it seemed clear that he'd heard our music and had asked for us to be on the bill, which was both surprising and flattering. Me and Dominic cornered him and quizzed him about what obscure B-sides they'd be playing. None would be the answer. It didn't occur to us how weird a move playing super obscure songs at a big London show would be. We must have seemed like a gang of excited puppies but they humoured us nonetheless.

I didn't have the highest expectations about how many people would be watching us. The opening slot at any gig can be a tough one and I was just happy to be playing at such a prestigious gig, but when we walked onstage I was astounded by how busy it was. There were a lot of people there. Certainly far more than we'd ever played to before. Our music had always managed to sit well in the places we'd played up until that point, but I didn't know how it would work in a such a big place. When we started our first song, our soon to be released third single 'Helicon 1', it felt like something magical happened. All of my nervous energy transformed instantaneously to a kind of focused excitement and it really felt like we belonged on that stage. Probably in no small part to Jamie's expertise, our music was absolutely filling the room. When 'Helicon 1' ended we got a rapturous round of applause. I was made up. London audiences can be pretty sniffy at times but the people there really seemed to be connecting with us, which was all the more remarkable as no one had heard that song yet. The rest of the set seemed to fly by. In some ways it actually did because our nerves had made us play a good bit faster than normal. We ended the set with our big noise jam closer 'Stereo Dee' and its almost traditional racket of feedback. We left the stage with the sound of the guitars still ringing from the amps. Ally went over and turned our amps off and when the commotion finally subsided we could hear the applause from backstage. It couldn't have gone any better.

We watched Broadcast and Gorky's, who were both fantastic. Later that night we met up and they were really nice folks. We'd asked Pavement if we could watch their set from the side of the stage and they graciously agreed. I'd never been on a big stage like that before and watching one of my favourite bands from that vantage point was incredible. The sound wasn't ideal but seeing the audience's reaction to their music was amazing. One of their songs that we all loved was 'Here'. It's such a magical song. When they played it we waltzed around the back of the stage, out of sight of the massive crowds. Unfortunately for Martin, in the dark and a bit drunk, he didn't see the stairs and crashed down them. Thankfully he was fine. It would have taken more than few bruises to take the shine off the night. It was one of the best nights of my life.

10.

Chemikal Underground

Our third single, 'New Paths To Helicon' (the title nicked from one of my dad's poetry books) was going down a storm. John Peel was playing it a lot (though quite often at the wrong speed) and it was single of the week in both *NME* and *Melody Maker*. Stephen from Pavement had described us in an interview as 'the band of the twenty-first century'. I constantly felt like pinching myself.

One thing that wasn't going quite so swimmingly was my living situation. Since leaving college I was officially unemployed and the government was paying my rent. That was until I got summoned unceremoniously to the Job Centre one day. Completely oblivious to any issues, I sauntered into the meeting and was sat down at a desk across from two very serious people. 'Have you lost something, Mr Braithwaite?' Not having a clue as to what they were talking about, I said, 'No, I don't think so.' The man handed me a cheque for £200 from SRD. The royalties from 'Tuner'. We'd sold all of the copies of 'Tuner' and the cheque had been sent to my house. I had it in my pocket to take it to the bank and I'd dropped it in the Job Centre when I went to sign on. An idiotic move of biblical proportions. In the aftermath, for this indiscretion, all my benefits were stopped and I had to move back in with my folks. My flatmate Geraldine was also going to have a baby. That flat was many things but somewhere to raise a child most definitely was not one of them. I was fine staying with my folks, though, and they were happy to have me. I'd miss staying with Geraldine and Kenny; we'd really bonded in our time living together.

On the band front, one thing that we needed to sort out was a deal with a permanent record label. Lisa at Love Train had expressed an interest in signing us. She hadn't put any albums out yet, though, and we wanted someone with more experience. One label that we had a lot of admiration for was the Glasgow outfit Chemikal Underground that Paul Savage was involved with. They'd had real success getting Bis into the charts and they'd also put out an album by a band that had an incredible impact on us – Arab Strap. When we were recording 'Summer', Paul had let us hear their debut single, 'The First Big Weekend', and I can say with some confidence that I'd never heard anything like it. It told the story of a weekend the previous June. The same weekend we had played at The Garage and England beat Scotland. There were two guys in the band: Aidan and Malcolm, both from Falkirk, a town in between Edinburgh and Glasgow. Their lyrics told brutally honest stories about their lives. Musically they were into a lot of the bands we liked – Slint, Smog and the like. Chemikal Underground had signed them, and their debut album, *The Week Never Starts Round Here*, was something special. When I heard it I thought we'd have to go some way to do something as good. It was a real triumph and probably the first time I'd heard something that properly reflected my experience of growing up in Scotland. Irvine Welsh had done it through literature, but that was fiction. This was real life. They'd put out their record before they had even played a gig. I'd been at their first gig at King Tut's and it wasn't what I was expecting. They were all smashed and wearing ill-fitting suits. We became good pals over the next few years. It was great to meet folks with as much enthusiasm for getting melted as us and there was never a dull moment around them. They had a similarly mental group of pals who were great fun too. After getting to know Aidan and Malc we'd end up hanging out a lot. Usually in Nice N Sleazy's, staying till chucking out time and beyond. Being on the same label as the Strap was definitely something we liked the sound of.

In the background, without our knowledge, Colin had been talking to Paul and the others from Chemikal Underground about us moving to the label. Chemikal was run by the four members of The Delgados – Paul, Emma (Paul's partner), Alun (an outwardly serious person and erstwhile archaeologist who sang in the band), and Stewart the bassist (a big, uber-friendly guy who looked after the accounts). We'd known and liked them all from hanging out in Glasgow and had watched admiringly as they had grown their label from a bedroom endeavour to the point where they were getting records in the charts. As the four of them hadn't actually seen us play a gig, they all agreed to come and see a headline show we were playing in Edinburgh at suitably named venue The Attic (it was essentially the loft of a pub). We were all excited about being on Chemikal and wanted to make a good impression. With all the coverage we'd had for our singles so far, we actually managed to pull a decent crowd. Thankfully the gig went really well and they asked us after the show if we would sign. We were ecstatic and said yes straight away. Knowing that we had a label who would pay for us to make an album was a huge relief. But I was sad to let Lisa down because she'd been so supportive. One of the biggest lessons that Lisa had taught me was that it was important to say no. It was ironic that I would be letting her down when she wanted to sign us permanently. Other than Lisa, all the labels that had been in contact with us seemed really shady and probably just saw that we'd had some good press and hadn't really listened to our music properly. There was so much money in the music industry back then that loads of big labels were full of people who didn't actually like music and were just trying to make money. I think that if we'd signed to a big label, they'd have stuck us in the studio with a producer who'd have tried to mould what we did into something much more commercial. Fuck that.

Chemikal were real music people. Their office in the East End of Glasgow was also fifteen minutes from where we all lived. You could see Celtic Park out the window, which was nice.

Chemikal wasn't the only label showing interest in us. Our records had only been available as expensive imports in America up until this point, so when the US label Jetset got in touch it seemed like a great idea. The label, run by an English woman called Shelley Maple, proposed releasing a compilation of our singles to date, as well as our, at this point, extremely theoretical debut album, and bringing us over to the States for a tour. I'd never been out of Europe. In fact I'd only ever been on a plane twice – to Dublin and back delivering a telescope for my dad – so this was an amazing proposition. Shelley came across as extremely shmoozy but that seemed worth overlooking for the chance to go to the States. We should have trusted our instincts.

In spring 1997 we signed with Chemikal and got a publishing deal with Chrysalis, signed by a guy with the incredible name of Rich King. You couldn't make it up. The money from that meant we could pay ourselves a monthly wage. It was the first time in my life I'd had any regular income; great news for me but probably even better news for Glasgow's pubs, comic and record shops, because that's where all the money went.

That spring we embarked on our first ever foreign tour. A bunch of students from the Norwegian town of Bergen had heard our music and invited us to come to Norway for a run of shows. Having never played anywhere except Scotland, Wales and England we jumped at the chance. The trip was eventful from the off. The ferry from Newcastle to Norway doubles up as a floating pub for Norwegians because booze is ludicrously expensive in their homeland. Sensing the heightened state of exuberance from the other passengers we immediately got in on the act. Not content with just drinking beer we had taken to *snorting* it as well, eyes watering, convinced that this was an express route to intoxication. We weren't far from British shores by the time we were utterly annihilated. It was a wet day and the deck of the ferry was absolutely saturated. John was running about outside and kept falling over. We were amusing ourselves with our usual drunken idiocy when we realised that no one had seen him for quite a while and it suddenly occurred to us that he might have fallen overboard. Thankfully he had fallen asleep somewhere and materialised a few hours later. Losing a band member before even getting to the first foreign country we'd ever played would not have been a good look at all. We were all so drunk that we were behaving like total fools, falling out with each other and generally making mischief. I'd love to say that this was a lesson we learnt from but unfortunately that wasn't the case.

Having barely survived our ferry journey we arrived in the town that was to be our first port of call – Stavanger. The venue we were playing, Checkpoint Charlie, was also doubling up as our accommodation; we were sleeping on the floor of the venue. The tour was absolutely no-frills, but it didn't bother us. We were accompanied by some of the Bergen students who had booked the tour. They were amazing hosts. The gig in Stavanger was fantastic and we took advantage of our sleeping circumstances by staying up till the wee hours drinking.

We were driven around in two vans by the people from Bergen and stopped to look at waterfalls, fjords and snow-covered mountains in Norway's beautiful countryside. In the town of Bo we stayed in little cabins in the woods and enjoyed the most amazing view of the comet Halle Bop in the brightest, clearest night skies imaginable. Being away from Scotland, meeting new people and getting to play music was a real privilege.

The final night in Bergen was a total celebration. We'd had a write-up in the local paper and we asked Mari, one of the girls who'd organised the tour, to translate for us. It read:

For this music can put a human being in a trance like state
And give us a sneaking feeling of existing
Cause music is bigger than words and wider than pictures
If someone said that Mogwai are the stars I would not object
If the stars had a sound it would sound like this
The punishment for these solemn words can be hard
Can blood boil like this in the sound of a noisy tape that I've heard?
I know one thing, on Saturday the sky will crumble
With a huge bang to fit into the cave

We thought this was hilarious. We'd never heard such hyperbole applied to our music and didn't believe it could be serious. Back then I carried a dictaphone with me everywhere to record weird or unusual sounds, so I asked Mari to recite the piece and kept it, perhaps for future use. We were in a weird liminal space with the band: People were starting to take the music we made really seriously but it was as though we couldn't face the reality, despite us being deadly serious about what we were doing. I think it's in the Scottish character to downplay achievements and go to any lengths not to look conceited. We were really ambitious but weren't looking for praise. We just felt what we were doing was worth hearing and wanted to reach as many people as possible.

The Hulen student union in Bergen where we finished up the tour was a converted cave (as referenced in the newspaper article), where there was a real feeling of community among the students and the locals who attended. Everyone was so welcoming and we, in turn, were so grateful for their invitation. The gig was one of our favourites, and after we played we stayed up late drinking with the folks who'd invited us over. Our first foreign tour had been an incredible experience.

Having only released seven-inch singles up until then, we had been restricted by the fact that you could only fit six minutes on one side. So for our first record on Chemikal Underground we wanted to release a twelve-inch. By this point we had written quite a few songs and had decided on the three to put on the single. One was called 'Superheroes Of BMX', named after a book I'd found in a charity shop when we'd been in London recording our Peel Session. At the same charity shop I found a toy Robocop figure which made a whirring sound, and that also featured on the song as I held it up to the pick-ups on my trusty blue Telecaster. My parents had bought me that guitar when I passed my Standard Grade exams when I was fifteen and I adored it. We also recorded 'Stereo Dee', our set closer. We named it that because it featured the last section of one of our very first songs – 'D' – and the first section reminded us of Stereolab. What it really sounds like is Neu! but none of us had even heard them at this point. We were getting the influence second-hand. For the other track we asked our pal Aidan Moffat from Arab Strap to join us. We'd never had anyone sing with us apart from me, so this was a new experience. Aidan's voice suited our music perfectly. The song was a beautiful and painfully honest tale of lost love called 'Now You're Taken'. We laid down most of the single with Paul in Hamilton, but then recorded 'Stereo Dee' in Edinburgh at a place called Chamber Studios with Jamie Harley, who had done our live sound at the Astoria. For the cover, my sister Victoria took a photo of the Ferris wheel in Strathclyde Park, near Hamilton. It was something I drove past every day on the way from my folks in the Clyde Valley into Glasgow and I thought it looked so incongruous next to the motorway.

In April we played some really memorable gigs, including The Garage, twice, the first time as part of an all-day event organised by Lisa from Love Train. On the bill that day were brilliant bands like Hood, Prolapse, Ligament, Urusei, Bob Tilton and our pals Eska. The following week we went abroad again to play a festival in Mauron, France, with most of the other bands on Chemikal alongside our old friend Alex from The Blisters new band,

The Karelia, as well as about thirty fellow Glaswegians in a bus. It was utter carnage. The ferry was like the one to Norway but on steroids. Loads of people presumed missing, certain label mates lobbing chairs off the side, all culminating in an encounter with the police when we disembarked. The whole weekend was insane. We were welcomed graciously by the small town and it was bedlam, but great fun. The novelty of being able to drink as much beer as we wanted wasn't wearing off. Things were getting pretty chaotic. At the end of the month we were invited to play at The Garage again, this time for a live broadcast for the Peel Show alongside Gorky's Zygotic Mynci and Kenickie. We decided for some reason to play in our pyjamas that night. We'd thought our set had gone well, only to find out that the start of 'Helicon 1' had been too quiet for the radio and an emergency tape featuring an Oasis song had started up instead. This wouldn't be the only time it would happen to us. We were either too loud or too quiet.

Our new EP was called *Four Satin*. We wanted to call it *For Satan* but didn't want to upset Martin's extremely lovely Catholic mum, who was still letting us rehearse in her house. Our love of horror films and the residual trauma of most of the band's Catholic upbringing was never far away. For the release of the EP we were going on our very first headline tour. The climax of the tour was in London, again at The Garage, but this time it was our own gig. It seemed mental that we were now in a position where we could play to 600 people. We would have our own van, which was to be driven by a guy called Ross. Ross also doubled up as our stagehand and had suffered from severe burns when he was a kid. Even though his hands were damaged he could still string a guitar far better than me. We also had our own tour manager, an extremely affable, big chap called Jaffa. Jaffa was a pal of The Delgados from Motherwell and he'd filled the role for both them and Arab Strap. We felt extremely professional for the first time. Another perk of being the headline band was that we got to choose the opening bands. For the first part of the tour we had Macrocosmica, the new band formed by Brendan O'Hare, ex-Teenage Fanclub and Telstar Ponies. In the middle we had Arab Strap, and for the last part we had Navigator with Arab Strap rejoining us at The Garage for the final night. It felt like our opportunity to become really established. With our pro touring party and its cast of great opening bands, we were all set. What could possibly go wrong?

Just before the tour we had a one-off gig in East Kilbride, a satellite town half an hour from Glasgow. We'd been contacted by a guy called Lee Cohen who was working for a company which made cover art for famous derivative English chart bands down in London. He had been asked to try out a new video camera and offered to come along on tour with us to test it out. He seemed keen and we agreed for him to tag along with us and film the shows. After soundcheck me and Dominic headed back to Glasgow to pick him up. Unfortunately, we were waiting for him at the train station when in fact he'd come up to Scotland on a bus. After realising our error we rushed up to the bus station to find a diminutive Jewish-American kid with bushy eyebrows and an impish grin. He was relieved at not having to sleep in a bus station and jumped in the car with us as we rushed over to East Kilbride just in time to get onstage. That night was also memorable because it was the first time we played a song that would go on to define us in a lot of ways – 'Mogwai Fear Satan'. We'd had the three-note drone delayed guitar part for a while but it was only when we thought to change the chords underneath that it really came to life. It had pretty much no structure other than building then falling, only to come back in a frenzy through a series of not-always-successful nods across the stage. The song was loose as hell but it had the makings of something special. The gig in East Kilbride was fine but what we were really excited about was heading out on tour.

Lee stayed with me at my folks for a few days before the tour. He'd been in London since finishing university in Texas and was glad to be away from his place of work, which sounded like the worst Britpop cocaine nightmare imaginable.

With Lee and his video camera in tow we headed off for the first date of our tour. Spirits could not have been higher and it felt like the culmination of two really exciting years.

Having almost always been the opening band up to this point, our strategy was to start drinking as soon as we got to the venue, and even though we were now the headliners this hadn't changed. The opening band for the first leg of the tour was Macrocosmica. Brendan, the frontman, was without doubt the most fun person any of us had ever met. He'd been around the world playing music and sharing stages with Kurt Cobain. He was also a maniac when it came to drink and drugs. It'd be unfair to say that he led us astray, but he certainly wasn't a calming influence. Someone had brought some acid on the tour and we had taken it all after a few days. When it was finished, Brendan would go into the crowd and just shout as loud as he could, 'Does anyone have any acid?' We'd loved watching Macrocosmica and had really bonded with Brendan.

The final night Macrocosmica played with us was in Bedford. Lee had a bong with him and we decided to get stoned. Myself and weed had never agreed. I'd always get really paranoid and feel sick, but this was very much a 'just say yes' environment. We got so mashed that Dominic was sick and I struggled to get through the gig, such was the inner turmoil I was experiencing. That night we invited Brendan onstage to play extra guitar on another new epic jam that we'd introduced into the set, named after its biggest influence, Slint. We were all sad at the end of the night that they were leaving, Brendan in particular. In a moment of elation we decided upon a solution: Brendan could just join the band and that meant he wouldn't have to go home. It was decided! He was the fifth member of Mogwai. I drunkenly called an extremely confused Colin and told him the news. The next day, two thirds of Macrocosmica drove back to Glasgow and Brendan stayed with us. The tour was going great. The gigs were full, we thought we were playing well, and we had a new band member.

Brendan's first show as an official member of the band was also the first ever festival we played, Essential Festival in Brighton. The headliners were The Levellers, Space and Babybird. You be the judge as to how essential they were. Since my experience at Reading six years earlier I'd dreamt of playing a rock festival. If only the bands had been a bit better. We were due to play early on the fifth stage, which was headlined by Monaco, a Peter Hook side project. As a Joy Division obsessive I was really excited about getting to meet one of my idols. All completely giddy with excitement we started drinking as soon as we got there. Playing our first festival seemed like a special occasion so we again played in our pyjamas. I'm not sure the mainstream Britpop fans knew what to make of the five inebriated Scots in their nightwear summoning this hellish racket. Thankfully we played not long after we got there and managed to perform OK. Brendan had only been in the band for a few days so just played along on guitar on most songs or held down a key on a little Moog keyboard. His enthusiasm was infectious though. The sun was shining and we were having the time of our lives. We'd started speaking in slogans like MOGWAI YOUNG TEAM, NEW MOGWAI NEW DANGER. Things were very messy but we felt like we were on top of the world. After we played we went to the press tent to do some interviews and did a pile on, a playground game where one person gets jumped on by the others. I can't recall the press conference too clearly, but I do remember that we broke a fence. Towards the end of the day, as the sun started to go down, I eventually summoned the courage to go and talk to Peter Hook. I accosted him and muttered something about his music changing my life, and he replied to say that my nose was bright red and I needed to get some sun cream. He had a point.

Our next gig was in Brighton itself, but we had a day off in between. We spent the day getting smashed. Lee was in his element and had captured a lot of the ensuing bedlam on his wee camera. Brighton being a fun seaside town, we went down the pier to go on all the rides. It was after coming out of the ghost train that Lee proclaimed: YES! I AM A LONG WAY FROM HOME. We weren't as far away as he was but it felt that way.

Our next gig was a DIY all-day affair, a million miles from the big sanitised festival. We shared the stage with old pals Trout and Bob Tilton. As great as the music was that day, our spirits were tempered when we heard the terrible news that Timmy Taylor, the singer from Brainiac, had died in a car crash. Not only was Timmy a lovely person but it looked to everyone that Brainiac were on the verge of mainstream success. It was scary to think that someone we'd shared a stage with the year before was no longer around. He would be dearly missed.

After Brighton we headed north again to Middlesbrough. What was already turning into a *Lord of the Flies* situation was about to get even worse when the next opener showed up – Arab Strap. The Strap had never been on tour before and took no convincing to join in our idiotic circus. Aidan and Malcolm were joined live by Gary, a quiet guy on bass, and Dave Gow, a bona fide nutter on drums. As far as getting fucked-up goes, they were pros. Arab Strap were having a great time of it. Guinness were about to use one of their songs in a TV advert and they were being courted by a load of labels eager to lure them away from Chemikal Underground.

The Strap brought poppers with them. From then on, as well as being continuously drunk, we were all pretty much either out of our tiny minds on amyl nitrite or drinking as hard as we could to get rid of the bastard of a headache they induced. Aidan mastered a technique where he would monitor our stage nods for when we were going to come in really loud in 'Mogwai Fear

Satan' and 'Like Herod' (the new name for 'Slint'), and then take a huge sniff just before the deafening part. For our part we would place the poppers tactically on our amps and take blasts between songs. It was fucking chaos. Jaffa our tour manager was all-in on the ride as well. It had reached the point where waiting for the promoter to bring the rider seemed like too long for us to start drinking. The solution was to get a massive stash of beer in the morning to bring to the venue. Our catchphrase for it was 'tipsy for soundcheck'. Somewhere along the way Brendan had found a small loudspeaker that also played some tunes. Many of them wrong. One of my strongest memories of that tour is of Brendan playing the French national anthem on the horn with about one in five of the notes being correct. It never ceased to be amusing.

Everything was amusing.

The night of the gig in Gloucester was the night the Guinness advert featuring the Strap's music was on the telly. Rather than shy away from the rampant commercial exploitation of their music, they embraced it by miking up a TV on stage and getting everyone to watch it. To celebrate, we all got extra wasted and Dave stole some massive conga drums. They got a bit klepto sometimes. Usually porn mags. The congas were unusual.

The following night, in Colchester, we were playing in a converted church. Behind the stage was an altar. Brendan had obtained some Es and demonstrated to me that swallowing them wasn't the only way to ingest them. He proceeded to crush them up and snorted them off the altar. I'd never taken E before and was higher than the fucking sun. Some pals of ours who ran a fanzine and had been to loads of early gigs came that night and I could see that they seemed somewhat surprised by the general mood of the tour. Things were getting really unhinged. We'd listened to nothing but a best of Black Sabbath tape I'd bought in a charity shop and, in my mind, we were on some kind of touring rock pilgrimage and were the spiritual heroes to Butthole Surfers and MC5. In actual fact we were a bunch of dysfunctional kids drinking too much and doing daft shit like boiling and eating snails in Travelodge kettles. At the Birmingham show Dominic's big brother Mark came along. I'm fairly sure he was horrified. We were disintegrating day by day, becoming more and more feral. Things were only going to get worse though. We still had to play London.

We spent the drive from Bristol to London drinking and taking the last of the acid. Chants had replaced conversations. We'd become the Mogwai Young Team and would incessantly chant:

MYT

MYT

MYT

We were out of our tiny minds and convinced that we were on a holy mission to cure the world of dreary rock and roll with the majesty of our music. As we entered London we passed Buckingham Palace and, as proud anti-monarchists, we booed the gargantuan building. I'm certain the Queen was not hanging out the window to see if any Scottish teens were voicing their disapproval. Jaffa saw an old woman and shouted, 'Two weeks to live!' All boundaries were gone. Arab Strap had been off the tour for a week, replaced by the far meeker and probably horrified Navigator, who were less keen on joining our bacchanal. The boys from Falkirk were coming back tonight though. For the big finale.

We greeted Aidan, Malc, Dave and Gary like long lost brothers returning from war. Playing our first proper headline gig in London was a big deal, but to us it had become the final ritual of a month-long rite. To say that the music had taken a back seat would be an understatement. We'd pretty much stopped soundchecking. We'd accepted chaos as a lifestyle choice.

Alun and Stewart from Chemikal Underground came down from Scotland, as did Colin. Colin looked fairly shocked at the general state of us. The gig had sold well and our agent Mick was coming down. Far from being appalled, Hendy (as we called Stewart) and Alun got in on the action by getting smashed with us all.

The dressing room was to the side of the stage in The Garage and from the get-go it had become a party room. Arab Strap having to leave the party to play seemed like an irritating interruption to the reverie. Our eyes were most definitely not on the ball. Brendan bounded onstage when the Strap were playing to give them all poppers. We were already entering debacle territory and we hadn't even played a note.

When we hit the stage we were mental factor twenty, out of our tiny gourds on booze, acid and poppers. I was in a heavy delusionary state. The space between what I thought was happening and what was actually happening was a chasm. With our new songs we felt we were on top of the world and about to create history. The songs *were* good. We were just too fucked to play them properly. There were moments of lucidity. I remember looking over at John during a new song, 'Long Way From Home' (named after Lee's Brighton proclamation), when I noticed that we were playing different chords. John gave me a look back as if to say, 'Does that matter any more?' It was a fucking riot. There was something weirdly infectious about the rammy though. The crowd seemed to be into it, from where I was standing at least. It was as if our new feral ways were contagious. At one point Aidan and Malc came onstage to desecrate a broken amp of theirs by pouring a pint of Guinness into it. A tribute to their new place in the world of advertising. We later found out that it just had a broken plug. As we conjured our mayhem, Stewart and Alun sat at the side of the stage bathing in the madness and doubtless happy at so many people coming to see two of their bands play. As far as I was aware we were trailblazing psychedelic warriors, using noise as a weapon to bring down the system.

The gig ended in pure chaos. Feeling that this was the culmination of the greatest rock and roll tour of all time, we smashed up our instruments. Brendan handed out bits of them to the baying crowd. This was Hendrix at Woodstock stuff. Or so we thought. We stumbled off the stage, not sure if we'd played the best gig of our lives or completely fucked our short careers in music.

After the gig Colin pulled me aside to tell me that Mick had not been amused and had left before the end.

When I awoke the next day with the mother of all hangovers, Colin told me we had to go and see Mick at his office. With my head feeling like it had been brutally assaulted, I made my way to Camden. Asgard, where Mick worked, is a big agency and very, very proper. Lots of dark wood and marble. They managed the singer Tanita Tikaram and she had a workout set up in the lobby. It all felt very surreal, not unlike when I used to get hauled up at school for wearing too much black. To say that Mick wasn't happy would be an understatement. I don't recall the exact words but 'disgrace' was used a lot. Reality and sobriety hit me like a tonne of bricks. What had felt like a righteous mission was in fact just us being morons. We had something really special going on and were in severe peril of destroying it before it even really started. Our next gig was in America. I had a lot of thinking to do on the long plane ride.

When I got home, I felt like fucking death. I was still working as a receptionist at my mum's surgery and had the added problem of removing the nail varnish that we'd all taken to wearing. Not being in the best of states mentally, I didn't consider using the aptly named 'nail varnish remover'. What I did instead was shave it off, which was as painful as it was stupid.

A few weeks after the tour, a fan who'd been at a lot of the shows and recorded them sent us a compilation of the best bits from her recordings.

We sounded fucking awful.

11.

Mogwai Young Team

A few days after The Garage debacle we flew to America for our first gig outside Europe. Ever since I'd fallen in love with music I'd wanted to go to New York. Images of the city were burnt into my mind from movies like *Taxi Driver* and *Ghostbusters*, and I felt that I knew the streets from hearing Dylan and Lou Reed sing about them. So much of my favourite music came from there: The Velvet Underground, Public Enemy, Patti Smith, Sonic Youth. The list was endless. The yellow cabs, steaming manholes and towering buildings were iconic. It was the spiritual home of rock and roll and getting to play there with Mogwai was a dream come true. We wouldn't be going with Brendan though. Brendan had some other commitments, and the fact he didn't have a plane ticket didn't help either. I was worried about playing without Brendan because he'd become an integral part of the band in the short period he'd been with us. He brought an energy and confidence that we all totally bought into. Even though Brendan wasn't coming, Colin was. There was no chance he was going to miss a transatlantic excursion.

Most of the band stayed in London after The Garage gig because the New York flight was from Heathrow. Martin went home for a few days and just managed to get on the plane to America by seconds, not knowing that he needed to check in again for the second flight after he'd flown to London from Glasgow. Visas weren't an issue because none of us had them. We would be sneaking in under the guise of tourists.

Spaceships Over Glasgow

After navigating immigration we stepped out into the street and the first thing I couldn't believe was the heat. It was like being blown in the face by a hairdryer. Sometimes a city can hold a grip on your imagination and reality can suffer by comparison. This wasn't like that. New York had every aspect of the romance that had existed in my head. Grimy but unique. One of the things we were most excited about were the huge bottles of beer that we'd seen in hip-hop videos. We acquired these as soon as we could, though they didn't quite live up to expectations because they'd go flat and gross way before you finished them.

Our trip had been organised by our new label, Jetset, and as well as playing our first gig we were to play in a record shop and do a radio session. We were greeted off the plane by a young guy who worked at Jetset called Daniel Kessler. Daniel was a smartly dressed guy who was half English and got our sense of humour way more than most Americans. He was a great host, and after getting to know him a bit he told us that he had his own band called Interpol. He took us to our decidedly unglamorous hotel where we met the rest of the Jetset people. The friendliest of them was a smiley guy with floppy blond hair called Sam Brumbaugh, who seemed excited to meet us and knew so many people in New York. He was friendly with the guys from Pavement and Dave Berman from Silver Jews. Shelley the label boss was a different proposition altogether. She could put on the charm but it was clearly all business. There was definitely something about her that made us uneasy. After getting some Mexican food with the label people we went out for drinks at a bar on the Lower East Side called Max Fish. We had to go somewhere Sam knew the owners because John was only nineteen and still a couple of years too young to legally drink alcohol in the US. Being out in New York felt like a waking dream, like something that would happen to other people. I felt incredibly lucky to be so far from home, somewhere I'd always dreamt of going, with my friends, making music.

The next day was our first performance on American soil. In a video and music shop. Mondo Kim's video shop was on St Marks Place on Manhattan's East Side and was unlike any other I'd ever seen. It had every weird and obscure movie and documentary you could think of. It was also a record store and we were to play on the shop floor. We set up our gear and got ready to play to the handful of folk who either wanted to hear us or just happened to be there. Just as we were about to start playing, a group of people came into the shop. They stood out because they were a similarly pasty shade of blue as ourselves and most definitely did not look like locals. As they got closer we all realised that we knew them. It was our friends Mig, Stevie Dreads and Ulriki, who we knew from Nice N Sleazy. They'd timed their New York holiday so they could come and see us. It was amazing to see friendly faces and it definitely put us at ease. The real thing was the next day though.

Our first gig proper in America was underneath the arches of the Brooklyn Bridge, part of a festival of shows called 'Music at the Anchorage'. Other bands playing that week included Sonic Youth and Main, Robert from Loop's new outfit. We were to play with the drone band Bowery Electric. I was a huge fan of theirs and excited about sharing a stage, but I was nervous about playing without Brendan and it felt weird soundchecking in his absence. It was the first time I'd ever experienced jet lag and the feeling of nausea and exhaustion added to what was an already surreal experience. The crowd for the gig didn't look anything like the type of people who would come and see us at home or anywhere else in Europe. People here looked so . . . refined. Sharp-dressed people with thick-rimmed glasses and books tucked under their arms. I think the highbrow nature of the event alongside us being an unknown entity had attracted a crowd of intellectual hipsters. We went onstage to briefly check our equipment before we started and I was quite surprised to see that no one even turned to face the (somewhat towering) stage. As we started playing, people didn't seem remotely interested in what was happening. I was bewildered. It was only after we really turned up the volume that the audience realised we were the band. I'm guessing that our attire of tatty tracksuits and football tops wasn't what they expected an instrumental art rock band from Glasgow to look like. Once they realised that we were in fact the band, they responded well. The gig was a success and it felt like people in America were appreciative of our music. Once they knew who we were at least.

We departed America the next day with great memories of our first trip and a promise from the people at Jetset that we would be back sooner rather than later. They wanted us to do some dates around our as yet unrecorded album, which we were planning on releasing in the autumn. This was July though, and we hadn't recorded a single note.

Back in Scotland matters turned urgently to the recording of the album, the only issue being that we didn't have enough songs. Joy Division had never released a single from an album and, as a Joy Division obsessive, I was adamant that we shouldn't either. That left us with only a handful of songs available to record. Those songs were some of the best we had written, but that didn't compensate for the shortfall in material. Not letting the fact that we were woefully lacking in songs get in the way of the plan, we reunited with Brendan and went into the studios in Hamilton with Paul Savage to get started. The recording sessions for our singles had been pretty intense because we only had a limited time to record. So we'd been studious, starting early and working late into the night to get everything done; recording an album, especially one that we were pitifully ill-prepared for, was a different situation entirely. Brendan, having made records with Teenage Fanclub and Telstar Ponies, was a big help talking us through the process, but on the flip-side the partying culture of the spring tour had seeped into our studio environment and things were getting a bit messy. The stress and pressure of coming up with an album in a relatively short space of time may have been a factor, but in reality we were generally just a bit of a mess.

Once we were set up in the studio we got to work straight away. All I could think about were the debut albums by the bands I'd grown up with – The Velvet Underground, the Mary Chain and The Stooges. We'd barely recorded a note and I already felt a huge weight of pressure on my shoulders. It was all very well being bratty kids putting out singles, but debut albums were something permanent, the foundations for a legacy. We'd told anyone who would listen how important our music was and how it compared to certain other bands. We had to come up with the goods or we were in danger of looking very stupid. I was worried that it could all be over before it had even really started. Our lifestyle at the time wasn't helping either. Barely a day went by in the studio without some kind of intoxication. The studio was next to a supermarket and the day wouldn't have long started before someone popped over to get wine or beers. Not to mention the occasional acid tab or bong session. At the back of our minds we knew we were in a bit of a hole and getting smashed seemed as good a way as any to get through it.

We started by recording the songs that we *could* play. Not that there were many of those. Two of the main songs on the album, 'Like Herod', and our new set closer, the rather epic 'Mogwai Fear Satan', were totally loose and proving a lot harder to record than we'd hoped. These were analogue times and computers were pretty scarce in studios, certainly the ones that we frequented. We were recording onto tape and what you played was what ended up on the song. Tape was expensive, too, so doing loads of takes and choosing the best one wasn't really an option either. Pro Tools hadn't been invented yet, where music can be edited and fixed beyond recognition by an engineer. 'Mogwai Fear Satan' in particular was a nightmare to record because it varied so much in length. One version that we recorded with the additional drumming of our friend Pete Gofton from Kenickie was almost twenty-two minutes. Paul said there were too many mistakes and he taped over it to make sure we didn't use it.

I'd love to hear it now, but Paul made the right decision at the time. We eventually nailed it and had the idea to get someone to play flute on it. I knew that one of my mum's colleague's daughters, Shona Brown, was a flautist so we asked her. She was only fourteen years old. God knows what she thought about the state of us but she did a great job.

Little did we know that there was another flute player in our midst, someone who would go on to have a huge impact on us – Barry Burns. The studio was also a rehearsal space for local bands and we got really friendly with a couple of guys who were left in charge of running that side of things, Eddie Farley and Barry. They both played in a band called Junior Funktion and were some of the funniest guys we'd ever met. They amused us by showing us a game they'd invented called 'face pellet', which consisted of someone throwing a hacky sack in a darkened room and seeing whose face it hit. The game escalated as larger and larger objects got thrown. The final iteration of the game was called 'Life Ender' and used a bowling ball. Thankfully that game never got past the conversational stage. As well as being highly entertaining company, Barry was also a great musician. He lent us his piano for a few songs and showed us how it worked by playing a note-perfect rendition of the introduction to 'Light My Fire' by The Doors before announcing that the song was shite. We liked that. Having a piano was a lifesaver. The three piano tracks (one each by John, Brendan and me) really helped the record. Brendan had written his in Colchester at the fateful night with the altar. There had been a scathing *NME* review of our shambolic gig in London a few months previously that had described him as a 'Gibbon Without Portfolio'. We called the song 'With Portfolio' as a bit of a retort. We'd taken to spending time in the rehearsal rooms trying to work on new songs before we started recording, in an attempt to get ourselves into some kind of shape. We really should have taken a few months off to write some more songs but everyone was dead set on getting the record out that autumn. There was a fear that everything would disintegrate if we didn't. We'd been lucky up to that point and no one wanted the spell to disappear, but the cracks were beginning to show. People's nerves were fraying and I was definitely not at my best. The stress seemed all-encompassing. Thankfully we managed to get away from the studio to let off some steam.

Our second festival after Brighton was close to home, Scotland's infamous T in the Park. The festival was becoming a mecca for teenage hedonism and we fitted right in. We were playing the Evening Session stage, compered by Radio 1 DJ Steve Lamacq. Steve had played us a few times but had made an offhand remark that we 'weren't the kind of band that you would pay your last fiver to see'. Not being ones to take something like that lying down, we retaliated by being mean about him the next time we did an interview. Steve is a good sport though, and after introducing us he gave us all a pound each. We've been friends ever since. The gig itself was intense. The new songs were ferocious. We had been playing them over and over in the studio. The gig felt important but we knew that what was really crucial was making sure our album was great, and it felt like we were still a long way off that.

After a few weeks of fairly high-pressure recording, we left to play the Phoenix Festival and decided to make a weekend of it. Urusei Yatsura were also playing so we shared a van down with all of our equipment (and our tents). Unlike the festival in Brighton a few months earlier, the Phoenix Festival actually featured a lot of music we liked. As soon as we arrived we headed off to see Spiritualized, featuring one of my Spacemen 3 heroes, Jason Pierce. They had recently released the wonderful *Ladies and Gentleman We are Floating in Space* and they were absolutely immense. The weekend was a blur of hedonism and a lot of chemicals. I remember watching Aphex Twin play inside a Wendy House flanked by bodybuilders while my brain did somersaults on my first experience of ecstasy and coke. Our gig was quite odd. We played really early and it felt like both us and the crowd weren't quite awake yet. On the final night I watched, enraptured, as David Bowie played to a massive crowd. Afterwards in the VIP bar I saw Bernard Sumner from New Order and, in my chemically-infused state, went straight up to talk to him. It turned out he was even more wasted than me and was convinced I was related to Alan McGee, the boss of Creation Records.

Back in the studio the next week, things weren't getting any easier. A heavy metal band had defaced my Joy Division poster that I'd put up in the control room, which didn't help my mood any. The effects of the weekend hadn't calmed our nerves and the constant pressure of having to finish the record was getting to us. The ad hoc rehearsal/writing sessions in the practice room were becoming quite fraught. Brendan had an idea for a rock song that wasn't at all where I saw the record going, and I was far from diplomatic in letting him know. One time Martin got so frustrated working out a drum part that he threw his stick and it caused the tube light to explode. The process seemed to be taking an age and we weren't sure what we were doing was any good. The new songs seemed OK but without having the time to test them out at gigs it was quite hard to tell. We didn't have a record but we did have a name, *Mogwai Young Team*, referencing the gang graffiti which adorned every other wall in Scotland. The band had become more of a gang than a musical endeavour of late and we were all-in. In solidarity we all shaved our heads and Martin, John and Brendan got the MYT logo we'd designed tattooed on their arms. We all had new names too. For some reason I was Plasmatron. John was Captain Meat because he was constantly on the hunt for new carnivorous delicacies. Martin was Bionic because of his Pacemaker. Dominic was Demonic. Brendan was The Relic because he was the grand old age of twenty-six, which seemed ancient to us. We looked like members of a cult. The strain was beginning to show and the stress of making the record was taking all of the fun out of the band. We were simultaneously bound together and falling apart.

We wanted the record to be different so we tried to add as many unusual elements as we could. We recorded a coin being tossed as percussion for one song and trains leaving the station just metres away from the studio for another. In one recording we prank called Colin to tell him that the band was splitting up. The fact that he didn't realise it was a joke says more about the state of the band than his levels of gullibility. For the opening song we put Mari's reading of the hyperbolic Norwegian review at the start. At this point we still thought it was hilarious. We also enlisted Aidan to do a duet with me, aptly based around a relationship falling apart. Slowly but surely, as the deadline approached, we realised that we had enough songs for an album, but none of us were sure about what we'd done and there was a real feeling of unease around the band. What should have felt like the culmination of everything we'd done so far felt weirdly like an opportunity missed. We toyed with splitting the album up into two mini albums, but Paul said that it worked well as a single record. Eventually, using everything bar a couple of experimental pieces, we had an album. It took quite a while to sort out the running order, especially as none of us had ever done it before. We handed it in to Chemikal Underground and waited to see what people's reaction would be. For the cover we used a photo that Brendan had taken of a bank in Tokyo, a city none of us bar Brendan had been to.

With the album finally finished, it felt like a weight off all our shoulders, though there was a nagging doubt that, having made it in such a rush, it wasn't what we had hoped for. Our ambitions were so high that even with all the time in the world we might not have achieved what we were after.

During the recording we got word that we had been invited to play Reading, the same festival that I'd seen Nirvana play as a young teenager six summers before. As well as Reading we were also playing Pukkelpop in Belgium and the Lowlands Festival in the Netherlands the same weekend. It was the same run that had been documented in Sonic Youth's *Year Punk Broke* film which me and Dominic had bonded over. We'd whiled away hours imagining playing those festivals and now we were about to do exactly that.

The first was Lowlands, a massive Dutch festival. The drive took a few days, including a ferry trip. Being a new band without an album out, our slot was comically early, onstage before noon. By now we were getting used to the big festival stages and played pretty well considering how knackered we were. Being on so early also meant that we could start drinking as soon as we got to the site. We got on it early doors and were fairly smashed by lunchtime. It was around then that we were approached by some people backstage who were giving away Levi's jeans to all the bands. There was some kind of promo on for jeans that you shrunk yourself and they were showing this off by having bathtubs backstage that you got into with the jeans on. Still all being fairly impoverished and utterly smashed, there was no way we were going to turn down free clothes so we got in on the act with great aplomb. It was around then that the guys from Pavement appeared. They were surprised to have missed us but were all too happy to join us in our epic drunken quest. I wonder what they thought of our transformation from wee, quiet shy kids into whatever-we'd-become in those seven long months. Whichever way, they were all too happy to join in. Festivals in Europe were always pretty accommodating when you asked for your drinks rider to be replenished, but things definitely took a turn for the better when we learnt that one of the headline bands – Blur – would not be playing, which meant that their exquisitely stocked dressing room was not going to be used. With that in mind we joined forces with Pavement to utterly annihilate Blur's rider. As a band, Blur epitomised the kind of vacuous nationalistic pop that we despised, so getting mortal on their champagne only seemed right. The whole thing felt surreal. That night I watched Pavement play one of the best shows I've ever seen in a huge tent. They were utterly mesmerising.

The next day at Pukkelpop was a bit more subdued due to our Lowlands hangover. We left soon after we played to get to Reading the night before our show, and the ferry home was particularly lively. With drugs largely legalised in Holland we'd bought a load of psychedelic mushrooms at Lowlands and knew that we needed to get rid of them before going through customs in Dover. We were only familiar with the wee skinny ones that grow in Scottish fields so didn't really know what we were in for. We took them before getting the ferry to England. Ferries are weird enough at the best of times, but this was another trip entirely. By the time we got into international waters we were out of our fucking minds. I tried to put a brake on the expressway to insanity by drinking more. It didn't work. When we arrived at Reading we were so fried on booze and mushrooms that we barely knew who or where we were. We'd stayed in hotels in Europe but for Reading we were camping. At this point we had also taken to eating baby food because it was cheap and easily available.

After quickly setting up our tents we immediately decamped to the backstage bar and continued getting smashed. We were a mess and I could see in the eyes of the people we met that they thought we'd gone off the rails. The Garage gig a few months back had already raised a few eyebrows. Back then, Reading was the only major non-mainstream music festival and it was the last big weekend for everyone involved in music in the UK. We'd become quite notorious for being mouthy in interviews and had been far from restrained in sharing our less than complimentary views on other bands and musicians. Being in a bedraggled, drunken and drugged state in an enclosure full of every indie musician in the country was a recipe for disgrace. We were loud, obnoxious and full of ourselves. People down south tend to wince anyway when they hear a Glaswegian accent (which is probably a symptom of every murderer, crook or hoodlum on UK TV being predictably cast as a Glaswegian). The fact that we were in reality nice boys and couldn't even fight sleep didn't seem to matter: people were avoiding us like the plague. By doing gobby interviews and getting a bit more drunk than was advisable we'd earned a bit of a fearsome reputation. After a few hours of berating passing musicians we decamped back to our tents. Tomorrow was a big day. Our first performance at Reading. Our Nirvana moment. Or so we hoped.

The one issue about being bratty regarding other musicians is that once in a while you meet them. When we were in our dressing room getting ready to play our show in Reading, a guy from a band (I honestly can't remember the name) came in and asked why I'd been so mean about them. I was brutally honest and said I'd never heard them, I just presumed they'd be crap. From the get-go I was inspired by the interviews of Ian McCulloch, Robert Smith, Julian Cope and the like, so I'd become a one-stop shop for pithy, snide put-downs of other bands. It'd become a bit of a shtick and, probably egged on by the fact it was getting printed, I was doing it more and more. It took me quite a while to realise how petty this was, but at that point I was in the thick of it. I suppose it was because our music had been so unfashionable when we started that I thought we really had to fight for our place to be heard among the commercial and, to my ears, more flippant music. Even by this point, when people seemed eager to hear what we were doing, it still continued. In a rallying cry against the music world in general, I told *Melody Maker*: 'We will take you on and destroy you.' And I meant it.

We played quite early at Reading but not quite the before-noon slots that we'd had the previous two days. We were on mid-afternoon and the tent seemed reasonably busy by the time the moment came for us to play. We were sandwiched in between a band called Snug and the new Britpop outfit led by former Ride guitarist Andy Bell, Hurricane #1. We'd been listening to a lot of the completely over-the-top hair metal band Manowar and we came on to one of their songs narrated by Orson Welles. It wasn't subtle. We played like our lives depended on it, thrashing at our guitars till our hands bled. During the noise section of 'Like Herod', Brendan and I jumped into the photo pit. We were writhing about on the floor, smashing our guitars against each other pretending they were light sabres, conjuring a ferocious racket. I was living the dream, ignited by seeing Nirvana there six years previously. There was a huge bucket of water for the bouncers to hydrate the crowd and Brendan dunked his plugged-in guitar into it. An extremely dangerous move. Things tended to get a bit dangerous with Brendan. He was something else that day. Playing his heart out and being even wilder than usual. We ended the show with 'Stereo Dee', pounding our guitars mercilessly before leaving the stage to a wall of feedback and dying amps. The gig was an absolute triumph and we left the stage feeling like we were on top of the world. We partied into the night, at one with the universe and anticipating the next steps in our holy adventure.

What we didn't know was that it would be the last time Brendan played with us as a member of Mogwai.

A week later we were back in Glasgow and about to do our first ever 'feature' interview for the *NME* with the writer Keith Cameron, a fellow Scot. We all got on with Keith and were very much at ease in his company. However, the cracks in the band were turning into fissures. The stress of the recording had taken its toll and some factions were starting to form. Brendan hadn't been happy with the way I dealt with things. I was no doubt extremely focused and my manner could leave a lot to be desired at times. I had a tendency to be quite tyrannical and I'm certain he wasn't the only one getting annoyed. We did the interview the day after a night out had got a bit messy and I had been thrown out of the art school union (I can't remember what for but I'm sure I deserved it). We did the interview in the pub – where else? – spending most of the time telling jokes about the recently deceased Princess Diana and berating other musicians. We were all getting along fine until later that night. Arab Strap, our label mates and by now real-life mates, were doing a show in the tiny Nice N Sleazy and we positioned ourselves right at the front. By the time the Strap came onstage we were mortal drunk. I was in front of the stage and Brendan was standing to my left alongside John Robb, the writer and singer of The Membranes. Brendan and John, old pals, were catching up but it was all I could hear. I asked them to be quiet a few times and, having my requests fall upon deaf ears, I totally lost it and told Brendan where to go. At first he thought I was kidding, but when he realised I wasn't, he went bananas. He stormed up the stairs to the left of the stage and lobbed a drum stool at me. Thankfully it missed me but almost hit the utterly bemused John Robb. When I got home later that night my dad said to me, 'There's a message from Brendan on the answerphone.' He looked slightly perplexed, which led me to believe that the message was not the usual kind. In the message, Brendan said he'd quit the band and told me quite clearly what he thought of me. He didn't miss me. It might have been the case that I'd fired him first. To be honest I don't remember and I'm not sure it mattered. He was no longer in the band.

Unbeknownst to me, the rest of the band had met up with Brendan and he had told them his plan. I'm not sure what was said but the upshot of the meeting was that only Brendan would be leaving. It had been great having Brendan in the band but there had always been a feeling of impermanence to his tenure. As unsure as we were about our album, I don't think that we would have been able to make one at all without Brendan. He was an experienced musician and a veteran of several albums, and his guidance had been invaluable. The fact that his leaving had been triggered by an altercation with me didn't feel great, but I'm convinced that if it hadn't been that, it would have been something else further down the line. The relationship had run its course and, now that we were back to being a four-piece, we had an album under our belts that we had to tour.

Our Young Team would live to fight another day.

12.

Ivy League Adventures with Pavement

We didn't have to wait too long to embark on our first adventure without Brendan. With our debut album, *Mogwai Young Team*, about to come out, we had been invited by Pavement to open for them on a string of dates in America. We were also booked to do a few headline shows of our own while we were there. Our first American tour!

We flew into New York and were greeted by the guy doing sound and tour managing for us, a small, rather serious, hippy-ish guy called Mike. He seemed relaxed enough and we were assured that we were in safe hands. Coming along for the ride was our pal Lee Cohen.

The drive up from Manhattan to the first gig in Burlington, Vermont, was lovely. The summer was fading and the trees were a million different shades of orange. It was truly beautiful. The gigs Pavement were doing weren't in the most obvious of cities and they were doing it in a fairly low-key way. They had a van instead of a tour bus and a crew of just two. Deb Pastor was their driver and tour manager, and they had one roadie, the hilarious Hull native Andy Dimmack. We had a load of mutual friends with Andy and really enjoyed his company. We'd bonded with the Pavement guys during the drunken demolition of Blur's rider in Belgium and were eager to spend time with them, and of course to watch them play. For soundchecks they would muck about doing covers of Velvets and Zeppelin songs. The gig in Burlington was in a small hall and Pavement coming to town was clearly a big deal, as it wasn't on the normal route for most tours. When Stephen sang a line mentioning Vermont the crowd went mad; the whole tour had amazing energy. Pavement were a band at the peak of their powers but were clearly doing it for fun and going to places that they fancied playing rather than embarking on some crazed quest for fame and money. They treated us really well. We were pretty much broke and, probably realising this, Pavement started to donate their deli tray to us. God knows what we'd have eaten if they hadn't hooked us up. Possibly each other.

A few nights into the tour there was probably the strangest night of all, at the Campus Club in Princeton, the famous Ivy League university. I'm guessing this show was well paid and probably what the rest of the tour was founded on. The only issue was the exclusive nature of the venue: only students at the prestigious university could go. As happy as I'm sure the Pavement guys were with the fee, they definitely weren't happy about only playing to privileged kids, and the number of heartbroken Pavement fans outside, unable to get in, was a source of serious disgruntlement. Our dressing room was in an ornate library, full of ancient books and mahogany. There was a beer tap too, which we were exceedingly happy about. It had a window that led to some grounds outside and Bob from Pavement took it upon himself to sneak as many of the shut-out kids in through the window as possible. The gig was a surreal affair.

Pavement were a big band and we weren't the most obvious openers for them. Some nights we'd go down great but other times people were a bit perplexed. From time to time people would heckle us, but it didn't bother us. Pavement felt like our big brothers and would pass on sage advice, like how using your shoe as an ashtray would stop them smelling. Or so Bob told us.

The final night with Pavement was in Athens, Georgia, on a night that also coincided with Dominic's twenty-first birthday.

That was cause for celebration and, it being our last night on tour with Pavement, we made sure to have a party. Sadly our show wasn't that memorable and we had to restart a few songs, which wasn't ideal. That night Michael Stipe from REM tried to get one of our CDs for free from the merch stand, but Deb, ever the musicians' champion, told him to get stuffed. Surely he could afford ten bucks.

After we said our goodbyes to Pavement we embarked on some of our own dates. Unlike the Pavement shows, these had been booked by our label and not a booking agent, and it really showed. The first gig in Detroit went well enough, but it was the next day that things started to unravel. The label had an offer for us to get on the bill with a band called The Seelies in Boston, but the show fell on the night after we played in Chicago, where we were also doing an in-store. The drive from one gig to the next was over fifteen hours, leaving us almost no time to get there. We were used to some tricky travel scenarios but this was another level. To exacerbate things we'd had a breakdown on the way from Detroit to Chicago so we were already sleep deprived. The chilled-out mood of Mike, our driver, was crumbling rapidly as the stress of the situation started to really get to him. The show in Chicago was at the infamous Lounge Ax venue, which had been graced by so many of our favourite bands like Tortoise, Shellac, Smog and the like. When we got to the venue we asked where the rider was and were told that they gave out drink tickets instead. Unused to this way of doing things, I immediately asked the barman what the strongest drink I could get with my ticket might be and was informed that it was a drink called a Long Island Iced Tea. The name seemed harmless enough and I proceeded to consume as many of them as my tickets would allow. I got very drunk. Very quickly. I managed to play the show, just. I was legless though, and honestly in no state to travel. Travel we must, however, and with no sleep we got in the van and trundled our way to Boston because the label insisted it was too important an opportunity to miss. I could not stop puking. I was a mess and had never experienced alcohol poisoning like it. By lunchtime, as the sun was starting to bake, we stopped at a McDonald's to get some food. I couldn't eat but relished the opportunity to wash my vomit-encrusted face. I got about two metres into the restaurant when I saw a six-foot poster for a burger called a Big Cheesy and it set me off again. I was a sunburnt, sweaty Scottish mess puking in every state between Illinois and Massachusetts. Seeing the sorry condition I was in, my bandmates offered $5 to whoever would make out with me, and one of them obliged.

By the time we got to Boston we were an exhausted shambles. Sleep-deprived and, in my case, suffering so badly from booze poisoning that I would have been better placed in a hospital than on a stage. However, we'd been promised by the label that the gig would be worth it. Was it fuck!

The following night in New Haven, Connecticut, Shelley from Jetset came along. After the endurance test that we'd suffered we weren't particularly pleased to see her. We'd got shifty vibes from her from the start and the growing animosity had been compounded before the tour during a particularly grim conference call when she lost her shit after finding out that she'd have to license *Mogwai Young Team* from Chemikal Underground because they had paid for the recording of the album. With Shelley that night was someone who was familiar to me, an English guy called Barry Hogan. Barry was a concert promoter in London and I'd actually been at the first show he ever put on: Tortoise, Snowpony and Flying Saucer Attack. He was friends with Shelley and had come up for the gig alongside Daniel and Sam from Jetset. Barry had a ferocious sense of humour and was great company. At times back then we'd find it a bit of a struggle finding people to party with. That wasn't an issue with Barry. We got on straight away and he was an instant convert to the cheap pills we'd taken to buying from gas stations called Pseudoephedrine, more commonly known as truckers' speed. We'd take a few before we went on and it would make the gigs way more intense. Mick, our agent, worked with a different promoter in London but Barry was really keen to be involved. Mick was a loyal guy, though, and Barry would have to wait a bit longer for us to work together.

The final night of the tour was back in New York at a venue called Brownies. We were playing with a great band called American Analog Set. The gig was packed and it felt like we were really on the verge of something great. Bob from Pavement came onstage and played some extra drums on 'Mogwai Fear Satan'. It was gloriously shambolic, exciting and fun.

Before we flew home we had a few more engagements. Jetset made us sign what felt like a million posters to be given away with albums, and also got us to record endless radio IDs where we'd say, 'Hi, we're Mogwai and you're listening to KRWTF', or whatever. They also got us to do another in-store, this time at Other Music in Manhattan. I'd been an avid record collector ever since I could remember and this was hands down the best record shop I'd ever been in. They had every good and weird record imaginable, and the staff were incredibly helpful and accommodating. We set up on the floor and played for half an hour before we headed to the airport to catch our flight. This was the week before our album came out and it felt like there was something magical in the air. We'd settled into life post-Brendan without too much fuss and were glad to have made it to the end of a pretty trying tour relatively unscathed. It felt like we'd shed all the drama and were back to just making music and having fun.

Safely on UK soil we eagerly awaited the release of the album. Back then reviews could make or break a record and I nervously waited to see what the verdict would be from the music papers. When the reviews landed they could barely have been better. John Mulvey in the *NME* and Sharon O'Connell in *Melody Maker* both lauded the record and described it as a triumph. A new website in America called *Pitchfork* gave it 9.7 in their bizarre Olympic diving-like scoring system. We felt like we'd dodged a bullet. I thought that our record fell short but in truth I think my expectations were so high that it would be almost impossible to achieve what I wanted, even if we'd had all the time in the world. Albums are a snapshot in time and as flawed as our debut was, it was a perfect document of that crazy, exciting, demented period we'd lived through. All I'd wanted from our music was permanence. Music that wouldn't be forgotten a few weeks later. I think we'd managed to achieve that no matter how flawed it was.

We held a release party for the album in The 13th Note and it was a fittingly messy affair. And it actually wasn't even just a release party. It was a signing party. Even though they had been putting out our records since the early part of the year, we had still never signed a contract with Chemikal Underground and were going to do so at the party. All of our pals from Glasgow, Belle and Sebastian, Arab Strap and our Chemikal Underground bosses, The Delgados, were there. Even Brendan came along to put the messiness of his departure behind us. The reaction to the album had taken us by surprise and we thought we'd really got away with it. In the toilets that night, the four of us made a pact, swearing that we'd never mess up again like we felt we had with *Mogwai Young Team*. We swore that our second album would stand alongside the all-time greats. It was drunken daftness but there was an air of seriousness about it. We cared about the music more than anything else. We had no idea if what we did next would truly be great, but by hell we were going to do our very best to try.

The day after *Mogwai Young Team* came out we were on the radio, doing a live session for the ex-journalist, now DJ, Mary Anne Hobbs on Radio 1. Aidan was joining us to sing 'R U Still In 2 It?' and we took the opportunity of being in London to go and see Rachels, an incredible band formed by the members of the Louisville outfit Rodan, who we adored. The gig was promoted by Barry Hogan and it was a great chance to catch up with him again. Barry was as entertaining as ever and used the opportunity to badger me about letting him promote the Mogwai shows. Rachels were stupendous. Watching them play their delicate chamber music was the perfect way to celebrate our first record coming out. I was blissfully unaware of the effect it would have on my life in the years going forward. I was a kid, really, and only saw things from week to week.

On the day of the session, while me and Aidan were already in London, the rest of the band travelled down from Glasgow with the equipment. With nothing to do until the band turned up with the gear, Aidan and I whiled away the day in the pub. By the time the rest of the band materialised we were fairly wrecked. Mary Anne is a true music connoisseur and unbelievably passionate about what she loves. She was a massive Arab Strap fan and had been beyond effusive about the records they'd released. Because of Mary Anne's exuberance about Arab Strap, we had a running joke that she had a crush on Aidan. In our inebriated state I teased her about it on the air. She took it in good humour, though, and our set went quite well, especially considering the state that me and Aidan were in.

The following month we went to Europe for a handful of gigs and our final shows of the year in Glasgow and London. The European gigs consisted of one in the Belgian town of Leuven, and then four as part of a package tour of France organised by the legendary French music magazine *Les Inrockuptibles*. Also on the tour were the Welsh band Stereophonics and the Scottish soul singer Finley Quaye.

The gig in Belgium was a total embarrassment. It was held in an arts centre in the town most famous for the beer Stella Artois. The show itself went fine but the perk of getting to drink as much Stella as we wanted was one that I indulged in a tad too liberally. After we played, on top of the buckets of strong Belgian lager we also had a bottle of Goldschläger spirits, which we were drinking with gusto in the van. I was adamant that I could finish the bottle and proceeded to do just that. Unfortunately, in doing so I had forfeited the use of my legs and, as I left the van to go back to the dressing room, they gave way under me. The venue had a huge glass wall which separated the street from the gig-goers who were in the bar downstairs. As I fell out of the van like a drugged elephant, every single one of the people who one hour earlier had been watching us play could see me in all my glory falling over and struggling (and failing) to stop my elasticated trousers from falling down. It was an absolute scene.

The following day was the first date of the *Les Inrockuptibles* tour. Musically it was a real mismatch. The Stereophonics, like us, were a new band but that's where the similarities ended. They were very much radio rock and their music couldn't be further from ours. If the tour had been in the UK we would have probably been bottled off, but the French are a far more accepting and cultured lot and no one batted an eyelid. The Stereophonics were nice guys and we got along fine, though the differences between us were marked. Before they played they would practise their harmonies by playing the Extreme song 'More Than Words', with the whole band singing along with Kelly, the singer, and his acoustic guitar. For our pre-gig ritual we would sniff as many poppers as we could and listen to 'Raw Power' by The Stooges at ear-splitting volume. Finley Quaye never turned up, which meant that both us and Stereophonics got to play a bit longer. From the first night it became clear that the French took music really seriously and had a real connection with us. The gig in Paris at La Cigale was wonderful. It's a big, old theatre like the Astoria where we'd played back in January, and it absolutely suited us. The difference now was that people actually knew who we were and the reaction from the Parisian crowd was incredible. Ever since then we've always had a great connection with Paris.

The final night in Toulouse was in an amazing venue called Le Bikini, which had a swimming pool at the back of the venue and the best food we'd ever been fed at a gig. The November weather was a bit chilly to swim but the venue and its fantastic hospitality made a huge impression on us.

With the stress of recording the album behind us, and relishing the positivity shown towards it, we felt in a really good place. We'd written our first new music since the album, an eleven-minute epic that played with the quiet/loud dynamic in a way we hadn't quite pulled off thus far. It started with just the guitars and continued at a barely audible level until the bass came in like a juggernaut, followed by the drums and the whole band, only to unwind for the last few minutes as it fell back to silence. It was called 'Christmas Steps' after a street that we'd seen in Bristol. It felt great to have some new music that wasn't attached to our very early days or our tumultuous album. We were looking forward with determination. To round the year off we had two headline gigs in London and Glasgow, both of which felt significant. Other than at T in the Park, we hadn't played in Scotland since the start of the year, and so much had happened to us in the meantime. We really felt like a different band after the various experiences we had shared over the previous twelve months.

Our hometown show was in The Arches, a nightclub-cum-arts venue built around the railway arches of Central Station. The gig in London was at ULU, a student union synonymous with iconic gigs. It was a good bit bigger than The Garage where we'd had the eventful show earlier in the year. We knew that we'd fucked up then and wanted to make amends and establish that we were, in fact, a serious band and not some drunken circus act. Probably because of our age and the way we looked, people in Glasgow didn't take us particularly seriously and eyebrows were raised when we said we were playing The Arches. We definitely wanted to show that there was more to us than daft antics and tracksuits. Both shows felt like opportunities to right some wrongs and establish ourselves.

The first of the shows was in London. The gig had sold out in advance and it felt different to those we'd played before. Our album had been well received and there was a sense of anticipation that I'd never noticed before. Conscious of the utter clusterfuck at The Garage show we decided to eschew drinking before we played. Another reason for this was it was to be the first time we played 'Christmas Steps' and it wasn't the easiest song to play. It was hard enough to play sober, so playing it drunk would be to pointlessly invite disaster. Our friends in the brilliant band Hood were opening for us, and it felt like the first time a gig of ours was a real occasion. We opened with the ten-minute monster 'Like Herod', which definitely set the tone. We were sober and focused, unwilling to let things slip from our grasp. As well as 'Christmas Steps' we also played another unreleased song called 'Waltz'. I felt that some of our earlier music had been a tad one-dimensional and wanted our newer songs to have a bit more to them. Having quieter songs in the set really worked too, and the gig felt like a big step up for us. We didn't feel like lucky kids any more. The experience of the Astoria with Pavement at the start of the year felt a million years ago. Now we were confident on those bigger stages because we had the music to back up our bratty claims.

Aidan had travelled down with us to sing 'R U Still In 2 It?' After the show we partied hard and Aidan definitely suffered for it the next morning, puking his guts up into a plastic bag on the tube to the general disgust of the appalled commuters.

For our final show of the year we were back in Glasgow. Like London, this felt like an occasion. Pretty much everyone we knew would be there and we felt the pressure to play well. Before The Arches, all of our Glasgow gigs had been in bars, and this room held four times as many people as any of those places. We'd started to get reviews in the broadsheet newspapers and all of our parents would be coming along. We definitely didn't want to mess up.

Martin is a huge football fan, and as a Glasgow Celtic supporter his moods would be largely dependent on whether they won or lost. When hanging out with Martin I'd go along to Celtic

Park from time to time if he had a spare ticket. In an effort to predict Martin's mood, I'd taken to checking on the results so I could see how approachable he'd be from day to day, and it soon came to my realisation that I also cared if they lost. I've supported Celtic ever since then. On the day of The Arches gig, Celtic were playing in the League Cup final against Dundee Utd. Martin wasn't happy about missing the game, especially as Celtic had had a pretty rough time of it in the preceding years with their city rivals Rangers having been dominant for most of the decade. Martin has always been 100 per cent dedicated to the band, though, and knew that the gig was important.

As well as all our parents, Brendan came along, as did Barry from the studio. Barry was dating a workmate of Adele's called Ailidh and I was hanging out with him a lot. The crowd was full and pretty rowdy. Like London we introduced quite a few new songs into our set and the boozed-up Glasgow audience weren't quite ready for that, with Aidan having to fulfil the role of librarian by coming to the mic and asking folk to be quiet. For the last song of the set Brendan rejoined us to play extra drums on 'Mogwai Fear Satan'. Reuniting with Brendan felt brilliant, even if it was only temporary.

As we were leaving the stage I went to lean against a curtained wall, only to find out that there was in fact no wall behind the curtain and I fell eight feet or so off the stage and onto the floor. I was bruised but so happy with how the gig had gone, as well as the news that Celtic had won the cup 3–0.

What a year.

13.

'Ambient Hard with Hard Bits'

Like 1997, we started 1998 back at the Astoria in London. Things were the same but completely different.

We were invited again to play as part of the *NME* Brats series of gigs, only this time we weren't first on, we were second headliners. Playing before us were our pals Arab Strap and headlining were the Welsh band Super Furry Animals, whose music we all loved. My girlfriend Adele had been invited the previous summer to sing with Arab Strap on a song and she would be singing with them at the gig. It was great to be able to spend time with her because most of the time there wouldn't be room in the van, or anywhere for our friends or partners to sleep. There was barely any room for us, truth be told. We decided to make our trip to London a bit of a holiday and went down a few days earlier so we could see a few of the other shows. By this point we didn't have to stay on floors and were instead staying at a hotel, The Columbia. The Columbia was well known for being a rock and roll hotel, kind of like the cantina in *Star Wars* but with musicians instead of aliens. The rooms were cheap, which was probably the main reason bands stayed there, but they were also happy enough to keep the bar open till all hours which definitely appealed. Whether the bar stayed open pretty much depended on who was working there, but more often than not someone would be willing to keep selling drinks till the crack of dawn.

We were following our Astoria show with our first trip to Ireland and a UK tour. Joining us on those dates were Aerial M, the new band of the Louisville guitar player from Slint, David Pajo. I'd met David a few years earlier when he was on tour with Tortoise and they popped into The 13th Note looking for somewhere to eat, and we'd stayed in touch. Aerial M were playing one of the Astoria shows opening for Stereolab, with whom David had also had a stint playing bass. Over the years I'd bump into David and the Tortoise guys and we always hit it off. They were funny, down to earth guys and incredible musicians, with none of the aloofness you might expect from legendary musicians. Getting to play with one of our musical heroes was one thing, but having their band actually open for you was utterly surreal. Aerial M were majestic when they opened for Stereolab. Tony, the young Black kid playing drums, was next level amazing. On bass was the glamorous Cassie, whose boyfriend Tim played the other guitar. We quickly introduced ourselves after their set and said how much we were looking forward to the tour starting the following week.

The other show we went to see was Spiritualized. Things had changed for them a lot since we'd seen them at the Phoenix Festival. Their album *Ladies and Gentleman* had been a huge critical and commercial success and they were the one band that people were most excited about seeing. I had a weird experience before they came on when one of their crew ran out to the bar to ask me how the Spacemen 3 song 'Suicide' went. They were going to do a live jam of the song with the actual band Suicide, who were in town to play at Meltdown, but apparently could not remember how the riff went. I was happy to relay the information about the two-note riff and was excited to see the show. Spiritualized were incredible. They'd grown as a band and created an incredible psychedelic wash of sound that really blew me away. I'd been a Spacemen 3 fan since I was a kid and was so happy to see Jason do so well. I loved Suicide too. Their music was so singular and powerful. They'd massively influenced so much of the music I loved.

That night back at The Columbia everyone seemed to be there. We were hanging out with David and the Aerial M guys and Arab Strap. Adele noticed Martin Rev and Alan Vega from Suicide and we went over to talk to them. They were lovely guys and seemed genuinely happy that musicians so much younger than them were excited about their music. We weren't the only ones wanting to talk to them. An older, dishevelled guy with floppy brown hair was there as well. When I heard him speak I realised he was a fellow Scot, and it took a few minutes before I recognised William Reid from the Mary Chain. It was late and it'd be fair to say that everyone was pretty drunk. William was really trashed though. We ended up hanging out till the wee hours, William regaling us with tales in Arab Strap's room. It got messy and it became clear that William wasn't in a good way. Still, only a year earlier we'd been terrified about getting on a stage bigger than a foot tall and here I was hanging out with some of my musical heroes.

The headline band on our night were Super Furry Animals, who were great. We'd met a few times and they seemed like real kindred spirits. Their sound guy, Michael Brennan, an enigmatic Fifer with a penchant for tall tales and excess, was also doing our sound. Even though he was only a few years older than us, he'd been doing sound for loads of great bands since he was a teenager: Slowdive, Elastica, Babes in Toyland and even the Ramones. He was super affable and great company; like us though, he was a bit of a maniac and never turned down any opportunity to party. Michael had a story about everything and was great at putting you at ease. He was also a brilliant sound engineer with an absolute understanding of what it was we were trying to achieve with our music. Also along for the tour was Ally Christie, our guitar tech. Michael and Ally would have a constant back and forth. Driving us on the tour in his own van was a big, outwardly stern guy called Stevie Broadfoot who had been a bouncer in King Tut's and gave off the vibe of someone you shouldn't mess with but was in fact a gentle soul. He'd converted the van himself and, with its seats hung on chains that converted into bunks, it had the vibe of a DIY sex dungeon on wheels. Along for the ride as well was a pal of Martin's called Gav, who was there to sell our merch. Gav was daft as a brush but also really excited about getting away and having an adventure.

It was astonishing how much things had changed in a year. This time when we looked forward to playing the Astoria we did so with confidence rather than trepidation. In that year we'd written, recorded and released our debut album, but we already had eyes on the next one. With this under our belts the experience of playing to the big London crowd was so different from the year before. When we started any of our singles or songs from the album the audience responded by clapping in recognition. Our new songs had long, quiet spells in them and I was concerned that we'd lose people's attention, but thankfully that wasn't the case. Even the unheard 'Ex Cowboy' went down great. The Super Furry Animals were (and are) a brilliant band but are definitely a lot more immediate than us and had a string of songs that had been all over the radio. For the finale of our set we played the by-now-traditional 'Mogwai Fear Satan', joined on drums by Aidan from Arab Strap. The song usually gradually faded to nothing but that night we all started playing louder and louder, building to a cacophonous crescendo. It felt like a release and a celebration. The twelve months since our first tentative steps onto that stage had been huge, challenging and transformative.

After the show we partied long into the night with the Super Furries. Their singer, Gruff, was really inspiring, charming, smart and humble, not qualities you associate with rock singers, particularly in the nineties when the exact opposite was usually the case. Loads of bands were lairy morons. There was a lot of money in the music industry, and you didn't have to look far to find some coked-up idiot talking utter crap. It was actually quite hard to find people in the industry who actually liked or had any particular knowledge of music, such was the ubiquity of wankers.

After London we travelled across the sea for our first gigs in Ireland. In Dublin we played with an amazing psych-rock trio called Wormhole, who we'd played with before, and in Belfast we shared the stage again with our old pals Backwater.

Once we'd finished in Ireland we headed back to England to start the tour with Aerial M, who we bonded with immediately. At the gig in Oxford someone brought some acid. After the show I was skateboarding around the beer glass-strewn dancefloor, high as a kite and in my element. All of us were wasted and we embarked on a wild psychedelic experience after the show, in the Travelodge we were all staying in. Tony the drummer's eyes went all black like a demon and he built a tent out of all the furniture, then we stayed up all night full of utter nonsense, glowing with camaraderie. It really was the best time because unlike the year before we were more focused on the music, and people being familiar with our record made it all the better.

Our last show with Aerial M was in Leeds at a legendary venue called the Duchess of York. It was sad to say goodbye to them but we left them as great friends, having had one of the best run of shows we'd done to date. Next stop was Europe, but first we had to play in Edinburgh at The Liquid Rooms, the biggest gig we'd done so far. The gig was superb and we were treated really well by the girl working for the venue, a Scottish girl with a Canadian accent and bleach blonde hair called Grainne. She was really helpful and had a great sense of humour. Her dad, like mine, was from Hamilton and we had a lot in common and made an immediate connection. After the gig we all went out till late in the night, partying with friends old and new. It felt like a great way to end what had been a brilliant run in the UK. And then on to Europe.

Before the tour had started, Colin had come to where we were rehearsing in Maryhill (with five of us now, we'd outgrown

Martin's bedroom) and talked us through the tour. The European dates seemed pretty far apart from each other and it was suggested that it might be a good idea to do them in a tour bus. Stevie, our driver, was adamant that we could manage fine in his van though, and we accepted that. He said that there were 'one or two big drives' to contend with. When we actually got to Europe we realised quite quickly that Stevie's optimism had got the better of him. The drives were insane. It was the norm for us to only manage a few hours' sleep in whatever motel we'd got to after the show. With all of us having to exist on hardly any sleep our nerves were starting to fray. We were extremely tired. The venues in Europe treated you far better than the UK, but there were some cultural issues we had to contend with, as far as some people on the tour went. The night after playing a great show in Paris, we played another good one in Bruges in Belgium, after which Gav our T-shirt seller ran into the dressing room to proclaim that he'd sold everything. 'Everything? Are you sure?' I said, only for Gav to affirm that he had indeed sold every single T-shirt we had with us. It was then that we worked out that he didn't realise Belgian Francs were not the same value as French Francs and he had sold all of our T-shirts for about a tenth of what they would normally go for. Things with Stevie were getting a bit strained too. He could be quite stern and it was causing a bit of stress.

In Paris we were invited to go on a mainstream TV chat show, which turned into a surreal experience. Robert De Niro was on explaining why he was returning his French knighthood after a false accusation of being part of a prostitution ring. He was speaking through a translator and things were clearly very tense with the hosts. I'm sure us appearing to play at deafening volume in between the to and fro didn't help things either. The other musical guests were the pop group Aqua promoting their hit 'Barbie Girl'. They were a friendly bunch and we hung out for a bit after the show. The big bald guy from Aqua asked Stevie what kind of music we made and he replied, 'Ambient hard with hard bits', which amused us greatly.

About halfway through the gruelling run we had a day off and decided to spend it in the Eastern European city of Prague. We had just arrived in Prague when Stevie made a wrong turn and decided to rectify his mistake by reversing a long way down the road, a manoeuvre that was somewhat of a speciality for him. Gav was in the passenger seat, and when Stevie rhetorically asked, 'Where are all the cars coming from?', Gav pointed down the road and said, 'Over there.' Delirious with exhaustion, we were in stitches at Gav's reply and before long the whole van was in a fit of giggles. Gav took severe umbrage at what he perceived as us laughing *at* him and told us to shut up. However, the more he told us to stop laughing the funnier it got, and eventually in a fit of rage Gav punched and smashed in the windscreen of the van. It was a Sunday. In Prague. So much for a relaxing day off. Michael managed to calm the situation and we all went out for dinner while poor Stevie searched for someone to fix the van. On the way to dinner, Michael (who was a big stoner) went looking for weed and managed to get a knife pulled on him. Eventually we found somewhere to eat and it was one of the nicest meals I'd ever had. Not only that but it cost hardly anything.

Things weren't going well with Stevie. The massive drives and his somewhat Victorian communication skills were causing a rift between him and the band. After a gig I asked him to lend me a pen to get a friend's phone number, and he said no. I kept asking him and he kept refusing, and eventually I lost the plot. My patience was running thin and I could have a fiery temper at times. Eventually Stevie lent me the pen but it all seemed really unnecessary. There was a gap between the first leg of the tour and the second and we decided that we should try someone else for the second half. As great a guy as Stevie was, it just wasn't working out. We weren't the band for him and he wasn't the tour manager for us.

The tour was massive and, bar a few weeks off, lasted the first five months of the year. We were all in a rotten state of exhaustion so decided to get a tour bus for the final leg, which meant we could sleep while travelling and be in better shape to play the gigs. Well, that was the plan anyway. Simon Smith, who had been the drummer for The Wedding Present, was our new tour manager. He was a bookish, bespectacled Yorkshireman, an affable chap who gave off an aura that you should not, under any circumstances, get him angry. Something of a Leeds Bruce Banner. Simon had considered becoming a park attendant but had decided to go into tour management as that had been his forte when in The Wedding Present. With our shiny (and expensive) tour bus and our new tour manager, we embarked on our final run around Europe. What could possibly go wrong?

Fucking plenty it would seem.

When we got to Italy things got a bit weird. A pal of ours called Kiko, a pharmacist who now presented a show on MTV, came to hang out with us for a few shows and brought some pharmaceutical gifts: bottles of Valium and various painkillers. After our final Italian show in Bitritto we had a few days off before playing a gig at the Bikini in Toulouse, where we'd played with Stereophonics a few months before. With some time off we decided to partake in Kiko's gifts. Of course, I was an extremely willing participant. I can't remember much about what happened next, though I have a few hazy memories. I remember John in a service station filling a bowl of chips pretty much to the brim with olive oil. I remember listening to a mix tape that Adele had made me featuring 'God Only Knows' by the Beach Boys on repeat. While rolling about semi-comatose in this state, things were getting extremely weird with Gav. He'd become really aggressive in his fucked-up state and Simon had had to hide the drugs from him. This didn't go down well and he'd developed a toxic paranoia. He was sharing a room with Martin, who'd heard him on the phone to someone back home saying that he was going to kill him. The next day we found him in a wheelbarrow next to the hotel. Simon realised that things were not at all good with Gav and got him a flight home and sent him off to the airport.

When we arrived in Toulouse we were shocked and astonished to find a remorseful Gav in the dressing room, having apparently missed his flight.

I was barely in any state to play a gig and spent much of the day trying to climb fences. Unfortunately I had to do an interview with *NME,* who had flown a journalist over from London to do a feature on us. We did the interview with the somewhat bemused writer Victoria Seagal and somehow managed to play the gig. The interview had been an unholy mess – I regaled her with an a cappella rendition of 'Frozen' by Madonna while she tried to ask serious questions about our music. I would try to avoid prescription drugs from thereon in. To her credit, Victoria didn't mention the state I was in; she could have had a field day but clearly saw we were just daft boys and thankfully concentrated on writing about our music.

A few days after that debacle we went to Madrid to play the Festimad festival. We got in the night before and made the most of it. The Cramps, one of my favourite ever bands, were playing and I was thrilled about seeing them. Our bus was full of booze that we'd accumulated from the month on the road and we made sure to party that night. The Cramps were unbelievable. The drummer played with bones as sticks and the singer, Lux Interior, climbed the PA like some kind of demonic horror movie Iggy Pop. Poison Ivy, the guitar player, was coolness personified. She is one of my guitar heroes and was on fire that night. They finished their set with a version of 'Surfing Bird' that lasted about fifteen minutes with Lux climbing underneath all the stage cables and rising up like some kind of Swamp Thing. It was hands down the greatest rock and roll show I've ever seen. Backstage I introduced myself to them as Plasmatron. Giddy from the amazing show, I

got absolutely annihilated on booze. Our friends Ash were playing the stage we were due to play the next day, and during their
set I climbed up the scaffolding only to be chastised severely by
the stage manager. Back at the bus my excesses caught up with
me and I puked everywhere, so hard in fact that all the blood
vessels around my eyes burst, which resulted in my face becoming so blotched that I resembled a lizard. A sweaty Scottish lizard
in human form. The next day when we arrived to play, the stage
manager saw me and said I wasn't allowed on the stage after my
antics. Thankfully Simon assured him that I really was meant
to be there, so we got on and played, hungover and sweating
buckets in the Spanish heat.

As summer approached, so did the festival season.

The weekend of Benicàssim was epic. Benicàssim is in Spain,
next to a beach town frequented by tourists. Back then it was
the biggest for alternative rock, with Sonic Youth, The Jesus and
Mary Chain, Björk and Primal Scream all performing. We were
playing before Tortoise on the second stage on the Sunday. With
so many bands we liked on the line-up we decided to make a
weekend of it. The festival is notorious for hedonism and as well
as a backstage swimming pool there was a guy appointed by the
festival to cater for all the bands' pharmaceutical needs. Our old
pal Kiko was also there in a similar capacity. From the get-go it
was carnage. Being in Spain next to the beach with so many of
my favourite bands playing was incredible. Adele had come out
for the weekend and we had the best time, swimming in the sea
during the day, hanging out at the pool backstage and watching
bands. It was also the first time we met Primal Scream. They
had been one of my favourite bands since I was a kid and it was
great to meet Bobby and Innes. Bobby was super friendly and
clearly happy to see another Glaswegian band doing well. At that
point Primal Scream had Mani of The Stone Roses and Kevin
Shields from My Bloody Valentine in their ranks. As a live force

they were visceral. These were guys we'd grown up idolising and it was amazing to spend time with them. At that point Primal Scream were nuts. One of their crew was on hand at all times to make sure that they had speed. They were constantly wasted, taking Dexedrine as if they were sweeties. Martin, a huge Stone Roses fan, as well as someone who avoided drugs because of his pacemaker, even ended up taking an E because it was chucked in his mouth by Mani. The whole weekend was a narcotic haze. I remember floating on my back in the pool, looking at the stars and listening to Sonic Youth play 'Shadow Of Doubt', out of my mind, thinking that things didn't get better than this. By the time our set came around we were frazzled. We knew that the company we were in meant that we had to perform. We were on before Tortoise, who were our peers, and surrounded by so many of the bands that had been the reason we'd picked up guitars in the first place. We played with a focused ferocity, performing many of the songs that would go on to make up our as yet unrecorded second album. We felt that we were on the crest of a wave, about to really make our mark. After we played we watched Tortoise and then Primal Scream absolutely obliterate a massive crowd on the main stage. It felt like it wouldn't be too long before we'd be up there.

Around that time I got my first and, to this day, last tattoo: a *Mogwai Young Team* logo on my arm – an amalgamation of the three letters, MYT, in the style of the famous Glasgow gangs that inspired the album title. Martin, John and Dominic (and Brendan) all had the same tattoo already, and I was assured by my lying bandmates that it doesn't hurt . . . but sadly that was not remotely true. It hurt like hell. I'm still glad I did it though. I've since become aware of sigil magic and I've no doubt that us dedicating ourselves to our music in this way had an effect on the band.

The preparations for our second album were really starting to take shape. We had loads of songs that we were happy with and had been rehearsing religiously every day we were not on tour. The question came up about where to record it. Recording it in Hamilton again didn't seem that great an idea as the distractions of being so close to Glasgow hadn't worked out that well for our first album, so the folks at Chemikal Underground suggested a solution. They'd just had their record mixed by Dave Fridmann, the Mercury Rev bass player, and it had turned out great so they suggested we go over to America and record it at his studio, Tarbox, in upstate New York. The latest Mercury Rev album that Dave had made, *Deserter's Songs*, was one of the best records released that year. Me and Dominic were huge Mercury Rev fans, particularly their early uber-psychedelic druggy noise *Yerself Is Steam* period. Dominic had put 'Carwash Hair' on the mix tape he'd given me when we started the band. We agreed to look into it and they arranged for me to have a phone call with Dave.

When I spoke to Dave, far from him being some psychedelic wizard-type character, he was just a lovely down to earth guy. When I suggested that I wanted the drums to sound like Led Zeppelin, he retorted, 'Well, if he can play like John Bonham, I'll do my best.' He knew our music already and had so many of the same musical references that it seemed like a perfect fit. The other bonus was that we got to go to New York. How glamorous, we thought! At this point we didn't realise there was a huge difference between Manhattan and upstate New York. We were soon to find out! Anyway, the plans were made. We were to record our second album with Dave at Tarbox.

In the meantime, we had a few more live engagements to deal with. Manic Street Preachers asked us to open for them on a short tour of ballrooms in seaside towns to coincide with their new record. Despite not being massively into the Manics' music, I loved their confrontational attitude and their intellect. The venues were also ones that we were unlikely to get to play ourselves so it was a chance to perform to a new audience.

The first gig was in a ballroom in a seaside town in the north of England called Bridlington Spa. Back then I took my skateboard everywhere with me, and as soon as we got to the gargantuan ballroom I immediately took the opportunity to skate around the massive wooden floor. Mid-skate I became aware of a rather unnerved voice telling me to stop. It was a guy built like a tank who it would turn out was the Manics' bodyguard. 'You can't do that!' he shouted at me. I asked him why not, and despite him never furnishing me with an adequate reason I decided he wasn't worth messing with. But that was the only interaction with anyone associated with the Manics that wasn't great. They were unbelievably kind to us and went above and beyond in looking after us. Their fans were another matter entirely. They had a kind of devotion the likes of which I'd never witnessed: obsessed and more than a little weird. I suppose that explained the scary bodyguard. Their devotion didn't, however, extend to the courtesy of wanting to watch the support band, particularly ones whose music eschewed the verse/chorus anthem stylings of their idols. We went down like a lead balloon. Port Talbot in Wales was the worst; we really got hell there. Dominic is a really laid-back guy and it takes a lot to get him annoyed but he got so fed up that he mooned the entire crowd. The only night where we got anything close to a decent reception was in Scotland, at the Caird Hall in Dundee. I was happy to be there because it was one of the places I'd seen The Cure a few years back.

It was also notable as the first time we were joined onstage by Barry Burns. Barry had played with us a couple of times but never onstage. He had joined us for a session we did with the legendary producer Arthur Baker, famed for producing New Order's 'Blue Monday' and the hip-hop classic 'Planet Rock' by Afrika Bambaataa. Arthur was a fan of our music and had seen us a bunch of times and become a good friend of the band. He was working on a collaborative album and asked us if we'd do an interpretation of the Jewish hymn 'Our Father,

Our King'. Excited to be working with someone like Arthur, we jumped at the chance. Our version was pretty epic and ended up becoming a live staple. Arthur came up to Hamilton to record it and we asked Barry if he would play flute on the track. As the songs started to take shape for our second album, it became apparent that a lot of them would benefit from having piano and keyboard. In Dundee, Barry came up and played flute on 'Mogwai Fear Satan'. The tour was so much fun, mainly because we were constantly out of our nuts the whole time, taking ecstasy like sweeties, often during the gigs. The waves of insults from the mall goths in mascara were like water off a duck's back, were a duck to be a Lanarkshire native out of it on ecstasy. One night someone shouted at me, 'Stuart, you are so fat because you sit and eat cheesecake all day.' I understood the bit about being fat but the cheesecake part mystified me. I had never tried cheesecake, believing it to be made of actual cheese and thus disgusting. Dominic assured me that cheesecake was in fact really nice. I tried some the next day, and lo and behold it was great. I would like to thank that belligerent Manics fan for the sage culinary advice. The Manics were very big on the visual element and didn't have any of their amps onstage. I remember one night climbing onto Nicky Wire's bass cab in an eccied daze and having a nap.

Having been woefully unprepared for the recording of our first album we went to great lengths for that not to be the case on album two. When not on tour we rehearsed constantly and even went into the studio in Hamilton and Cava in Glasgow to record demos. We were booked to record in America in November and every spare minute we had was spent making sure we were in as good shape for it as possible. As one final bit of preparation we booked a gig in Nice N Sleazy to play a set heavy with new songs to road-test them before the trip. As well as the gig in Glasgow we also had a short run of shows in America in between the recording and mixing of the album.

Around then we made the decision to ask Barry to join the band. We asked him to come with us to America but he couldn't straight away, so it was just the four of us that flew out to start the record with Dave. Barry would join us a week later.

Before we went to Dave's, we flew to New York to play at the famed CMJ festival, a showcase for Jetset Records, who we had decided we wouldn't be staying with for our new album. It quickly became apparent that this had very much been noted. Adele had come out to New York having never visited the city, looking forward to spending a few days there before I went upstate to start recording. The first issue was the accommodation. Colin hadn't told us where we were staying, which seemed a bit odd, and we soon realised why. Jetset had booked us into a YMCA, but Colin somewhat unconvincingly tried to tell us that it wasn't like the normal ones. None of us had ever stayed in a normal one, so God knows what *they* were like. When we got to the building, the first warning sign was the bullet holes in the front door. That wasn't good. The second sign was when we got in the lift and there was a fairly troubled-looking woman who had what was clearly semen in her hair. The rooms themselves had a definite jail vibe and, along with that, we had to share a bathroom with about twenty other rooms. Adele, quite rightly, was pretty upset and we left to stay on Sam Brumbaugh's couch. It was clear that Jetset weren't going to spend one penny more on us than they absolutely had to. Sadly, it wouldn't be the last time they let us down – they pretty much stopped paying us any royalties we earned soon after we left the label.

The CMJ gig was bedlam. On the bill that night were other Jetset bands like Edith Frost and the incredible Prolapse, featuring dual singers: tall Scottish Mick and tiny blonde Linda. The minute venue was packed to the rafters and it was almost impossible to get anyone in. The dressing room was the beer cellar downstairs and we were having a drink with the other bands waiting to play when a familiar face appeared from nowhere,

Simon Williams, the *NME* writer who'd got us our first review. He'd climbed through a manhole on the street to get into the gig. It was great coming back to New York, and people seemed to really know our music. The place was a sweaty mess and our new songs went down really well. After the gig we met some of the people from Matador Records, the legendary New York label who'd released Pavement and The Jon Spencer Blues Explosion. They were keen on working with us and didn't have a shifty vibe at all. They certainly didn't seem like the kind of folk that would stick you in a janky hotel, which was enough for us.

We got the first inkling that upstate New York wasn't the same as regular old New York when we had to get on a plane to fly to Buffalo. Maybe the others had, but I hadn't bothered to look at a map and had pretty much no idea where we were going. When we landed in Buffalo and collected our bags, we went outside to get picked up and got a big surprise. There was a stretch limo waiting for us. We felt like actual rock stars. After checking that it was in fact for us, we got in. The hour-long drive to the studio felt great, soundtracked by Led Zepplin's *Houses of the Holy*. We were buzzing to be travelling to the studio in such salubrious fashion. It turned out Chemikal had booked it for us because it was the most cost-efficient way of getting us there. I suppose there probably aren't that many celebrities in Buffalo.

We were met on arrival by Dave, his wife Mary and their two tiny boys, Mike and John. They were incredibly welcoming and had stocked the kitchen with food and drinks for us. The studio was in a renovated Amish house which, to my horror-obsessed mind, was eerily reminiscent of the haunted house in the Amityville movies. As you walked in, there was a kitchen which opened out onto a massive live and control room. The studio was full of paraphernalia relating to the bands that had recorded there, predominantly The Flaming Lips. They had collected loads of weird and wonderful instruments, toys and other psychedelic knick-knacks which were on display and available to use. We'd never been in a residential studio and were relishing the chance to concentrate fully on our music without distractions. And as far as distractions went, there were NONE, the studio being in the middle of fucking nowhere. After we got our bags in, Dave and his family bid us goodnight and we settled in. The following day we'd be setting up our instruments and making plans, and we couldn't wait to get going. It felt like this was the beginning of something really special.

Once we were set up, we got into it straight away. We didn't have loads of studio time so we worked really hard and spent every second we could on the music. We recorded pretty much everything live and used as many of the cool toys that were lying around as possible. Being in a house in the woods was amazing for productivity. Our only excursions were to the shop, which was a fifteen-minute drive away and, as well as selling food and drink, also sold hunting gear like knives, guns and camouflage clothing. We really were a long way from home.

After a week Barry showed up. He slotted in straight away, adding Fender Rhodes piano to the ballad I'd written, 'Cody', about a childhood friend of mine who'd got himself in a bad way with drugs and ended up in a psychiatric hospital. One day on the studio piano Barry came up with a song which really worked. I added some orchestral chimes to it and that was it: Barry's first Mogwai song. We stole a headline from the *Weekly World News* ('Oh How The Dog's Stack Up') for it. A lot of our song titles came from that trashy US supermarket tabloid because we found it hilarious. Dave was also having a positive effect on the record. His presence was so calm and he was always open to possibilities. He'd put everything into the studio and, with the success that Mercury Rev and The Flaming Lips were having, was seeing it pay off. The nearby town of Fredonia was where he'd grown up and it was so great to see someone build something that completely suited them without any kind of industry pandering.

Most producers go to London, New York or LA to build their careers but Dave had done it completely on his own terms. It was something we aspired to as well.

Once the tracking was down we headed off to play a few gigs before we started the mixing. Tour-managing us for the dates was our pal Sam Brumbaugh from Jetset and his friend Mike Fellows. Mike was a great guitar player, having been in the legendary DC hardcore band Rites of Spring. He was super relaxed, bordering on comatose, and was going to be my guitar tech. Also along for the ride was a diminutive ginger girl, a few years younger than us called Alanna Gabin. Alanna lived in New York (on Sam's couch) but was originally from Florida. She looked exactly like Peppermint Patty from *Peanuts*. Alanna had grown up in the skating scene and knew a lot of the actors who'd become famous through the Harmony Korine movie *Kids*. We got on really well. She was going to sell our merch on the dates, and we'd go on to become really close friends over the years. We had an immediate connection and I felt that she understood me in a way that not many people did.

We went back to Manhattan for two more shows at Brownies, supported both nights by my psychedelic heroes Bardo Pond. It was the first time we'd met them and we had an immediate connection. The two guitar players, brothers Mike and John, were lovely, as was Isobel the singer and Clint the bassist. They had a totally great attitude and loved playing super loud, far-out psych-rock but had none of the associated pretentiousness. They were immense live, creating massive walls of wailing guitars with Isobel's dreamy vocals and flute over the top. I couldn't believe that they were opening for us. Sharing a stage with one of the bands that had inspired us when listening to Peel was a real honour. When the venue was empty and we went onstage to get our guitars, we saw that the front of the stage was loaded with piles of empty cough bottles. Clearly it wasn't just us and Bardo Pond getting into the spirit of psychedelia.

After the tour, we got into the job of mixing the album back at the studio. We had loads of songs and knew that deciding which tracks to put on the record wouldn't be easy. We also had to work out a name for the album. It was Barry who told us about a gang that his dad had been in as a teen called The CODY. CODY standing for Come On Die Young.

Come On Die Young it was.

Our friend, the *NME* journalist Keith Cameron, was in New York interviewing the Beastie Boys, and since we thought (mistakenly) that he was in the same vicinity, we decided to invite him up to the studio. This arrangement was made before we realised that the studio was hundreds of miles from New York City. It's a bit like finding out someone is in Birmingham so inviting them up to Glasgow for a night. Keith was happy to be invited though and made his way on a flight from NYC to Buffalo to hang out for an evening. Celtic were playing Rangers that day back in Glasgow and, in the pre-internet times, Martin had to call home to find out what the score had been. When his sister told him it was 5–1, Martin immediately presumed the score favoured Rangers. When she confirmed that it was in fact Celtic who'd won, we were elated. To celebrate we decided to get as much green (lime) and white (grape) flavoured MD2020 wine as we could muster and have a party. It was biblical, and in full swing by the time Keith arrived somewhat bedraggled from his journey. The next day we had one of the most brutal collective hangovers I can ever recall. John invented a sandwich, a variation of a BLT with cheese, and named it 'The 5–1'. We played Keith some of the mixes and he seemed to like them. We had a lot of respect for Keith and his endorsement made us feel confident about what we were doing.

Recording at Tarbox had been a memorable experience and their hospitality had made us feel like a part of the Fridmann family. They were such warm people and had just as daft a sense of humour as us. The experience of recording with Dave had been so great and we were sure that we'd be back.

Back in Scotland we listened to what we'd done, finalised the tracklist and had the album mastered. For the cover we used one of the many polaroids we'd taken during the recording, of Dominic making a scary face, which we colourised so that he looked the demon from *The Exorcist*, a film that we all loved.

We felt in a great place and had managed to learn from the mistakes we made on our first record. I was excited for people to hear what we had done.

14.

We Do Like to Be Beside the Seaside

Since we'd started the band the *NME* had been really support-ive, showcasing us at their annual Astoria gigs and giving us really good write-ups, the exception being a completely justified kicking for our shambolic Garage gig. In 1999, with the release of *Come On Die Young* on the horizon, things stepped up a gear. We were once again invited to play the Astoria but this time we were headlining. As headliners we also had a say on the bill that night, choosing the legendary Louisville singer Will Oldham, aka Bonnie Prince Bill, Clinic and Bob Tilton. Bob Tilton was a particular coup as they were famed for not playing at venues with stages and the Astoria most certainly had one of those.

As well as inviting us to play what was to be our biggest ever headline gig, *NME* were also going to interview us in Europe for a feature that could potentially land us our first ever cover. Get-ting on the cover of *NME* was a big deal. Most weeks they had arena bands like Oasis or 'next big thing' London indie bands, so having a band like us seemed pretty unlikely and a bit of a victory for the underground.

First up though was London and the Astoria. Barry was now an official member of the band, which meant he had to do all the things we all considered to be normal, such as photoshoots. After the soundcheck in London we had to do some press shots, so, clad in a load of Kappa clothes that our friend Kiko had sent up for us, we walked out to the front of the venue to have our pictures taken. Barry was mortified because everyone walking past was staring at us, presumably wondering if we were famous. We were used to feeling like prats in public and having to do this kind of shit relatively often. Barry would soon learn that feeling like a prize goon was just something you had to put up with. To us it had become fairly normal.

The gig itself felt like a real occasion. This was huge for us. We were so sure that our new record was something special and the opportunity to play the new songs to so many people seemed massive. We even made *Come On Die Young* T-shirts to sell four months ahead of the album's release. The opening bands were great. Bob Tilton really owned the big stage. They were such a visual band and seeing them in a venue like that felt totally right. Their singer, Simon, flailed about like a man possessed.

Our set felt like a total triumph. We started with the new song 'May Nothing But Happiness Come Through Your Door'. It was one of our quietest songs but has a gradual build-up halfway through that never quite goes full tilt. Barry was a brilliant addition. His Fender Rhodes and organ parts transformed the song and, in general, he just made everything we did sound better, playing flute on 'Helicon 2' and extra guitars on 'Mogwai Fear Satan' and 'Like Herod'. It had only been a few months, but it felt totally right having him in the band.

After the show we partied with our friends. Bobby Gillespie and Kevin Shields were also there. Hanging out with these guys at a sold-out London show months ahead of the release of what we believed was our best music to date felt incredible.

Straight after the Astoria show we left for a short run of Scandinavian dates which would also serve as the background for the *NME* feature that might result in our first cover. The gigs were in Stockholm, Oslo, Vordingborg and Copenhagen. Joining us from *NME* was our friend James Oldham and a photographer called Eva Vermandel. We didn't know Eva but we instantly got on. She

Top: Me and Victoria being amusingly dressed babies. Lanarkshire, 1976.
Bottom left: Dungaree fever. Haircut by my mum as I had an irrational fear of hairdressers. Lanarkshire, late 1970s.
Bottom right: Mum and me in fetching plasticky jackets. Lanarkshire, early 1980s.

Top: Me holding my first skateboard with Mum, Dad, my cousin Claire and our dog Lady. Lanarkshire, mid 1980s.
Bottom left: Me with my first musical instrument, a Casio SK-1 keyboard, at my parents' house. Lanarkshire, mid 1980s.
Bottom right: Me and 'Wee' David Robertson. Edinburgh, 1993.

Top: My sister Victoria rocking the goth look on her bus pass. Early 1990s.
Bottom: Me with David Robertson and Ally Anderson, from my college band,
Deadcat Motorbike. Edinburgh, 1994.

Top: Adele and me in all our early 90s goth glory. Lanarkshire.
Bottom left: Eska days. Me with Colin Kearney, Kenny MacLeod and Chris Mack.
Glasgow, 1996.
Bottom right: Mogwai polaroid. Dundee, 1996.

Top: John, Dominic and me opening for Urusei Yatsura. Somewhere in the UK, 1996.
Bottom: Carnage at The Garage. Dominic keeping me hydrated while Aidan Moffat helps out on drums at the front. London, 1997.

Top: Martin Bulloch, Dominic Aitchison, Colin Hardie, Matt Gilfeather and me on our first trip out of the UK. Norway, 1997.
Middle: Martin's anti-Blur artwork on fencing at T in the Park festival – the letter E is just out of shot on the right. Kinross, 1999.
Bottom: Exuberant Barry Burns after our first Barrowlands gig. Glasgow, 1999.

Top: Me and Robert Smith backstage after we opened for The Cure
at Hyde Park. London, 2002.
Bottom: Mogwai press shot, dressed as Inuits for some unfathomable reason.
Troon Beach, 2005.

Top: Mum, Dad and my sister's husband Jared Earle, with our dog Moxy. Lanarkshire, 2010s.
Bottom: Me and Elisabeth on holiday. Thailand, 2011.

was clearly a brilliant photographer. We even got her up onstage to do some guitar feedback at the Copenhagen show. For James's part we dared him £100 to eat a whole jar of garlic cloves. I can't recall how it even got mooted. He did it though, and we paid up. Everyone except Martin, who never pays up.

When it came to the interview James wanted to speak to us all together as well as doing one-on-one interviews. For mine, James spelt it out that for the feature to get on the cover there had to be a 'quotable element'. From the word go I'd been really mouthy in interviews and castigated other bands, politicians, football teams, any moving target really, non-stop. There had been an element of attention-seeking to it, trying to make noise so people would notice and take our music seriously. Now that we had reached the stage where people had acknowledged what we were doing, I didn't feel the urgency to do it so much. It became clear from talking to James, though, that this was what they were after. I wanted us to be on the cover so I was slightly torn. With a modicum of arm-bending, I succumbed and gave an uber-gobby interview by coming out with a lot of hyperbole, patent nonsense, withering put-downs of others and lofty claims about ourselves. I was slightly wary of how the interview would turn out.

With the Scandinavian dates done, we headed Stateside. Having left Jetset we were now officially on Matador Records, who had invited us to go and play in New York at Bowery Ballroom, a prestigious venue near where the legendary CBGBs had been in the Bowery. The Bowery had been a famous slum in the seventies and eighties but was now starting to change into the fancy area that it is now. Joining us that night was our old Jetset pal Daniel Kessler's band Interpol, and Sophia, the latest project by Robin Proper-Sheppard from The God Machine. Playing in Sophia that night was Adam Franklin from Swervedriver. Both Interpol and Sophia were fantastic. Afterwards we all headed to Max Fish. Scott McCloud from Girls Against Boys was there along with Sam, Alanna, Mike Fellows and a bunch of the folks from

Matador. The Matador crowd were great. The two bosses, Chris Lombardi and Gerard Cosloy, were brilliant characters. Lombardi, a gargantuan monster of a man with a vociferous appetite for hedonism, was a non-stop human party, and Gerard Cosloy, the quieter of the two, was equally great to spend time with. He'd been involved in releasing early records by Dinosaur Jr. and Sonic Youth, among others, so it was a real honour that he wanted to work with us. Their publicist, Nils Bernstein, was hands down the funniest American I'd ever met. He had an amazing sense of humour and a massive stockpile of brilliant stories. He'd been Kurt Cobain and Courtney Love's nanny as well as their PR when he'd worked at Sub Pop. Not only were the Matador folk brilliant to hang around with but they clearly loved our music. Jetset had seemed way more interested in how they could make money *from* us, rather than the music itself. There had always been an air of shiftiness with them, but it was the complete opposite with Matador. We partied long into the New York night with Lombardi's credit card behind the bar. We had found some great friends and, in Matador, people who really got our music and were totally supportive of us. There was a romance to New York that I found intoxicating. The energy of the place was infectious. Everywhere you went something great was happening. The people there really got us. Their sense of humour was much closer to ours than in other parts of America. It felt like home.

After NY we got ready for the imminent release of the album, and we were invited to record a session for Steve Lamacq's evening session show back at Maida Vale. We did two of our new songs, 'Chocky' and 'May Nothing But Happiness Come Through Your Door', as well as two older songs, 'Helicon 1' and 'Like Herod'. 'Like Herod' consisted of about five minutes of pure noise for the second half and we thought it was subversive and fun to get this onto early evening Radio 1. The version we recorded was almost twenty minutes long. While in London we also did another photo session for *NME*. The photos Eva took were great but apparently weren't quite what they were looking for in terms of a cover. I translate this as 'the band looked like shite', which we almost certainly did. We didn't care what we looked like and it showed. The photographer for the new session was a guy called Steve Gullick, a legendary photographer responsible for some iconic shots, notably of Nirvana. He'd taken amazing photos of the Reading show in 1991 when Kurt jumped into the drums. We first met Steve in a random building in London somewhere and he immediately disarmed us with his base sense of humour. We had a pretty childish, guttural sensibility as it was, but Steve blew us out of the water. He was fucking hilarious. Getting a band to have a good time while they're getting their photo taken isn't the easiest thing to do, and this was his strategy.

One of our first photoshoots consisted of some twat asking us to hate the camera. There was only one thing we hated, and it was him. Unsurprisingly those photos were rotten; all of us had facial expressions that screamed, 'Who is this prick?'

With Steve we were immediately at ease and he managed to get a few decent shots. Steve also had a pretty experimental technique using weird cameras, lenses and film to make them look different. In the end we did get the cover of *NME*, though rather than it being a normal cover, it was billed as the No Sell Out Issue, with us appearing alongside other folk who apparently weren't sell-outs, like Fugazi and the comedian Bill Hicks. For the cover they used a shot Steve had taken of me making the same face that Dominic had pulled for our album cover. The interview had, as I'd feared, turned out a bit embarrassing though. One of the quotes that James had pried out of me was that us being an instrumental band was as important as Bob Dylan confronting racism in the sixties. It was weapons grade horseshit, and I knew it. It was pretty ironic that it was in the No Sell Out Issue because I had pretty much sold out by saying something that was complete nonsense to get a magazine cover to help the commercial prospects of our album. The nineties weren't a great time for irony.

To promote the record before its release, Keith Cameron, Martin and myself went on a 'media tour' of sorts around the UK, travelling by train and doing press conferences where we would play some of the album to students and local journalists before Keith interviewed me. On quite a few occasions the young journalists would take the opportunity to have a go at me for daft stuff I'd said or be cheeky about the record. I was fine with that though. As a connoisseur of cheek I was always happy to see someone else taking up the art form. I recall on the trip both Keith and I taking a pill just before ordering a curry, and then staring blankly at our plates as we lost our appetites completely as the E took hold.

The night before the album came out we played the Virgin Megastore in Glasgow. The shop stayed open till after midnight for people to buy the record. Both us and Chemikal Underground were pulling out all the stops to try to make the record do as well as possible. The record shop gig was surreal. We'd done in-stores in America but they usually consisted of us tinkling away in a corner while bemused shoppers perused the jazz section. This was different. We were on a proper stage and it felt like everyone we knew was there. Our friend Noj, a wee cheeky guy from Lanarkshire with a mod haircut, worked in the shop and really looked after us, letting us all get some CDs as payment. We were still at the stage of asking more about free stuff than how much money we got paid. It would take us quite a while to realise that actual payment was in fact better than 'free' stuff.

We had a party on the day of the album release. It was a predictably messy affair. We hired the G2 nightclub and got our friends Barry Hogan and Keith Cameron to DJ. Keith played 'I Want To Dance With Somebody' by Whitney Houston, which went down a storm with the annihilated crowd. As well as the DJs, we hired a guy to do karaoke. On the night everyone got smashed with all our friends from Glasgow and beyond in attendance. Chemikal Underground put money behind the bar and it disappeared quickly. There was a real feeling of euphoria around the release, in stark contrast to the record itself, which was anything but euphoric – it was bleak. We had managed to do exactly what we wanted with it. It felt like the culmination of a lot of hard work and had gone a long way towards exorcising the ghosts of disappointment that I'd felt in the wake of our first album. The reviews were good for the most part, though there were a handful of complaints about our swerve towards minimalism. I love music writing and have a lot of time for journalists, but I'm often bemused when criticism is levelled against music for what it is not, rather than how successfully it has managed to be what it actually is. With music you are trying to achieve what you want, whether you successfully manage it is the issue. To say something is at fault because it is not what you (the writer) want it to be is ludicrous.

All the hard work paid off. *CODY* went down really well and we even managed to get in the top 30 in the UK charts. It felt a long way from packaging singles at my mum's house.

After the *CODY* launch party, back at Aidan's, in what was by then the normal all-night soiree that followed any social event, Barry Hogan told us about an event he had coming up in a few months. In conjunction with Belle and Sebastian he was organising a festival in a holiday camp called the 'Bowlie Weekender'. The bill had been put together by Barry and the Belles. I loved the idea and wanted to go along. It was suggested that, as we were going to be there anyway, we should do a secret set, to which we wholeheartedly agreed.

Set in a holiday camp in a beach town in the south of England called Camber Sands, normally used by families, the 'Bowlie Weekender' had a completely different atmosphere to most music festivals. As well as the slightly surreal setting, the other big difference was the complete lack of separation between the bands playing the festival and the attendees. The accommodation for everyone was chalets. There was no backstage to speak of, and as the bands chosen by Barry and Belle and Sebastian were all really good, most of them stayed for the whole weekend, creating a real sense of community, which is rare at the mainstream festivals. Loads of the bands playing were from Glasgow: Teenage Fanclub, The Delgados, The Pastels and Camera Obscura. It also seemed as though half the city of Glasgow had decamped down there for the weekend and there was a palpable sense of reverie. Other bands playing included The Flaming Lips, Broadcast, Sleater-Kinney and a band from Canada whose music I'd fallen in love with, Godspeed You Black Emperor, who made instrumental music on a grand scale. Their first record, *F Sharp, A Sharp, Infinity*, was incredible. We'd played a handful of shows together and got on really well. Their music was serious but off-stage they were a lot of fun to hang out with. That was a recurring theme, actually. I tended to find that the more seriously a band or singer took their music the more fun they had when they weren't playing. The converse was also often true. I remember we played with a band that looked like they were having the biggest party of all time when they were onstage, but when not performing they instantly transformed into a bunch of misanthropes. There must be something in it.

The weekend itself was a riot. It had been a long time since an event like this had taken place and everyone was in their element. I'd grown up reading about the Futurama festivals in the late seventies and early eighties, and this was as close to those events as we'd get. Our gig, just a few months after the release of *CODY*, was brilliant, and with so many of our friends around the partying was epic.

As the summer approached we headed back out to Europe to play some dates, one definite highlight being a handful of gigs with Low. Ever since that night in Edinburgh I had become a massive Low fan and was so excited to play with them again. Incredibly it would be them opening for us this time, though that didn't matter a jot. As well as being an amazing band, they were really lovely people. Their latest album, *Secret Name*, was their best to date and hearing those songs live was a real pleasure. Embarrassingly, however, at the airport on their way home, they were stopped and searched by the German police – after spending so much time in close proximity to our stoner band and crew, the stench of weed had alerted the drug dogs.

We then learnt that we had been invited to perform at the legendary Glastonbury Festival; not only playing but closing the whole festival on the second stage. It was a real honour and would without doubt be our biggest show yet. Knowing what a special occasion it was, we went out of our way to make sure the show was as epic as possible. Our lighting engineer, a gobby southerner named Nick Jevons, had a plan to make a specially designed stage and light show. He made banners for the stage saying Stage Left, Stage Right, Drums, Barry, etc. and we hired an unbelievable number of lights and mirror balls. It was the first time we'd put a lot of effort into stage design and this definitely seemed like the kind of occasion to go to town on. We'd had a great year already but this was something else, playing to tens of thousands of people at one of the world's biggest festivals. We'd gone from not knowing how our music would fit on stages bigger than a few feet wide, to playing on some of the biggest. It genuinely felt like a dream.

Glastonbury is more of a city than a festival. There are people in every direction and the sheer number of tents was awe inspiring. Our friends Super Furry Animals were playing on the same stage as us on the Saturday night. They had people in alien outfits, designed by the artist Pete Fowler, who would come onstage with them for their finale, 'The Man Don't Give A Fuck'. They asked if any of us fancied donning an alien costume, so me and Martin volunteered. Their show was immense, with the massive crowd going bananas for their futuristic psychedelic rock. Dressed in an alien costume, I experienced being on that massive stage for the first time. In a moment that will live with me forever, as we stood on the stage, someone, presumably having lost their way or their mind, drove a van right through the middle of the crowd. Thankfully, and somewhat miraculously, no one got hurt during the madness. It made what was an already surreal experience ever stranger. I'd never been to a festival as big as Glastonbury and standing on a stage in an alien costume in front of tens of thousands of people was about as mad as it could get.

The next day, the day of our show, was a daze. Closing the festival was extremely daunting. We had always believed our music belonged on big stages, but I had never really thought about the reality of it until it actually happened. Tons of our friends were there. Arthur Baker came and filmed us, as he did at a lot of our shows back in the day. Our old friend Sam Brumbaugh was there as well and agreed to introduce us, in a silver cape of course. The hours before we played seemed like something from a dream and we were very nervous. I think Dominic might have actually been sick, but when the moment came and we got onstage, everything clicked into place. We opened with 'Mogwai Fear Satan', starting with the guitar gently building into a crescendo. Then, when the drums came in, it was clear the crowd were on our side. Me, Barry and John had hatched a plan to take some E about halfway through the show. It wasn't the wisest move in retrospect, but I suppose that, in our minds, we were in some way being professional by not taking them before the gig. When we got into the second half of the set I started coming up and my legs felt like jelly. There was a small moment where I thought I might lose it but, like getting a skidding car back under control, I managed to keep hold. While we played 'Helicon 1' I remember staring out at the oceans of people and just feeling completely at ease. It might have been the E but it felt like a truly perfect moment. We finished with 'Like Herod' and the cacophony of apocalyptic noise that we'd taken to ending it with. The crowd had been amazing, especially considering that for many of them it would have been the first time they'd heard us, never mind seen us play.

After we played, it was a total celebration. We were deep in backstage bacchanal when someone came up and asked if me and Dominic wanted to go on the radio. Radio 1 had been broadcasting from the festival all weekend and John Peel had requested an interview on air. Despite being drunk as hell and wasted on E, I said yes. I'd last seen John Peel the year previously when he was in Lanarkshire filming a TV show called *Sound of the Suburbs*. The Delgados had mentioned to him that the hotel he was staying at was a five-minute walk from my parents' house so he got my number and invited me down for dinner. It was really kind of him and he was wonderful company. He'd always been so supportive of the band and I didn't want to turn him down now, whether I was out of my gourd or not. Mary Anne Hobbes, another big supporter of the band, was on too. Me and Dominic sat in on the show, blethering away to them both, blissfully unaware of the masses listening at home. I remember at one point, Jools Holland was playing a song on a piano next to us and it dawning on me how utterly bizarre the whole experience was. I've very little recollection of it, but what I do recall seems like something from a dream.

In the week after Glastonbury we were asked about doing a new T-shirt to sell at our appearance at T in the Park in Scotland. We had never been big fans of Blur – I thought they were OK musically but when we saw Super Furry Animals support them in Glasgow, they had bank adverts on the screens in between the bands and it felt extremely wrong. Their anti-American English nationalism also grated, as did their fake cockney accents. Back then it'd be fair to say they were the antithesis of what we felt was good in the world of music. Earlier in the year we'd been offered a festival but because of the travel the only way we could do it would be if Blur let us travel back on the plane they were hiring. They said no, which in hindsight was no surprise as I'm sure we were castigating them in every interview we did at the time. That was probably the moment when what had been a withering dislike of Blur escalated into a full-blown detestation. Our T-shirt seller at this point was called Valerie Deerin, an old pal from Lanarkshire. She was definitely not someone who suffered fools. Valerie held a similar disdain for Blur and so when the question was raised as to what our new T-shirt should say, Valerie declared, without hesitation: 'Blur Are Shite'. We all thought this was really funny and agreed to make said shirt using the *Come On Die Young* font on a grey T-shirt. It was super childish but I honestly didn't think anyone would really notice.

They did notice.

On arrival at T in the Park it appeared that our daft T-shirt had most definitely attracted some attention. Blur were the headliners on the main stage at the same time as we were playing the tent. What had seemed like a particularly childish prank now seemed a fairly big deal. What we should have done was sell the T-shirts and never mention it again. But readers, that is not what we did. I was asked for a quote for a story about it by *NME* and I didn't hold back. I said that not only were they shite but having a qualification in music I could prove it. All patent nonsense of course, but to those not familiar with my somewhat acerbic sense of humour it probably read like I was some kind of malevolent psychopath. Blur were (and are) far from my favourite band, but it really wasn't worth all the hassle that ensued. For weeks the music press letters pages were full of furious Britpop fans aghast at the temerity of anyone casting aspersions on their heroes. The whole debacle added a sense of surrealism to what should have been a pretty standard show.

There was some other drama before the gig when Andy Dimmack, my guitar tech for the night, was felled by one of the plethora of mirror balls that we had adorning the stage. Thankfully he escaped with nothing worse than a sore head. My parents came along that day and as well as bumping into a quite spectacularly spangled Arab Strap, who'd just been for a drug-fuelled ride on the fairground, were probably rather perplexed over the palaver we'd conjured. Martin added to the drama by spray-painting 'Blur Are Shite' on the fencing surrounding one of the stages. We'd be endlessly amused as we saw various anagrams of the slight around the country for years to come as the panels were redeployed at other festivals. I recall my mum saying to me that we shouldn't feel the need to be saying stuff about other bands because people really liked our music in its own right. She was of course right, but I was too young and daft to hear it. Commotion apart, our show went really well. It was a real homecoming after a great start to the year. We had sold a lot of T-shirts but possibly at the expense of a lot of people taking our music seriously. I'm not entirely sure it was worth it, as funny as it was at the time.

After all, who really gives a fuck what Mogwai think about Blur?

15.

Take Me Somewhere Nice

Two days after T in the Park we played a secret show opening for Godspeed You Black Emperor at the G2 in Glasgow, joining them for the encore and an epic jam. It was a blast playing together and we celebrated late into the night at a club that Chris from Belle and Sebastian was playing, Northern Soul. They were sublime dancers and it was great to find kinship with other musicians from so far way.

The summer had been full-on and things weren't getting any quieter. There was an intensity to everything happening and my lifestyle was increasingly chaotic. There was barely a night out that didn't end up becoming a few days out. Aidan from Arab Strap had bought a flat in Glasgow's West End and it became something of a home away from home for us and all our pals, particularly on Sundays. A new club night had started in Glasgow's famous Sub Club a few years earlier called Optimo. The two DJs, Keith (aka Twitch) and Johnny Wilkes, would play no wave, electro and techno music to a packed room full of people who didn't have anything to do on Monday. This appealed to us particularly because our Mondays were largely free and the music was off the scale. We'd all get totally mashed on E and head up to Aidan's where me and him would listen to miserable records and talk nonsense until the pubs opened the next day, at which point we'd head back out and keep drinking. The band was going great but I wasn't dealing with it in the most grounded manner. In fact, I was a mess. My shit was barely together and it was beginning to show. My relationship with Adele was suffering because I was smashed most of the time. I think the band's modest rise to fame had gone to my head. Arab Strap were in the process of leaving Chemikal Underground to sign for EMI and our success had been noticed by some other suitors as well. It felt like a real period of change. Up to this point we'd been on an inexorable upward trajectory. Other labels had been in touch about working with us on our next record and the attention was definitely inflating my ego.

That summer, I headed back to Benicàssim festival, but not with Mogwai. Arab Strap were playing and Adele was singing with them, and Barry was helping out on keys. Their pal, John Mauchline, whose DIY songs interspersed the tracks on *The Week Never Starts Round Here*, had the poisoned chalice of tour manager. At that point Arab Strap on tour was more of a circus than anything else. Along for the ride as well was Malcolm's then girlfriend Lauren Laverne, the singer from Kenickie. Things had been pretty unhinged at Benicàssim when I'd been there to play with Mogwai, but this was on another level. It was bedlam. The line-up had changed a lot since I'd first been there and was now a lot more mainstream. This meant there were fewer musical distractions and more opportunities to get wasted.

On the first day, me and Adele went to the beach. We had a really nice day but things started to get weird when we bumped into my pal and guitar tech Ally Christie, who was there with Bis. John from Bis was with Ally and we could see that he was in some distress. There was a go-kart track on the festival site and John had managed to crash his and do some serious damage to his scrotum, needing to get stitches. Back at the festival site things were taking a definite *Apocalypse Now* direction. Everyone was completely fucked. The Delgados were playing and the awkwardness surrounding the fact that Arab Strap were about to jump ship probably only exacerbated the drinking and drug-taking. On the Saturday, Arab Strap were playing second to last in the tent. That day, word came in that they'd had an offer to play at another festival in Portugal on the Sunday, as a last-minute replacement for The Jon Spencer Blues Explosion. They would be playing in between Ocean Colour Scene and James, two fairly up-beat bands, but not ones to turn down a good offer, they said yes. I had a ticket back to Scotland but Adele, not wanting to travel without me, volunteered me to be the guitar tech and go with them. It seemed like a reasonable proposition and Arab Strap agreed. There was only one flaw in this plan: I could not guitar tech. For the last few years I'd had my own guitar tech and, before that, had tricked John into changing my strings and tuning my guitar by telling him that I couldn't do it. This left me in a pretty bad position to fulfil the role. I didn't want to let them down though, so I agreed.

Getting to Portugal was a farce in itself. The flight was really early and corralling everyone out of the hotel was an utter palaver. Dave the drummer hadn't been to bed. I'm not sure anyone had. Dave emptied the contents of his toilet bag out, which was filled with all the miniatures from the minibar so he could keep on drinking on the flight. Poor John the tour manager somehow managed to get us to the airport, checked the gear in and got us on the flight. It was chaos. We were all drunk and it felt like the scene from the end of *Gremlins* when they trash the cinema. It was as if the party from Benicàssim hadn't stopped.

It was a long drive from the airport to the festival, by which point everyone's hangover was starting to kick in and the realisation that I was about to guitar tech for Malc and Gary, the bass player, was hanging over me like a particularly ominous cloud. Everyone started drinking again as soon as we got there. No one seemed particularly concerned that the slot was between Ocean Colour Scene and James, two big crowd-pleasing acts that couldn't be any more different from Arab Strap. Aidan's lyrics are raw and personal and the music really centred around that. There are no singalong moments, no ritualistic mass handclaps. Definitely not traditional festival main stage stuff at all and certainly not a good fit to be sandwiched in between two party bands.

In preparation for the gig I got all of Malcolm's guitars and Gary's basses and tuned them using the electronic tuner. I was reasonably satisfied that everything was going well and had assumed that my only other role would be to hand Gary or Malcolm a spare guitar if they broke any strings. With everything set up I waited at the side of the stage alongside Lauren and Adele. The band were fairly inebriated but that was par for the course. It was all looking good.

Until they started playing.

It only took a few seconds for me to realise there was something deeply wrong. Everything was completely out of tune. Either that or Gary and Malcolm had lost control of all their digits and abandoned the concept of musicality completely. It was utterly fucking horrendous. Barry, Dave and Aidan were all looking at each other, clearly wondering what the fuck was going on. It sounded catastrophic. It was then that it dawned on me that I had tuned the strings to the letters representing the notes, but I had completely forgotten about the concepts of flats and sharps. This meant that a good few strings (possibly all of the strings) were tuned to the wrong notes. Malcolm is a great musician and sorted it out himself, but Gary had learnt the songs by being told where to put his fingers and he just kept playing. It was horrific. I started sweating. I knew I'd fucked up. The anxiety over my massive fuck-up was not helped by the reaction of the crowd, who were not happy at all. Presumably hoping for something of a similar party vibe to the Blues Explosion (who Arab Strap had replaced), they were not pleased with this shitshow. The fact that it was an out-of-tune nightmare wouldn't have helped either. They were throwing things and heckling:

'You don't sing, you just talk.'
'Waste of cash.'

They weren't shy in letting the band know their displeasure. But Arab Strap just kept playing . . . By this point I felt that the world was collapsing in on me. Feeling jittery from the weekend's excess and the nightmare journey, this was more than I could handle. I ran to the side of the stage and started puking. Lauren was comforting me while the out-of-tune music vs heckler war raged on. Thankfully their set wasn't that long and they came off stage guilefully avoiding the missiles that were raining down. Far from wanting to beat me up, Aidan and Malc seemed reasonably amused by the whole affair, though that could have been an act to not make me feel so bad. That was my one and only experience of being someone else's guitar tech.

Portugal wasn't done with me yet though. The very next week I was back with Mogwai to play another festival. Surely it couldn't end as badly as the Arab Strap debacle, could it? Adele travelled out with us again and we regaled the rest of the band with the story of what had happened with the Strap. We were staying in a really nice hotel in the countryside with a pool and had a few nights off before we played the festival. It was a really great time.

Come the festival itself though, everything changed. Most of the other bands were metal or at least heavy rock. We definitely stood out and I'd seen from my experience with Arab Strap that Portuguese festival-goers weren't the most patient. I started to wonder if we might be the recipients of a similar reception to our Falkirk brethren. I was not wrong. Things were going fine when we started. The first two songs, 'Summer' and 'Small Children', went OK, though I could tell that there were murmurs of discontent throughout the crowd. Things came to a head when we started 'Christmas Steps'. Clearly people weren't happy that we didn't have any vocals, but the fact that we had a song that started with five minutes of near silence was the straw that broke the camel's back. People started whistling at a level that came close to drowning out the music. When we came in loud there were some modest cheers, but things got hairy again towards the end of the song which, like the start, is almost inaudible. The whistling and bottling continued until the very end. Our last song, 'Like Herod', ended with me screaming back at the crowd while the rest of the band pummelled their instruments into submission. We left the stage somewhat dazed but agreed that despite the gig it had been a lovely trip.

Back home, we were getting very close to making a dream come true. Our agent Mick and our new promoter Mark Mackie at Regular Music had concocted a plan for us to play our biggest hometown show to date. It was to be at the famous Barrowlands in Glasgow. At first we were fairly sceptical about doing it. After all, the most we'd ever played to in Glasgow was in a venue a quarter of the Barrowlands' size. Mick was adamant though, and Mark the promoter was confident. A small bespectacled guy with a huge personality, Mark was an infectious character. He'd cut his teeth booking bands like The Smiths at the QM union before being headhunted by Regular. Regular were the main promoters in Scotland and had put on most of the legendary gigs that I'd been to as well as lots before my time. The thought of playing the Barrowlands was scary but also enticing. After a bit of persuasion, we all said yes.

During some time off we'd recorded a new EP with our sound guy Michael Brennan. The EP, simply called the *Mogwai EP*, featured a lead track written by John and named after the film director Stanley Kubrick. The other tracks included 'Burn Girl Prom Queen', which featured the Cowdenbeath Brass Band, and 'Rage Man', the title taken from a tabloid headline about Michael after a road rage incident. The cover was by my old pal Neale. Me and Neale went around Glasgow taking photos of water towers and Neale then projected them onto screens and photographed them again. The last song on the EP, 'Christmas Song', was a beautiful piano-based song that Barry had written. Our gig at Barrowlands was to be part of a small tour to promote the EP. *CODY* hadn't been out for long but we were still going with our

Joy Division-inspired philosophy of not releasing singles from albums.

The gig in London was at the Kentish Town Forum, the largest we'd played to date. It was full and it felt like a real moment. I remember that night us all erupting with cheers when we discovered that there were people outside selling bootleg T-shirts. We'd made it! We were now worth ripping off. We sent Simon out to all the bootleggers for some free T-shirts, which they obliged us with.

London had been great but all our thoughts were on the Barrowlands. Finally, we'd be stepping onto the same stage where I'd seen the Mary Chain, PJ Harvey, The Cure, Sonic Youth and the like. But then I started to experience stress dreams about playing the gig. Something that continues to this day. I remember the first one vividly. I was in Nice N Sleazy and had been drinking all day. At some point during the dream someone appeared and informed me that I was playing the Barrowlands. I was legless but, with some assistance, made my way down to the gig. There was a big queue outside and people were looking at me incredulously because I could barely walk and was in no shape to play. The gig was an inevitable disaster and most of the people left before we finished. I still have variations of this dream all the time.

The date was fast approaching and it was all we were thinking about. Us playing the Barrowlands was seen by a lot of people in Glasgow as overly ambitious. It was certainly a punchy move. My biggest concern was that we wouldn't fill the room and I was nervous about that. Come the night itself I was a bag of nerves. As special guests we had invited Ligament, the amazing London noise rock band, and Spectrum, the solo project of Sonic Boom, of Spacemen 3. Both bands were tremendous but I was too uptight and stressed to really get into it.

When we finally got onto the stage everything changed. The place was full to the rafters and everyone was going nuts. We started with 'Superheroes of BMX' and throughout the first song I was just taking it all in. I'd always wanted to play there but, in all honesty, I hadn't expected it, and certainly hadn't envisaged us being the headliners. But here we were, performing to a packed crowd in the venue we'd been watching our idols play since we were kids. It was also unbelievably loud. These gigs were the first where we'd been in a position to bring our own PA and lights, and we'd really gone for it. It was so loud that it had gone beyond just being a musical experience and transformed into a physical one. I played the first song facing my amp in the dark, taking in the occasion but not quite coming to terms with what was happening. When we finished, I turned and faced the crowd to see everyone with their hands in the air. We'd never had a reaction quite like it. All my nerves disappeared instantly. The show flew by in what felt like an instant. Afterwards our dressing room was full of pals and family, everyone joyous at what had been an amazing homecoming show. There was an aftershow in the bottom bar of the venue and it was utter carnage. Everyone we knew was there and it'd be fair to say that almost everyone was wasted. The occasion had definitely got to a few of our pals and family members, and a good few folk had been evicted by the time we even made it down. Everyone knew it was a big deal and the mood was celebratory. The journey from that first gig at The 13th Note to the Barras had been epic. It also felt like it had happened in the blink of an eye.

There were a lot of firsts that autumn. We also made our first trip to the other side of the world to play in Japan and Australia. It was the farthest any of us had ever been. Japan was particularly alluring. I loved Japanese culture and had always wanted to visit. I'd also heard tell of the experiences that bands had had when they went there and I was fascinated to see if it was hyperbole. I'd recently read Julian Cope's fantastic book *Head On* and his description of the reception that The Teardrop Explodes received there was wild, boarding on Beatlemania. I didn't expect that but was curious nonetheless.

We had an issue before we went, in that Michael our sound

guy had double-booked us with Super Furry Animals and wasn't going to make the trip. The further problem was we'd already bought his plane ticket. Thankfully the perfect solution was at hand. Michael's dad, Mick, rather helpfully had the same name as Michael, did live sound and was available to come in Michael's place. We'd met Mick before and we all loved him. A good bit older than us, Mick was super experienced and despite being in his fifties had an enthusiasm that would put most teenagers to shame. Mick hadn't been to Japan before and was totally up for it. The twelve-hour plane ride was longer than we had experienced before and it wasn't a dull affair. We'd been told that the best way to deal with long flights was to take Valium and our old pal Kiko had managed to procure some. I'm sure the conventional wisdom is to take Valium and sleep through the entire flight. However, our excitement levels were through the roof and we had zero chance of sleeping, such was our state of frenzy. We had been drinking since we left Glasgow and were fairly far gone by the time it occurred to anyone to take the medicinal Valium in preparation for the plane ride. Mick in particular had been partaking of the whisky and was definitely on one. When we boarded the plane we were surprised to find that the flight was almost empty. As the sparsely populated plane began to taxi, Mick got out of his seat and pretended to surf. The patience of the incredibly polite JAL cabin staff was an early insight into the gulf between European and Japanese etiquette. Mick was clearly off his rocker, and that was not going to be the last of his antics. A keen weed smoker, Mick decided that since the plane was empty no one would notice if he smoked. The fact that he'd brought weed on an international flight was outrageous enough but what happened next beggared belief. He fashioned a weed pipe out of an empty coke can and smoked it under a blanket. I shudder to think what the repercussions could have been but amazingly the incident passed without comment. Different times, I suppose.

When we landed it became abundantly clear that we were a long, long way from home. Japan was mind-blowing, so different was it from anywhere we'd been before. The buildings looked like something from an unmade sci-fi classic, and everything was so clean. It seemed their technology was years ahead of anything we'd seen because all the teenagers were on phones that took photos and played tunes; it was like being in a movie. The time difference was also discombobulating. After the two-hour drive through the industrial outskirts of Tokyo and the sprawling metropolis, we ended up in Shibuya where we were staying and playing. The centre of Shibuya, with its famously massive pedestrian crossing, was wild. An immense neon jungle with something happening on every floor of all the buildings that stretched in every direction as far as the eye could see. Very few signs were in English, so who knew what was happening? But it all seemed other-worldly. The sounds, too, were incredible. Music was everywhere but it was tiny loops of electronic snippets of melodies and Japanese pop songs with their high-pitched, frenzied choruses. We met Koya, a young smiley guy who worked for our promoter, Smash. Our gig was the next night at a venue called Quatro. Our hotel was only a few streets away from the madness but felt a world away. On a backstreet lined with trees it felt like it was on a different planet. The hotel was small, incredibly clean and neat. After dropping our bags off we headed out for dinner. Going for dinner in Japan was a completely different experience. Firstly, all of the food was communal; secondly, there was a mystery as to what any of the food actually was. It was unlike anything I'd ever had but also absolutely great. Koya was a wonderful host and made sure we were all having a great time. We were in our element, so far away from home and about to play our first show in Asia, somewhere I'd always dreamt of visiting and playing. After a great night of drinking and eating we headed back to the hotel. I was so tired I felt like I was leaving my body. When I got back to my room I was asleep before I hit the pillow and conked out.

After sleeping like the undead I woke at an unholy hour and went for a walk. The ghostly quiet of the morning was in stark contrast to the seething madness that was Shibuya at night, the blinding neon and deafening sounds of activity replaced by a serenity that belied the concrete surroundings. The first thing that struck me was how safe it felt. Cities have a certain element of danger to them wherever they are in the world, but this was different. Everything was so calm. I wandered around the shut-up shops and restaurants for a while and eventually found myself in Yoyogi Park. It was quiet, too, but there were people there. Lots of people with dogs. Westerners with big dogs and Japanese people with small ones, and many of the dogs were dressed up in weird outfits. I also saw a guy with a sword practising some kind of martial arts. I remember thinking that if I saw a guy with a sword in a park in Glasgow, I'd probably phone the police! I was in love with Tokyo. Before heading to Japan my life had been increasingly messy and chaotic, and this moment of peace was so welcome. It seemed a long way from the chaos, not just in distance. Japan felt like a refuge. I'd never been anywhere like it, and I really hoped it was somewhere that I'd be visiting again.

The gig was that night and we had a lot to do in one day. Before soundcheck we had to go to the offices of our record label, Toy's Factory, to do some interviews. The first thing that struck me about the offices was the chaos. I had in my mind that everything in Japan was painstakingly neat and tidy, but if that were the case then these guys had clearly missed the memo. The place was a riot of paper and CDs. We were met by the guy in charge of putting our music out, a cheerful chap by the name of Shigeru who led me into the room where I was to do the interviews. Before the journalists arrived, I was met by my translator. She was really nice and when I told her that this was my first time doing press in Japan, she gave me a wry smile. When the interviews started I realised straight away that this was a completely different ball game from what I was used to back home, in Europe or in North America. The questions were straight-up intense, really cleverly thought-out and all showing a level of understanding and seriousness the likes of which I'd never really experienced. Certainly not with this intensity. If I tried to dodge a serious question with a silly answer, the writer would laugh and ask the question again. It was tiring but at the same time great to have come so far and to be taken so seriously.

After the interviews we headed to the venue and were met by a few fans who'd been waiting there to meet us. They were really polite and had brought us some gifts, stickers, sweets and even a jacket. It was so nice to get such a warm reception and we couldn't wait for the gig. The venue was immaculate, situated on the top floor of a shopping centre. You wouldn't have known it existed from the outside. Our small crew, which consisted of Mick and Ally Christie, had massive help from the local crew who knew in advance exactly what our stage set-up was and had everything ready for us to just set up and plug in. The gig was really early in comparison to what we were used to, onstage at 7 p.m. There was no support band and the plan was to go for dinner after we played. Koya told us the gig was sold out.

Before we played, the dressing room felt weird. We were all extremely jet-lagged and there was a surreal feeling to the proceedings. Playing in a shopping centre at teatime, 10,000 miles from home, felt far from normal. Finally, after what felt like an age it was time for the show.

We made our way onto the stage and were greeted by a huge roar. The room was packed and everyone looked so happy. We opened with 'Mogwai Fear Satan' and the reaction was breathtaking. When it got really loud people put their arms in the air as if trying to feel the noise with their hands. There had been other gigs where, in the middle of the song when it breaks down to just Martin playing on the floor toms and the rest of us barely playing at all, it was hard to keep time because the chit-chat in the room would make it hard to hear everyone. This was the complete opposite. People were so quiet we could hear our fingers moving along the strings. This was certainly the first time that had ever happened. Even at our best gigs there had been some people nattering away, usually at the bar. This was a completely different experience. We'd never known real reverence for our music before. Enthusiasm? Yes. But not actual reverence. It felt so special. The only shock came after the first song where, after a huge burst of applause, the crowd suddenly went completely quiet. As we walked over to change guitars the audience remained silent. It was weird but clearly just part of the respect that the audience show for artists in Japan.

Afterwards we all went out to celebrate into the night. Koya took us to another restaurant where we drank beer, sake and ate more mysterious food. We were all in love with Japan and had one more gig to play there before heading to Australia. The next day we got the famous bullet train to Osaka, travelling at over 200 miles per hour and taking only a couple of hours to get from Tokyo to Osaka, which is 250 miles. Osaka was slightly less sci-fi than Tokyo but incredible in its own right. Koya was from Osaka and told us that this was the more musical of the cities in Japan, where bands like the Boredoms and Shonen Knife were from. We had a few spare hours before soundcheck so we went for a look around. The area around the venue was a burrow of little shops selling everything you could think of; brilliant record shops, instrument shops and clothes shops. We stocked up on demented tat and got ready for the gig. The crowd in Osaka were just as great as Tokyo, and again we went out after the show with the Japanese crew for drinks and food. One of the roadies, a big guy with massive dreadlocks called Sasha, turned out to have been a roadie for the band who'd played the theme song for the kung fu show *Monkey Magic* we'd all loved as kids. Even though there was a massive language barrier we got on great with everyone we met in Japan. Everyone working with us had been lovely and the fans had been so kind. We left Japan with heavy hearts, hoping it wouldn't be too long before we returned.

And then, Australia.

None of us had ever been to Australia but it didn't have the same allure. Like most nineties teenagers we'd all grown up watching *Neighbours* and *Home and Away* and thought we knew what to expect when we went there. I had a pre-conceived and pretty basic idea of Australia as being a bit like Britain with sun. The differences with Japan were marked. Where Japan was reserved and polite, Australia was brash and intense. We were met by our Aussie tour manager, Michael, who was uber-friendly and determined for us to have as good a time as possible. This was the farthest any of us had ever been from home and the sense of discombobulation was combined with a feeling of being out of the glare of anyone we knew. People were so friendly here. The whole year had been nuts and this felt almost like a holiday. Back in Scotland it was starting to get dark at 4 p.m. and you couldn't leave your house without a jacket to protect you from the cold and wet, yet here we were wearing T-shirts and shorts.

Our first few shows were in Brisbane and Sydney. Brisbane was pretty low key but still a great show. Getting to Sydney seemed like a big deal. We were met by Aaron Curnow, a freckly surfer whose label, Spunk, were putting our albums out over there. He was incredibly friendly and chipper and really made us feel at home. We had two shows in Sydney, both at ex-servicemen's clubs. We were pretty perturbed by the numerous paintings of the Queen of England, which most definitely was not to our taste. One of the old guys who worked there also asked Martin to take his hat off before he came in, which didn't go down that well.

We were staying not far from the harbour, nestled among huge skyscrapers, about twenty floors up. The night before we had managed to procure some Es, which we were going to take before we headed out for a night's drinking. Me, Barry, John and Mick all took ours and sat around the apartment drinking small

Australian beers waiting for the pills to kick in. It didn't take too long before I started to feel distinctly odd. We used to take Es all the time – Barry and I even once took some before going to the cinema to see the Will Smith film *Enemy of the State* before soundcheck – but this wasn't the same feeling. My legs felt shaky and I started to experience a nostalgically weird feeling, kind of like a permanent yawn pulsating through my body. The conversations were starting to sound like snippets or samples chopped up. Everything had a jittery feeling. I was entering a dream-like state and didn't feel entirely in control of either myself or the situation at hand. I can't recall who said it first but in a fearful tone of voice, not unlike Han Solo pointing out that the Death Star was not in fact a moon, someone said that the E was not in fact E – we were all tripping out of our minds on acid. Time as a concept had ceased to exist. We were speaking to each other but it was hard to tell what we were saying or hearing. I'd taken acid loads when I was a teenager but this was different because back then I was completely carefree, whereas now I felt like I had the weight of the world on my shoulders. I was getting more and more paranoid by the second. I started to worry that someone was going to jump off the balcony. I kept asking people if they were OK and they would reply that they were, but in my paranoid state I thought they were messing with me. I was not having a good time. I needed to talk to someone who wasn't fucked. I somehow deciphered the calling code to the UK and started phoning people. The first person I phoned was Barry Hogan. The previous month Barry had invited Mogwai to curate the follow-up festival to the Bowlie Weekender – All Tomorrow's Parties – and we were right in the middle of choosing the line-up. We had some sorting to do and I tried to talk to him about bands playing the festival, but I had no anchor to reality and just started talking gibberish. The time zones were all out so I was calling people in the middle of the night. I called Adele but just woke her parents up. I was a mess. After a while I realised that I needed to get outside.

The room was suffocating me and I needed to be somewhere else. We were in the middle of a concrete jungle and the huge buildings felt like they were falling on me. I saw a taxi and hoped that it might be my escape. I got in the back and the guy asked me, 'Where to?' 'Take me somewhere nice,' I replied. The guy saw me – a sweaty, pale, wide-eyed maniac talking utter madness – and just drove me round the block and dropped me off exactly where I'd first got in. In my fevered mind I wondered if this was a sign. Was where I *was* actually nice? I made my way back to the room to find the others rolling about laughing having a brilliant time. I was still tripping hard and completely unanchored from any kind of reality. I decided to turn on the TV. *The Matrix* was on. I loved that film and thought that seeing something familiar would be a good way of pulling myself together. I was watching the film and feeling somewhat better about things. After all, I might be freaking out in Australia but at least I'm not being held prisoner with the rest of humanity by malevolent aliens using a computer programme to convince me that everything is normal. No. Things weren't great, but they weren't that bad. At one point in the movie a helicopter crashes into a skyscraper in a particularly dramatic turn of events. It was at this exact point that I looked out of the hotel window and saw THE EXACT BUILDING THAT THE HELICOPTER HAD CRASHED INTO. FUUCKK. I was in the fucking *Matrix*!! At that point I decided that surrender was the only option. I went to bed and put the covers over my head, waiting for the aliens to get me or one of my bandmates to jump out of a window, or something else hideously awful to happen. I drifted into a feverish trippy dreamscape, only to wake in a much more lucid state hours later. I thought about everything that had happened and realised that the simple and far less threatening truth was that they'd filmed *The Matrix* in Sydney, near our hotel.

The next day I still felt like someone had put me through a washing machine. The joke in Australia is that you are upside-down and that was exactly how I felt. At our Sydney show someone had met the guys who wrote our beloved sitcom *Neighbours* and we arranged to meet them. I was still tender from my horrendous and unwanted trip and tried my best to rehumanise myself with beer. The *Neighbours* guys were sound. To be fair, everyone in Australia was so friendly and almost completely without pretension. Very much like Scotland in many ways. They offered to write a mention of Mogwai into the show, which seemed incredibly unlikely. I'd actually forgotten about it for years, only to be called by my mum one day to say that my uncle Gus on the Isle of Lewis had heard us mentioned on *Neighbours* and was very impressed.

The remaining dates in Australia were something of a blur. I was still teetering on the edge of reality when we played in Melbourne – so tired, wired, confused and far from home. At points during the show I couldn't remember what band I was in. For a second I thought I was in The Stooges, only to click back into reality and remember that I was in fact in Mogwai. What a comedown! After we played I went for a walk around the beach. A girl who'd been to the show saw me and we walked and talked together for a while. She told me about her life, which seemed way more troubled and dramatic than mine. I realised at that point how lucky I'd been. I was being flown all over the world, doing exactly what I'd always dreamt of doing. I felt like I had been fired out of a cannon though. I'd got so into the pattern of making and playing music and getting as wasted as I possibly could. I never stood still and, as I stood on that beach pouring my guts out to a total stranger, I realised just how lost I was. I was too young and immature to do anything about it though. So I just kept going.

After Australia we flew to New Zealand to play in Auckland. By this point we were all done. The year had been an absolute whirlwind and we literally could not be further away from home. Mick had been relishing our instructions to make the gigs as loud as possible and, as this was the last night of the tour, he really went all in. That night the volume level was recorded as being

132 decibels, not far off the volume made by a jet engine when an aeroplane takes off. As well as being punishingly loud we also played for a long time to mark the occasion of it being our last show of the year. Our deafening gig pushed the two-hour mark.

Landing back in Glasgow was a shock. It was typical December weather and it felt like our bodies contracted when we landed, having been wearing T-shirts and shorts for weeks in Asia and Australia. There was also a real feeling of reality falling in like a ton of bricks. I was used to being on tour and everything that it brings. I was about as far from the present as you could be. The combination of never being home and being constantly wasted when back in Glasgow meant I wasn't being a very good boyfriend to Adele. We'd been together since we were kids, though, and didn't really know how to process it all. I certainly didn't.

At Hogmanay a load of us went out to the annual party Optimo threw, with Aidan and Malcolm from Arab Strap. The end of a century seemed like a massive event and millennial paranoia was everywhere. There was even talk that the millennium bug would stop Martin's pacemaker at the stroke of midnight. People thought the world was going to end and we certainly partied like it might. Full of E we danced into the night, and as was traditional we headed back to Aidan's flat to keep the party going until well into the morning. After sleeping on a couch somewhere, me and Adele headed back to where I'd parked my car to drive to Lanarkshire for the traditional New Year's Day family dinner. When we got to my car we saw that someone had smashed the back windscreen. With no way to get it fixed and in no real state to get it sorted anyway, I drove the half-hour back to my folks freezing and petrified.

The New Year had started with confusion and a clawing feeling in my stomach that everything was about to fall apart.

As it would turn out, that feeling wasn't far wrong.

Part Three
The Hard Part

16.

All Tomorrow's Parties

Superficially everything seemed to be going well, but you only had to scratch the surface to realise that this couldn't be further from the truth. I was not doing great at all.

We'd had a feeling for a while that things with Chemikal Underground were coming to an end. The band was getting bigger and our instinct was that we should move to a larger label. To be fair to Chemikal Undergound, they had done nothing wrong whatsoever but our ambition, alongside interest from others, had unsettled the band.

The first people to show real interest in signing us were the legendary Sheffield electronic label, Warp. We all adored the music that Warp put out and it seemed like a great fit. They invited us down to their offices in Sheffield to get to know them. We were all obsessed with a really random documentary called *Tales from a Hard City* that follows the lives of some Sheffield natives and were excited to find out that the two owners, Rob and Steve, actually knew some of the characters from the film. Rob and Steve were lovely guys with great stories. Steve in particular told us a story about getting into a press-up competition while on acid, which really tickled us. Rob was cool as well, although he did indulge in a pretty Olympic *faux pas* by telling a bunch of jokes about gingers without noticing the colour of Martin's hair. They were cool guys though, and it looked increasingly likely that they would end up being our new home. They gave us all Warp record bags, which we loved. We still lived for free stuff back then.

We were extremely close to signing the deal with Warp when we got word that there was another possibility: PIAS, who owned Vital, the distributor that Chemikal used, were setting up a new label, Southpaw, led by a fellow Scotsman John Niven, and they were keen on us becoming their first signing. Icelandic band Sigur Ros had signed to PIAS and were in the midst of a pretty meteoric rise. Another person we knew was also involved. Mark Mitchell, who helped out with Chemikal Underground at Vital, was on board and we had a lot of time for him. He really believed in us and having him involved felt like the kind of continuity that we needed. First of all we had to meet John Niven, the guy who wanted to sign us.

I met John in a fairly upmarket restaurant in Glasgow. He was a working-class guy from Ayrshire with a demonic sense of humour and a sharp wit. He'd previously worked at London Records and had actual hit singles like Mike Flowers Pops' kooky cover of Oasis' 'Wonderwall'. He was an indie guy at heart, having played in the jangle band The Wishing Stones before becoming a label guy. The first question I asked him was what his favourite record was. Without blinking, he replied, *'Marquee Moon.'* Being a total guitar nerd, I was very happy with this answer. John seemed ambitious and told me about the other bands he wanted to sign, many of whom I loved. It was looking like Southpaw (PIAS) was going to be our destination. The fact that they were going to give us more money than Warp also made the decision a little easier.

Even though we were about to sever ties with Chemikal, there were still a few things we had to do together. To celebrate five years of the label they had organised a birthday gig at The Garage in Glasgow, with all the bands on the label playing and John Peel DJing. The atmosphere was a little odd because even though we were all still friends, Chemikal knew we were leaving. Playing that night were ourselves, Arab Strap (who were also in the process of leaving for another label), The Delgados, Bis and new signings Aereogramme and Suckle. Despite the slight awkwardness

234

it was a great night and John Peel's DJing was brilliant. One old soul record he played really blew me away. I asked him what it was. 'Gladys Knight & the Pips,' he replied, with a look of slightly horrified bemusement. When I told him I'd never heard of them before, he looked appalled. John's not around any more but I'm sure he'd be happy to know that I now have many records by them.

As was normal, after the gig we all went back to Aidan's. Pills were gubbed and beers consumed. It was par for the course. When the sun came up someone suggested we go to the pub. There was a pub in Finnieston that would serve you beers as long as you also ordered some food. I was there with Aidan, Adele, Eugene from The Vaselines and Tony Doogan, the engineer. A motley crew indeed. When we got to the bar and the beers, rolls and square sausage arrived, Adele asked me if the rolls were a prize for staying up all night. We were all royally fucked.

The next month was the first ever All Tomorrow's Parties. As curators we had chosen the bill for the entire weekend. It was such an important gig for us so we decided to do a warm-up show in Edinburgh. The opening band at the warm-up, also playing All Tomorrow's Parties, was the Texan band . . . And You Will Know Us by the Trail of Dead. I'd fallen in love with them after hearing them on the Peel Show and was super excited to see them play. They were like a more punk rock Sonic Youth and apparently pretty wild live.

We'd been the ones to ask Trail of Dead over so we invited them to stay with us while they played their first gigs in Scotland. The night before the gig with us, they played a headline show in Glasgow. It was immense. They were a non-stop rock and roll whirlwind, perpetually flying about the stage, swapping instruments and ending their set with a cataclysmic freak-out, leaving the stage looking like it had been hit by a bomb. Half of the guys in the band – Jason and Neil – stayed with me at my parents. In the car on the way back from a gig in town we stopped to get chips at the train station in Hamilton. The Trail of Dead guys were totally down for having a good time, adorned in their usual garb of all-black tight jeans, shirts and cowboy hats. Hamilton train station can be a bit of a backward place at the best of times and the locals didn't know what was going on when these loud Texans in cowboy hats appeared. They probably thought it was a fancy dress event.

The next night in Edinburgh was great. Trail of Dead were amazing again. For our show we had hired a string quartet to play on songs like 'Christmas Song', our Jewish hymn 'My Father, My King' and a new song 'Take Me Somewhere Nice', inspired by my Australian meltdown, the lyrics reflecting my somewhat unsteady state of mind. We knew that our All Tomorrow's Parties show was important and this was our last chance to run through the songs before the festival. One issue we had at the Edinburgh gig was that the string players, clearly overcome by the spirit of rock and roll, had drunk a large percentage of the rider before the show. Maybe it was not being used to playing alongside such loud instruments but they weren't entirely in tune all of the time. On the off-chance that it was because they were drunk, our tour manager Simon asked them if they would please wait until after the show before they drank the rider.

Afterwards we all hung out at an aftershow organised by the promoter Keiron. Working at the gig was Grainne, the Canadian/ Scottish girl that I'd met the year before. She hung out with us all at the party. We were definitely starting to bond.

Before we even got to Camber Sands it was evidently clear that All Tomorrow's Parties was going to be pretty biblical on the hedonism front. The ATP main man Barry Hogan was a legendary partier, and with most of Glasgow in attendance and pretty much every band we knew playing, it was never going to be a modest affair. We were closing the festival on the Sunday night, and headlining the Friday were our Welsh friends Super Furry Animals. On Saturday night, incredibly, Barry Hogan persuaded Sonic Youth to play. Being part of an event with Sonic Youth was special enough, but having them play because we wanted them to was unbelievable. We had other bands like Labradford, Godspeed, Wire and Bardo Pond. Aphex Twin had also agreed to do an unannounced set and John Peel was DJing. We'd even chosen all the movies and TV shows to be shown in the chalets.

When we got to Camber the whole scenario was surreal. So many people we knew were there. The very first band to play were the Leeds band Hood. We'd played with Hood so many times and become great friends. They played the second stage which, although not as big as the main ballroom, was still substantial. When watching Hood, I remember thinking how great it was that they were playing to so many people. Everywhere you went you met someone you knew and it became pretty clear that certain chalets were the party chalets. The parties started on the Friday and didn't finish until the bouncers chucked everyone out on the Monday morning. On the second stage that day were Labradford. They had been a band that Dominic and I had bonded over since the first time we heard their music at David Keenan's 13th Note DJ night, Coulpourts. Their music is utterly transformative, completely without parallel, both the heaviest and the lightest thing you've ever heard at the same time. As the day went on, I oscillated between hanging out with friends and watching bands. Godspeed were amazing, as were the Super Furries. Seeing thousands of people watching musicians that we'd chosen was wonderful and surreal. By the time the bands finished we all congregated in the bar downstairs. It was like some kind of Walt Disney version of a pub from *EastEnders*. Our old pal Noj was playing records and it was bedlam. Everyone was wasted. It felt like such a celebration, like the party was never going to end. I remember going to the beach in the middle of the night with some people – I can't remember who they were – and feeling on top of the world. But in reality, I really wasn't.

I woke the next day with no idea how I'd found my way back to the chalet. I was a mess. I could barely recall half the night. I just knew it had been great. Reflecting back, helping organising that festival is one of the things I'm most proud of in music and I can barely remember a thing about it. Being part of something so wonderful and having blacked out for most of it isn't great. None of this occurred to me though. In my mind that would have been the position that almost everyone else I knew there was in. Perhaps they were? The next day kicked off with Ligament and Trail of Dead on the main stage. I remember seeing Kim Gordon from Sonic Youth watching Trail of Dead and almost pinching myself. Our Glaswegian touring mates, Ganger, were playing what was to be their final gig in the second room and Martin was joining them on the second drum kit. Later on the same stage, Brian McMahon from Slint's new band, The For Carnation, played before Shellac. On the main stage that night were Arab Strap followed by Sonic Youth. Adele was singing with Arab Strap. It was great watching her sing but I'd barely seen her all weekend. I'd been off on a drunken drugged haze wandering who knows where. Arab Strap played one of my favourite songs of theirs that night. The lyrics go:

I hear we had a good time
I hear I was a riot
I would've liked me a lot last night
I could've put me to shame last night

Arab Strap were fantastic as always. Next up were Sonic Youth. I adore Sonic Youth. Everything from their big pop hits like 'Kool Thing' and 'Sugar Kane' to their psychedelic freak-outs like 'Expressway To Yr. Skull' and 'Diamond Sea'. The way Sonic Youth could live in both worlds was massively inspiring to us. The way they blurred the lines between rock and roll, poetry and art was an inspiration. I love the fact that they could surprise you and were never predictable. This night they most definitely were NOT predictable.

Me and John were so excited about seeing Sonic Youth and took advantage of our position as curators to watch the band from the side of the stage. It became instantly clear that this wasn't going to be the typical Sonic Youth festival show. When I'd seen them play at Reading or Benicàssim, they'd always played a bunch of songs that people recognised. This clearly was not the plan tonight. They were playing the most freeform noise jams, wildly swinging between barely there minimalism and freak-out noise. At one point Kim Gordon started hitting her guitar with a trumpet. John and me absolutely loved it. Most of the crowd didn't seem to though. I suppose after two days straight of drinking and drugs, people maybe expected something a bit more upbeat on a Saturday night performance by the best-known band at the festival. Eventually they did play a hit of sorts, 'Sunday', and everyone went bananas. Sonic Youth showed that night that they were unpredictable and unconventional. Opinions about their show were mixed but I thought they were brilliant.

After their set the partying continued. Warp Records had taken over the smaller of the two rooms and Aphex Twin played an unannounced set. I'd been a huge fan of Richard D. James's music since hearing 'Digeridoo' all those years back at The Orb show. I'd heard his sessions on Peel and thought he was the best electronic musician around. His *Girl/Boy* EP was one of the best records I've heard in my life. I'd love to report on his set at ATP but alas I was so fucked I can't remember a thing about it. Everyone was out of their mind. Our soon-to-be label boss John Niven was there for the weekend too, and he, an arch hedonist at the best of times, was completely out of his gourd. He looked like he was having some kind of medical emergency. He wasn't just wrecked, he was 'does he need to see a doctor?' wrecked. Barry was also on one for the whole weekend. At one point I remember him wondering if he had taken enough E to get a hit from it when in fact he'd already taken so much that he could barely walk or speak.

The next day I felt like death warmed up. Two days of caning it had taken its toll. I was a shell of a man, and that night had to play what was probably the most important show we'd done so far. I was so proud of being part of the inception of the festival and having assembled such an amazing cast of musicians. It seemed borderline tragic for us to fall at the final hurdle by not putting on a good show to close the whole event. However, I barely felt like a human being, never mind a musician about to play the best concert of his life. The line-up that day was colossal. Playing before us were the recently reformed Wire, one of my favourite bands of all time, and before them was Papa M, the new name that David Pajo was playing under. Sophia were playing in the second room and Adele was singing with them. I watched the show and became completely immersed in the music. Robin Proper-Sheppard's music completely mirrored how I was feeling. His songs are so heartbreaking and personal and I was transfixed. After they played, in my state of nervousness and fragility, I didn't say anything to Adele about the performance. She was rightly upset with me. She'd always been there for me and this was a big deal, and I hadn't even offered the bare minimum of congratulations. I'm sure this was just the tip of the iceberg. I was a shit boyfriend, too wrapped up in my own life and not paying much attention to hers at all. We'd been together for so long, since we were kids, and I'd just really taken her for granted. I buried this as I always did by drinking. What should have been something momentous and to be excited about was approaching like an iceberg. I was a wreck. I could barely watch the bands before us because I was so nervous. I'd spent the whole weekend out of it and was haunted by fear as to what I'd done or said to people. Everyone was being so nice, but in my state I wondered if they were being genuine. My grip on what was going on was getting looser by the day.

After what felt like an age it was time for us to play. As an intro we played 'Lust' by Low over the PA. It had always been one of my favourite Low songs and they were one of the few bands we'd invited that weren't available to come and play.

> *Are you filled with anger?*
> *Are you filled with lust?*
> *Would it kill you to trust?*

When the lights went down and reflected around the room, dashing off the mirror balls onstage, I listened to Alan and Mimi's voices and tried to summon the inner strength just to get through the show. I was not in a good way. We opened with 'Punk Rock', the first song from *Come On Die Young*. It was just Barry and me playing alongside the recorded voice of Iggy taken from an old TV interview. My part couldn't have been simpler, just a few notes, but my hands were like jelly. As we moved on to the next song, 'Christmas Steps', I felt myself relax. It was as if the audience was carrying me along. When we got to our new song, 'Take Me Somewhere Nice', I had to concentrate so hard. It was the first time we'd played it live, and with the live string players accompanying us, any mistake would lead to the whole thing falling apart. As we were playing I had the epiphany that it was one of the best things we'd done up to that point. The strings sounded majestic and it felt like we had managed to meet the moment. Our final two songs, 'My Father, My King' and 'Mogwai Fear Satan', sounded huge. The weekend had been stunning and I was so happy to have been part of it, though I wish I'd been able to remember more of it.

The next day travelling back to Scotland was utterly hellish. Barry was in a bad way, as was I. At the airport I tried to use my bank card to get money out to buy a coffee and there was so much cocaine stuck to it that it wouldn't go in the ATM. My solution was to eat all of the congealed manky coke off the bank card, which obviously got me instantly fucked again. It was a never-ending cycle. We heard the news that TV star Jill Dando had been shot on her doorstep. It all seemed so surreal, like we were living in a dream that we needed to be woken up from.

It was a time of massive change. Chemikal Underground were more than just our label bosses, they were our friends. We'd got to know Emma, Stewart and Alun really well and thought highly of them. Paul was one of our closest friends in music and his involvement in recording us was huge and something we'd always be grateful for. We made the decision that we had to tell them we were definitely leaving face to face and arranged to meet them in The Griffin. It wasn't one of the bars our friends hung out in all the time. I'm fairly sure they knew that we weren't meeting them to give them good news. Telling them was even worse than I'd imagined. With Arab Strap having already left, us leaving would be taking away two of the bestselling bands on the label. After we broke the news there wasn't really much left to say. It felt like we'd really let them down, even though we were sure of our decision. What I've found in music is that the people you work with become more than just your workmates. You wouldn't be making music unless you really wanted to and that bleeds over to the people you work with. It's very rare that someone you work with doesn't become a friend and the people who you work closely with become almost like family. Leaving Chemikal felt like breaking up with someone.

I'd never gone through a big break-up. Me and Adele had been together since we were kids but that too was about to change. In the spring of 2000, we parted acrimoniously and I didn't deal with it at all well. Looking back, it's a miracle that we didn't break up sooner. We'd spent almost all of our adult lives together and when the relationship ended, I was a mess.

My friend Alanna Gabin was working in London and I turned to her. We'd become close over the years and she was someone that I trusted implicitly. I felt terrible and blamed myself for the relationship ending so badly. It was then that Alanna told me about unconditional love, that it didn't matter what someone does, if you love someone then there are no conditions. I'd been lucky to always have kind, loving friends and family around me, but it was only at that moment that I realised what love truly was. I was in a state and I didn't think I could handle being in Scotland, which wasn't ideal as we were about to start recording our third record for our new label. I just needed to get away. The proximity to the whole situation was suffocating me. I had to leave.

I asked David Pajo if he minded me coming to stay with him in Louisville for a bit while I sorted my head out. He kindly said yes and I booked myself a flight to America. I'd never really been anywhere on my own and just getting there was an ordeal. I'd never changed planes in America before and didn't understand what to do with my bags when I landed. I put my bags on the carousel and had to be told to collect them. It's a miracle they didn't just go round and round while I went to catch the next plane. I almost missed it anyway, as I totally zoned out at the gate.

When I got to Louisville, David was the perfect host. He had suffered a lot of ups and downs in his life and was a great friend to me. We'd listen to Leonard Cohen for hours, drink and eat pizza. One night David's friend Will Oldham came over. It was the happiest I'd ever seen him. He'd just come back from recording with Johnny Cash and he was so joyful and proud. The song they recorded, 'I See A Darkness', was a masterpiece anyway, but having it sung by one of his idols must have been incredible. One night we drove to Champaign, Illinois, to watch Tortoise play a secret show. They were trying out new songs for a record they were about to work on. I remember driving through the fields and seeing small glowing lights. I thought I was hallucinating and asked David what they were. 'Fireflies,' he told me. I had thought they were something from fairy tales. I had no idea that they were real. It was so strange and magical.

David had some gigs to do so I went up to Chicago to stay with my friend, Lee Cohen. Chicago was so like Glasgow and I was looking forward to spending some time there. I hadn't been there long, though, before I realised I'd left my passport in Louisville. Americans are super strict about ID so it left me a bit limited as to what I could do. Lee lived near a bar called the Rainbow that was the hang-out for most of the Chicago musicians, and he knew the owners so they let us hang out there even though I had no ID. It was attached to the Tortoise studio and they used the bar loo as a bathroom because they didn't have one in their studio. They must have thought I was stalking them. We'd go to see bands play at house shows and I got to know loads of the musicians there, like Rob Lowe from 90 Day Men and Ian from Don Caballero. Everyone was so cool and I was impressed by the sense of community among the bands, but everything has to come to an end and I headed back to Scotland to try to sort my life out.

Upon my return I went to a new festival at Glasgow Green, which seemed like a good idea because all my friends were going. I was in a mess about the break-up so going out and seeing some of my pals seemed fun. Loads of my friends like Trail of Dead, Teenage Fanclub and Primal Scream were playing. Backstage at the festival everyone was hanging out and it was getting increasingly messy. I wasn't in a good way and ended up completely off my head. I got chatting to Justine Frischmann from Elastica. She liked Mogwai and was extremely amused by our 'Blur Are Shite' T-shirts. Damon Albarn was her ex-boyfriend and I guess they weren't on great terms. I told Justine about my break-up and that I was having a bit of a hard time in Glasgow. Everywhere I looked reminded me about how things had ended with Adele and I was feeling a combination of shame and anxiety. Justine made the suggestion that I just get on their tour bus and go with them to the Reading and Leeds festivals, which were the same weekend. I didn't even have to think about it. I said yes. When I told my friends they all looked at me like I'd lost the plot. I met the other folk in Elastica: Justin the drummer, Mew the keyboard player, Annie the bassist, and a young Asian woman who was on the trip as a videographer called Mia. Mia was a sweet person who seemed utterly transformed when she emerged a year or so later as the rap star MIA. All of the Elastica people were lovely and seemed totally fine with having a random Scottish kid jump on their tour bus. I had been under the somewhat innocent impression that Mogwai were hard partiers, but it would seem that we were in fact complete amateurs because Elastica were on another level. Drugs of every kind materialised and things got messy in ways I'd never witnessed before. Justine held court and was one of the smartest, funniest people I'd ever met. Mew was great company too, and everyone was just having a great time getting trashed, listening to Lil Kim and Peaches. It was just what I needed. I'd been so absorbed in the rollercoaster that was my own life that I hadn't just had fun in what felt like an age.

The next morning I had the hangover from hell and a really hard time working out where the fuck I was. The answer, for the fourth year in a row, was that I was at the Reading Festival. Elastica's extremely accommodating tour manager got me a pass so that I wasn't chucked out of the festival as an intruder. The tour bus driver was less happy about me joining the party. It had emerged that he was a Rangers supporter and wasn't that happy that a Celtic fan was on his bus. It was the Old Firm Derby the next day and it didn't seem likely that we'd be watching it together.

Elastica were playing the main stage and I watched them from the side. They had a string of huge hits and it was great watching people go bananas for them. At one point Justine tried to get me to come on stage. I politely declined. After another full day of non-stop hedonism we got on the bus and headed to Leeds for a day off before the final show.

That day, against all the odds Celtic beat Rangers 6–2. I was delirious.

After the game I headed back to hang out with Elastica and, predictably, they all thought I was off my head for being so excited about a football game. It seemed that the weekend's excesses had caught up with Justine as she'd lost her voice. There was some serious dubiety about whether they would be able to play at the festival in Leeds the next day. Justine didn't seem too worried about it though.

The next day, Leeds was headlined by Primal Scream and Oasis. The Primal Scream guys were also ecstatic about the Celtic result. Justine's lack of voice had put the kibosh on Elastica playing but they all went along anyway. The partying had lost a bit of the frenzied edge from the Friday in Glasgow but was still going on. Primal Scream were incredible, with Bobby saluting Celtic's win from the stage. The band they had at that time was utter sonic annihilation. After the gig everyone decamped to the hotel we were staying at. As well as all the bands who'd played, Billy Duffy from the Cult was there. Disinhibited by drink and drugs I went up and told him that his playing on 'She Sells Sanctuary' was one of the reasons I'd picked up an electric guitar. The party continued well into the night. I was having a blast getting wasted with these luminaries, but I knew that it wasn't real life and that sooner or later I'd have to go home. I had to sort my life out and, even more pressingly, I had to start recording our new album.

17.

The Demon Hand

Plans were hatching for our third album at a furious pace. John Niven came up to Glasgow to talk to us about it, taking us all out to dinner at a bizarrely opulent Indian restaurant in Finnieston. Since returning from my Elastica holiday my life hadn't calmed down. I did however have a new place to live after having moved into our friend Mig's flat in Hyndland in the West End of Glasgow. John was already living there. It was handy for going out, which we did all the time. We were going to record with Dave Fridmann again and head over to Tarbox in upstate New York. In my frenzied state of mind, though, I had another idea which I was adamant about. During the meal, without prompting I proclaimed, 'I want to record my vocals in New York City.' John looked at me with the perplexed look of a parent whose child has just demanded every flavour of ice cream from the van and nodded along. It took a few minutes of me expanding on my plan and the huge significance and importance of said plan before he started to take me seriously. I'd been on one for a few months by this point so I'm fairly certain that the rest of the band barely blinked an eye. To his credit, with a good decade or so's experience of placating semi-deranged musicians, Niven agreed. We would start prepping the music in Cava in Glasgow with Tony Doogan, before heading to Tarbox to do the main recording, with Tony coming to assist. Afterwards, Barry, Tony, Dave and me would head to Manhattan for a fortnight to do extra overdubs and vocals. We would all then decamp back to Tarbox to mix the album. Before a note had been played, this was already looking like an extremely expensive record.

While back in Glasgow, I'd been able to calm my fevered mind by going out all the time. I'd go out drinking and seeing bands at night, and during the day I'd wander for hours at a time. The only constructive thing I'd do was work on the songs, but even that was taking a back seat now. One of the songs for the record, 'You Don't Know Jesus', had been written by the rest of the band while rehearsing without me when I was galivanting in America. Despite my lack of focus I had a definite idea for what I wanted the record to be like. In the few years since we'd started the band, the kind of music we made had become weirdly popular. Not popular as in permeating the mainstream but popular as in loads of new bands sounded very much like ourselves or Godspeed. I could see this becoming very tired very quickly and wanted us to try something different. I wanted the record to sound really rich and as far from the minimalist, austere atmosphere of *CODY* as possible. For 'Take Me Somewhere Nice' we asked an old university pal of Barry's, Michael Brolley, to do a great string and horn arrangement. We had actually recorded loads of songs at that first session in Glasgow and used many instruments we hadn't really experimented with before, like banjo and drum machine. We wanted to try as many different ideas as possible. I'm not sure there was a lot of coherence but it definitely sounded different to what we'd done before.

One day I decided that we should record a version of the Hendrix classic 'Hey Joe'. David Pajo was in town and played a killer solo on it. David also sang backing vocals on 'Take Me Somewhere Nice'. It was a weird time because it seemed as if the band had become a huge machine, but at the same time I was in no shape to really be making any decent decisions, and up until that point the rest of the band had looked to me to make a lot of those. I think Colin was struggling a bit as well. Previously he'd been working with Chemikal, who he knew outside of music and had a very personal relationship with, whereas now he was working with PIAS which was a massive multinational label. Everyone at PIAS was great, particularly Nic Shanks, a young woman who worked in the office with John and Mitch, but dealing with dozens of people instead of just a handful was a definite change and one that I'm not sure he ever got used to.

When we flew back to America to start recording, I could tell that Dave knew I wasn't in the best place. After a few days he took me aside and we had a chat. I told Dave that I was having a hard time dealing with the break-up and wasn't feeling great about myself. Dave gave me some advice that really helped and stuck with me. He said that everyone messes up and there's no point dwelling on what's already happened. I really valued that and I think it definitely helped me move on. Dave Fridmann is a man of few words but always worth listening to.

I was driving my bandmates nuts, though. I'd developed a passion for skipping and my sleeping patterns were all over the place. This was the infant stage of the internet and I was keeping in email contact with lots of people. The issue was that the only computer connected to the internet was in the bedroom where we all slept and it made a massive BONG sound when it was turned on. My skipping was also a problem. The house was wooden and when I would skip on the porch outside the kitchen, it made the whole place shake. After a few days this got so annoying that one of them, or possibly all, threw my ropes away. I think I should be fairly grateful that they didn't beat me to death with them. Tony Doogan, who was there assisting Dave, managed to scare the utter wits out of us one night. We had just seen the horror film *The Blair Witch Project* and referenced it quite often, seeing as we were stuck in a cabin the middle of the woods. One night Tony snuck out while we were busy and made little stone cairns outside every door. I was sure that we were in serious peril from an evil witch. Such are the powers of young, fevered minds.

On the music front everything was still going well. Barry was now a prolific songwriting band member and the songs he'd written were brilliant. He'd slotted into the band perfectly and his musicality was really bringing us up to another level. He also has the greatest skill for never taking anything too seriously, which can be helpful in an environment where people take the dumbest things so seriously all the time. With bigger budgets than before we had the time and resources to try a lot of different things out on this record and utilised Dave's studio really well. My head was still a bit of a mess but at Tarbox I was focused on the record and excited about what we were doing.

Then we went to Manhattan . . .

When I say 'we' I should say me, John and Barry went, along with Dave and Tony. We were staying in a place called Off Soho Suites, which was a pretty basic place near the Bowery. The studio we were recording in was called Sorcerer Sound and, for some godawful reason, was full of snakes and spiders in cages with the walls adorned with dried bodies of other creepy-crawlies. I'm fairly easily grossed out by insects but alas that was not much of an excuse for my absence. I barely went into the studio for the entirety of the trip. Basically, me and Barry just went on a colossal bender. By that point we had quite a few good pals in New York and my dear pal Alanna Gabin was always up for going out, and we'd got to know a lot of her friends like Matt Sweeney, Chloë Sevigny, and the band Gang Gang Dance. Sam Brumbaugh and Mike Fellows and the whole Matador crew were always up for a night out as well. I had money for the first time in my life and was single in the greatest city in the world. It was basically non-stop. Alanna and her pal Lizzie from Gang Gang Dance knew pretty much everyone in New York and it seemed like there was something happening every night. With pharmaceutical assistance we hung out all over the city. One morning as we were wandering back to the hotel around 9 a.m. we saw Tony and Dave leaving the hotel to head to the studio. While I'd be the first to admit that my efforts in NYC were beyond lacking, I did produce some music, recording the song 'Robot Chant', which consists of about fifty layers of feedback over a drum machine from an organ. Matt Sweeney came in to play guitar on one song. There was a plan for Chan Marshall (aka Catpower) to sing on that song but she told me she had lost the lyrics she'd written in a hotel in New Orleans.

More than anything music-related I have memories such as driving across the Brooklyn Bridge with Lizzie Bougatsis in her rickety car to find a bar aptly named Cokey's, where gangsters openly sold and took coke. I remember us both being wasted and driving back from our wired quest listening to 'People Ain't No Good' by Nick Cave. It was a surreal and amazing moment in my life. I remember staying up all night at a party with Alanna and the Gang Gang Dance crew and Matt Sweeney playing me Nina Simone's version of 'Hollis Brown' by Bob Dylan. It was so perfect. So visceral and raw. It's funny how remembering hearing a song can evoke such strong memories decades later but that completely does. One night we all left the city and went to a party hosted by Chris Lombardi from Matador at a house in The Hamptons called the Octagon House, built by an architect who had designed the house to represent all of the different parts of the brain. There were bags and bags of Es and everyone was wasted. It was like something from the movie *Rollerball*. I remember wandering into a room and seeing people doing a Ouija board, high as fuck. I've no memory of how we got back to the city.

Back in Manhattan, Sam Brumbaugh asked me if I'd do him a favour. He was hoping to make a documentary about the late country singer Townes Van Zandt and asked me if I'd play a solo set at a fund-raiser for it. Being mid-bender I wasn't in the greatest of shape to perform but agreed anyway, and I asked Barry if he'd join me. By this point my excesses were definitely catching up with me. I would grasp my right hand so the fingers reached the bottom of my palm with the thumb sticking out. To my fevered mind it would look like the face of a demon, and as

I looked at it I'd imagine there was something bad within me. I did that a lot in New York. *Look at my demon hand.* I was so wired and paranoid that I felt like I was being chased half the time. Evan Dando was playing the benefit as well and asked if he could borrow my guitar. He had learnt a bunch of Townes's songs and did an amazing set. Before I went onstage I was in full-on demon hand mode. I turned round to Barry and asked him in all seriousness not to laugh when I was singing. Barry looked at me as if I was literally insane and said, 'Why would I do that?' Why indeed? I was not in a good way. The show went great all the same, and I played 'You're Gonna Need Somebody On Your Bond' by Blind Willie Johnson. I'd first heard it on John Peel, and David Pajo had recently introduced me to some incredible blues music. Blind Willie Johnson's music was incredible, and his track 'Dark Was the Night, Cold Was the Ground' had been included in the Voyager probes which were on their way through the solar system; I loved the idea of aliens hearing his perfectly haunting song. There was something so honest and primal about that music and it really spoke to me. In my quieter moments I would listen to Skip James and Washington Phillips, their music soothing me, providing some respite and a glimpse of the redemption that I so badly needed.

While Tony had been in the studio with Dave every day, he had been partaking in the out-of-hours partying as hard as anyone. Him and Chris Lombardi had created a bit of a nihilistic bond and were causing all kinds of mischief. The night before we flew home we had one final, big night out and Tony got so smashed I pretty much had to carry him onto the plane; no easy task as Tony is a good foot taller than me. It seemed that New York had done a number on quite a few of us.

When we got back to Scotland, Martin and Dominic were very keen to hear the fruits of our labour and were none too amused to discover that all I'd managed to do was record one vocal (not particularly well) and a song that sounded like its sole purpose would be to make anyone in a room leave said room upon hearing it. I think what probably annoyed them more was that we'd clearly just had the time of our lives and they'd missed out on it. It is still frequently brought up to this day.

Cost did not seem to be issue. The album budget appeared to be pretty much unlimited and as we were scheduled to go back to Dave's a few months later, we were sure we'd get it all done then. No one was keeping track of the costs we were running up.

I'd stayed in touch with Grainne, the girl from Canada, ever since first meeting up in Edinburgh. One night in Glasgow at a terrible nightclub called Archaos we ended up hanging out all night with Grainne staying over with me. We were both extremely full-on characters, particularly back then, and from that moment on were inseparable. Adele had moved on too and was going out with a lovely guy called Scott Paterson. You'd like to think that with me having a great new girlfriend that things might have calmed down for me. Wrong. Grainne was a few years younger than me and was probably as hard a partier as I'd ever met. If she could play an instrument she'd have fitted right into Elastica. She was into drum and bass and we would go to clubs almost every night and get completely mashed. We hung out and partied every day until I had to go back to America to finish the record. The night before I was due to fly out we had a particularly messy night which ended with us both taking acid. I managed to get up just in time for the flight. A minor miracle in itself but when I was about to leave, I couldn't find my passport. I turned my bedroom upside down, then upside down again (it already looked like a bomb had hit it), but I could not find the bloody thing for love nor money. After having given up and my flight having long since left, my flatmate Mig came through to ask what all the commotion was about. He picked my bag up and there it was right underneath. I'd lifted everything in the place upside down apart from my bag, which was deviously concealing it.

After I sheepishly told Colin what had happened he advised that I go to the doctor's to get a sick note so I could claim I missed the flight because of food poisoning on insurance. When I went in with my spurious tale of food poisoning the doctor took my blood pressure and said it was abnormally high. Not a surprise really. I'd been on a bender for four months, high on acid and convinced that my hand was a fucking demon.

When I finally got to Tarbox and reunited with my bandmates, Dave and Tony, things were finally starting to feel a little more like what passed for normal. Thankfully Dominic, John and Martin were treating our extremely expensive and unproductive visits to New York as a matter of amusement rather than annoyance, and we were all hands on deck getting the album finished. We had recorded a load of songs, way more than we could possibly use, and were going out of our way to try something different on each one, some with admittedly more success than others.

Recording at Dave's place was wonderful but spending long periods of time there could make you feel a bit trapped. I'd taken up running and asked Dave if it was good to run near the studio. He said that Wayne from the Flaming Lips liked running and would take a stick with him and use it to hit any snakes that he encountered on his travels. Fuck that. I'd wait to resume my running routine till I returned to the relative safety of snake-free Glasgow.

One thing that we were becoming obsessed with on our time off from recording was a particularly stupid skateboard video that Alanna had passed on to us in NYC. It featured some of the guys who ended up finding fame on the *Jackass* TV show doing incredibly stupid stuff to amuse themselves. One stunt featured them paying the excess insurance on a hire car and basically destroying it. This wasn't any dumber or stupider than any of the other stuff they did but it must have planted a seed in our minds. When we were only a few weeks away from finishing the album, Colin flew over to see us with Steve Gullick in tow, who was going to take photos for the album campaign. Another ludicrous expense (Steve could easily have shot us in Glasgow) but hey ho. By this point we hadn't seen another human for quite a while and it seemed like a great opportunity to let our hair down metaphorically. My hair now only existed in metaphorical form as it had fallen out almost completely over the last year or so, no doubt as a consequence of the hideous way I was treating my body. Since meeting Steve the previous year, we'd become good pals and we took the opportunity to have a night out in nearby Fredonia. The bar that Dave and Mary frequented was called BJs and we were regulars there when recording. We'd become friendly with the staff and even made a tentative plan to do a show there before we left. It had been a good night and most of the band had gone out to BJs with Steve and Colin. We were fairly hammered and left at closing time, but when we got back to the studio we couldn't believe what we were seeing. In clear tribute to the CKY skate video, the half of our party that hadn't gone to the bar had taken it upon themselves to pretty much destroy the hire car. It was cabin fever, drunken idiocy at its finest. One (unnamed member) of the band was knee deep in the roof off the car when I saw him with a smile on his face, the likes of which I'd never seen before, or indeed since. It was ridiculous. Realising that we had a bit of a situation on our hands we drunkenly tried to plan our way out of it. Burning the car out was mooted but then abandoned when it was pointed out that people in America tend to do that when covering up homicides. Recreational car burning was very much a Scottish pastime. In the cold light of day it became abundantly clear that the scenario painted in the skate film was a bit more complex than just paying the excess for the insurance. The guilty parties had to pay to have the car fixed out of their own money. Thankfully Steve wasn't too put out by the whole affair and ended up taking some pretty great shots of the smashed-up car.

When not smashing up cars we were incredibly productive. Having Tony there was a huge help because we could keep on working even after Dave had gone home. Any idea we had we would try. Not being limited by time made a huge difference and we were trying to be as ambitious as we could. The song '2 Rights Make 1 Wrong' had so much going on, including banjo and electronics courtesy of our friends Remote Viewer, who had previously been in Hood. One thing we'd spent our advance from PIAS on was an old seventies Roland Vocoder. We all loved Kraftwerk and wanted to incorporate computerised sound into our music. A vocoder works by taking the sound from a microphone and synthesising it through a keyboard to create a mixture of the sound of the voice and the notes played on a keyboard. It was a way of humanising what we did and it suited our music perfectly. When we got the album finished we stayed true to our word and played a concert at BJs. Dave did our live sound, which was something he hadn't done for a very long time. Mercury Rev had played their first ever concert at BJs and it felt great to be part of that tradition.

We said goodbye to Dave and Mary and headed back home to Scotland. All of this time I'd been in America, I'd stayed in constant touch with Grainne and couldn't wait to see her again.

Upon landing back in Glasgow, me and Grainne spent all of our time together. She lived in a mad flat near the castle in Edinburgh with a girl that she worked with, and it was a full-on party house. We'd split our time between Glasgow and there and were pretty much out all of the time. It was only a few weeks after I'd returned from America that we decided to get married. We'd been pretty drunk when we decided this but the next day when we sobered up we agreed that we should go through with it, so we made tentative plans to get married soon. Grainne was incredible and I'd never been engaged before so it all felt super exciting. All of my friends thought I was mad, of course, but to be honest they thought I was mad anyway. This was just more evidence that I was, indeed, mad.

For one of the songs we'd recorded for the album we decided to ask Gruff Rhys from Super Furry Animals to sing on it. John Niven was exceedingly happy about the song with Gruff as the Super Furries were a big chart band at the time and he thought this combination would help get us on the radio. His face dropped like a stone, though, when he heard the song and realised that it was in Welsh. None of us had any particular interest in commercial success and hadn't even paid the slightest bit of mind to any of the murmurings that were going on in the background about plans for the album. All that we were interested in was making a good record. But what we should have been paying attention to was how much it was costing. Fair enough, PIAS had given us a hefty advance but what we hadn't really absorbed was that the money was a loan. Not just any loan. One that you paid back via your royalties. Our royalty rate was about 20 per cent, meaning that for every £100 we made in record sales only £20 went back to paying back the loan. Not that we gave a shit. We were having the time of our lives. We'd never looked too far into the future and were pretty surprised that we were even making a third album, never mind that it was on a big label and someone had given us a pile of money to make it. The whole thing seemed ridiculous.

Plans were coming along for the release of the record, but we didn't even have a name for it. Our contract stipulated that we could call it whatever we wanted so we started messing with John that we were going to call it the most offensive things we could think of. That was all well and good but we did have to call it something, and we had nothing. It might have been a reaction to all the fuss being made over the release but we genuinely didn't have a clue as to what to call the record. At some point someone mentioned naming it after our own record label, Rock Action. It seemed suitably obtuse so we ended up going with that. We thought we might replace it with something better further down the line but never got round to it. For the cover we hired

Andy Vella, who had done the cover for *Disintegration* by The Cure. Everything was stepping up.

To launch the album we decided to do a few gigs in Iceland. We'd never played there and it seemed like a suitably epic setting to unveil our new music. We spent a few days there and I was immediately taken by the sheer beauty of the place. In many ways it was similar to the Hebrides where I'd spent so much time visiting my mum's family, but it had its own grandeur too. The gigs themselves weren't 'just' gigs either. PIAS had invited half of the UK music industry to come and see us. Journalists, DJs and dozens of people from the label. We also flew our string players out. We had enlisted a live cello player, Carole Barber, into the band and this was to be her first show with us. It was a peak time for the music industry. A far cry from Chemikal Underground putting a few hundred quid behind the bar in Glasgow. CDs were selling for £18 a go by the bucketload and money was everywhere. Sending dozens of people from London to Reykjavík to see a band from Glasgow play must have cost a fortune but no one cared. It was an idea and people just seemed to enact them back then. Gruff and Cian from Super Furry Animals were also flown out to sing 'Dial: Revenge', the song they featured on.

We did a photoshoot near some snow-covered mountains and in the famous blue lagoon hot spring, despite being told by the locals that it was full of tourists' pubic hair.

As far as the gig itself went, I was terrified. Loads of the new songs had samples, and one in particular, '2 Rights Make 1 Wrong', where all the sampled drum machines came in about two thirds into the song. Every time we rehearsed it I'd be a ball of panic in case it came in halfway through a bar or not at all. This panic was entirely justified as some of those things happened reasonably frequently. I've never been so nervous before playing a show as I was that night. As well as the army of music industry folks there were loads of great Icelandic musicians there from bands like Sigur Ros and Múm. Messing up would have been a nightmare and having worked so hard and gone through so much this felt like the end of a journey as well as the start of another. So much had changed in that twelve months and this album was what had come out of the end of it. I remember that first night in Reykjavík for a few things. Firstly, when everything came in at the right time in '2 Rights', which I think is the happiest I've ever felt onstage. I think I'd focused on that one potential issue as the key to everything that had happened over the last year and turned it into a microcosm of whether everything in my entire life was going to go right or wrong: whether I'd be living with the demon hand forever, or not. It sounds silly now but when everything clicked in perfectly, I felt that everything was going to be OK. I still think of that moment to this day whenever we play that song and it makes me happy. After the first night we did our obligatory ten minutes of noise and some of the audience left with their fingers in their ears. Sensing that this might be a slight impediment to mainstream success, John Niven mentioned to us that we could maybe cut it down to about five minutes. The next night we did it for twenty.

The other thing I recall was that there was a round of applause when we played the first few bars of a new song. Not just a normal cheer but one that definitely intimated familiarity. I asked someone about it after the gig and they quite nonchalantly said that they'd probably downloaded an MP3 of the album. At this point my only knowledge of MP3s was from my sister's boyfriend, Jared, who had an MP3 player the size of a brick that held five songs and, to my mind, was the most useless object on earth, especially in comparison to my Sony Discman which was smaller, played CDs and sounded better. But this was something new entirely. It was explained to me that people could now download music without paying for it and listen to it on their computers. That didn't sound particularly good to me but I didn't give it much more thought.

After the gig there was predictably a big party, where it seemed like there were as many people as had been at the gig. The guys from Sigur Ros were effusive about our show. Everyone was in amazing spirits. Caroline our new cello player made the distinctly unwise move of buying everyone a round of tequila, which is an incredibly expensive thing to do in Iceland where a round costs more than a new car. Predictably I got far too drunk and when I got up in the middle of the night in my underwear, stepped into the hotel hallway instead of my own bathroom. One of my special moves. I've ended up naked in so many hotel lobbies over the years that I've lost count. I knocked on the door next to me to try to get back into my room and it was occupied by a guy writing a cover story about the trip for the *Sunday Herald*, a Scottish newspaper that my parents read. After shepherding me safely back to my room I asked the writer not to mention it in the article. He said he wouldn't but of course he did.

After Iceland we flew to Austin, Texas, to play at the Matador showcase at South By Southwest. The gig was in a massive exhibition centre and we were playing with our pal Steve Malkmus, who was launching his solo career after Pavement broke up. It was our first visit to Austin and I immediately fell in love. South By Southwest was a bit of a circus but it was evident that Austin was a special place. It was especially different from the other cities in Texas which tended to adhere much more closely to the clipped view of Texas as being brash and uncultured.

We played a gig in San Francisco and a writer for the *NME* came out to interview us, the force of nature that is Sylvia Paterson. Sylvia was great and really got us. Knowing that there was a chance that we would get the cover, I was my usual mouthy self and went on a rant about the state of the *NME* which was becoming a pale shadow of its former self, using misogynist imagery to sell copies and purposefully not putting pictures of Black rap artists on the cover in case it scared their readership. The *NME* threatened not to print the interview and Sylvia threatened to take it to another newspaper as part of an exposé of what had happened to the *NME*. I was also extremely mean about other bands, a habit I was finding difficult to shake off, this time saying that the singer from post-Britpop band Starsailor would 'rape his granny for a Brit award'. It was an appalling thing to say and one for which I would personally apologise to him for saying years later. I was yet to work out that acting like a dick doesn't really get you anywhere.

We had hatched a plan to launch the album a lot closer to home on the island of Bute in the seaside town of Rothesay, about an hour from Glasgow. Rothesay was where people from the west of Scotland traditionally went on holiday and we had planned to make it a day out running buses from Glasgow and back after the gig. It was a great plan but was going to cost us tens of thousands of pounds. That didn't even cross our minds because we thought it was a fun idea and we knew that our pals would love it. I look back now and think that perhaps buying houses might have been a more sensible way to spend the huge cheque that PIAS gave us but that would have seemed terribly adult and boring at the time. We just wanted to make fun things happen and play our music to people in unusual places at eye-watering volume. Opening for us in Rothesay was Eugene Kelly from The Vaselines. The same guy whom I'd seen jump onstage with Nirvana all those years back as a kid at Reading. Eugene was by now a good friend as well as musical hero and it was an honour for us to play with him. I'm not sure Eugene would have quite felt the same way by the end of the night; being our support act that night was a tough slot. By the time the people made their way from Glasgow on the buses and ferries and on to the island, they were pretty drunk. Patience was in short supply. I don't think I've ever seen such a wasted crowd. Everyone was having an amazing time though; it was one of those nights when the gig itself became somewhat secondary. We had wanted to document the event and had hired a mobile recording studio as well as a film crew to make a documentary about the gig. Only a few songs in it became pretty apparent that the gig was not going to be a classic, when a beer can hit Caroline's cello, which she was unsurprisingly fairly furious about. People have fond memories of that weekend but the gig itself was fairly poor. Everyone was so smashed and chatty it was hard to play.

After the gig we all went back to the hotel and the crowd headed back to Glasgow for a party. As well as the bus and the ferry we were also paying for a party that none of us even made it to. Afterwards, the hotel room where me and Grainne were staying became the party room. Everyone was on Es and there was loads of coke around. We partied late into the early morning and by the time everyone left our room the sun had come up. It was one of those nights where everyone talks all night and no one can remember a thing anyone said the next day because everyone was so fucked. I can't even remember who was in our room, even though I'm sure we were all best friends that night. In the aftermath of the party we found a sizeable bag of coke. With no idea whatsoever who'd left it we adopted a finders keepers policy.

The next day we all met up in the local pub to watch the Scottish cup semi-final before heading back home on the ferry and the train. A bunch of John Niven's old school pals from Ayr were there and they'd made the gig the central focus of one of the guy's stag weekend. They were all big Rangers fans and spent the entire game giving us a hard time. One of them, a big chap with an intense stare called Keith Martin, was particularly unnerving, one of the scariest guys I'd ever met. Years later I'd bump into him more often and realised that he was winding me up and was one of the smartest, nicest guys on the planet. I was so full of drugs and drink though that it's no wonder I found him a bit much.

After we watched Celtic win we all shambled our way back to Glasgow, then me and Grainne continued our journey back to Edinburgh. I was by now living in Edinburgh permanently because Grainne was working there. The Warp band Autechre were playing at The Venue that night and we both planned to go. Our plans to continue partying were also bolstered by the fact that we still had the massive bag of coke that had been kindly left in our room in Rothesay. The DJ who performed before Autechre was playing the most insane records I'd ever heard: a mixture of the fastest drill and bass techno and super fast metal. Pretty much a guy screaming over a drum machine. In my addled state I remember staring at a strobe and clicking my fingers trying to work out the time signature of the record that was playing. It was probably two records at once anyway. Autechre were amazing but Grainne and I were both in a state. We'd been taking coke now for almost twenty-four hours and hadn't been to bed. We went out drinking after the show, and when everywhere that sold drink had shut we headed back to the flat and took more coke. It was a fucking mess. Indie *Scarface* hell. We were both in a bad condition. Eventually we went to bed. It didn't seem I'd been in bed for that long when Grainne woke me up and said that she needed to go to hospital. It seems so painfully obvious now but at the time neither of us had a clue what was going on. Everyone we knew took coke and it seemed like such a normal thing to do that it hadn't occurred to us that taking it for days on end would be in any way dangerous. Grainne went to the hospital and was met with a series of justified eye rolls. We were assured that she would be fine and should cease with this kind of nonsense. It had been a wake-up call.

Days later I was back on tour. The schedule to promote the album was relentless. We had more gigs in England and Ireland before heading to Europe, then back to Japan and over to America again for months. I wouldn't have any time off until July, which is when we decided to get married.

One song we had planned to record for our album but hadn't quite got done yet was the cover of the Jewish hymn 'My Father, Our King' (or 'Avinu Malkeinu', to give it its proper name) that Arthur Baker had shown us years earlier. It had become a huge part of our live show with us playing twenty-minute plus versions of it to close our sets most nights. We wanted to record it as live as possible so decided that the man for the job was legendary sound engineer Steve Albini. We decided to record it in London with Steve at a studio that reeked of faded glamour. Steve was appalled by how filthy it was. Recording with Albini was quite daunting. Even though by this point we had made quite a few records, making one with someone with his reputation was a big deal. After all, Steve had made records such as *Surfer Rosa* by Pixies and *In Utero* by Nirvana. In the end it was one of the easiest sessions ever. Steve is funny as fuck and shared our sense of humour. He also has a great irreverence that puts you at ease. The recording turned out great and I left with a huge amount of respect for Steve. Not only as an engineer but also as the only person I'd ever seen eat nothing but Hobnob biscuits for three days straight.

My sister Victoria and her boyfriend Jared had moved to Paris. My parents both adored Paris and decided to time a trip to see Vic and Jared with our show at Café de la Danse in Montmartre, near their place. Before the gig we had dinner at one of the pavement cafes that line the streets. The gig was round the corner from Moulin Rouge, in one of the most colourful parts of the city. It was so nice to spend time with family. I'd been all over the place for the last year and I'm sure they were glad to see me a bit more settled. My dad in particular loved Paris and he loved that part of town. He was fluent in French and would spend hours perusing the second-hand bookshops looking for gems.

We had been having an issue that year with our volume, especially in Europe. It had been our mission to be as loud as possible for a while and our sound guy at the time, Ajay Sagar, was definitely on board with this. When we'd get really loud he'd mix us with the kind of ear defenders used for people directing planes on runways. It definitely wasn't for the faint of heart. With Paris being heavily residential it had a lot of local noise restrictions and we had an inkling that there might be an issue with the volume level that night. Ajay had a few tricks up his sleeve though.

Whenever the volume rules were applied to average volume, he would let me know and I would make sure that we played quite a few extremely quiet songs so that he could go to town on the really loud ones. Usually we got away with it. He bore the brunt of people complaining and usually managed to keep them happy enough. Not tonight though. We were getting into our by-now traditional encore song 'My Father, My King' when I noticed a commotion at the sound desk. There were bouncers physically trying to pull the faders down on Ajay's desk. Clearly diplomacy had failed. I looked around the stage and could see that the others had noticed as well. We continued playing but kept a keen eye on what was happening over by the desk. As we played we could see that things were getting out of control. It was when we saw the first punch thrown that we chucked our guitars on the floor and ran to Ajay's aid in what had escalated into a melee of sorts. I was so furious that someone would mess with our sound and hit Ajay that I completely forgot my parents were in the crowd. I was clambering past bemused Parisians when I felt a fairly firm hand on my shoulder. It was my dad. He said to me with a puzzled expression, 'What are you doing, Stuart?' Only for me to reply, 'I'm just going to brain this cunt.' Not my finest hour, I'll confess. I think by the time we got to the sound desk the whole thing was pretty much over, probably for the best as I don't think I'd be much use in a fist fight with a Parisian bouncer. All five foot five of me. The gig was over though, and the bouncers had robbed the crowd of the last ten minutes. Jared stepped up to the plate and explained to the crowd what had happened. The French, being a principled people, understood the situation and forgave us.

Me and Grainne decided to get married in Lanark, the town of my birth. The initial plan was to only have a handful of our family and close friends there. We went to the registry office the week before the wedding to see the venue. Of the two rooms available the smallest had all the charm of a funeral home so at the last minute we re-evaluated our plans and invited a few more of our friends. Dominic was the only one of my bandmates in town and he came along, as did my old pal, Neale Smith. David Jack was my best man. David McBride, one of the bosses at Regular where Grainne was now working, came, as did Arthur Baker who was in Scotland DJing that night. The ceremony itself was hilarious. The registrar asked very early on if we were related, which set Grainne off in a fit of giggles. None of Grainne's family were able to come over to Scotland for the wedding so we made plans to have another wedding in her hometown of Chatham, Ontario, later in the year. Grainne wore a beautiful vintage white dress and I wore a suit that my sister kindly bought me in Paris when I'd seen her the month before. I'd never worn a suit before in my life. It felt distinctly weird but definitely added to the sense of occasion.

I'd gone from being a mess who was scared of my own hand to being a deliriously happy married man. It had been a wild time.

18.

'A Sad Night for Football, but a Great Night for Music'

After we got married, me and Grainne settled down in Edinburgh. We moved out of the demented city centre party flat and got our own place in a quiet street in Leith. Grainne's new job at Regular Music was only a short walk from our house. We were close with the people from Regular: our promoter, Mark, and the accountant, David McBride, who by this point was helping out with Mogwai. They were both great people and spending time with them was fun. I was happy commuting to Glasgow, cycling to the train station and getting the train over to rehearse. We were enjoying life in Edinburgh, spending loads of time with our friends there or heading back to Glasgow for shows.

As the campaign for *Rock Action* wound down, a lot changed with the band. Things hadn't been great with Colin for a while and I think resentment was starting to creep in on both sides. For our part it had got to the point where anything at all that went wrong was blamed on him. I'm sure Colin was getting fairly sick of us too. It was a fractured relationship, but it still took us by surprise when Colin told us he wanted to quit. He'd been with us since we started and it came as a shock. With Colin gone we made the decision to manage the band ourselves. Most of the decisions had fallen to us anyway and a lot of the administrative side was taken care of by accountants, tour managers and lawyers, so it didn't seem that hard a task. I was a bit of control freak and quite fancied the idea of being all over everything to do with the band.

Around the same time, I received a slightly panicked call from John Niven. It seemed that PIAS' patience with him and his Southpaw project had run out. John had more than taken advantage of the free rein given to him by PIAS. The bottom line was that he'd taken the piss financially, living as if he was shifting millions of albums when that was far from the truth. They'd had enough and asked him to exit the building. The fact that our album, despite doing well, probably hadn't reached the heights that warranted the amount of money spent on it can't have helped matters either. It left us in a weird spot, signed on a big contract by a guy who was now no longer employed by the company. It's a story as old as the hills but certainly not one we had anticipated or knew how to deal with. Thankfully we had friends in PIAS, most importantly the boss, Kenny Gates, who liked our music and seemed to find us entertaining. More importantly he believed in us. Being 'dropped' was without doubt the boogie man in the music industry back then. Bands who'd been dropped may as well have had leprosy, such was the disdain people felt towards them. Whether you were under contract for a record label clearly had nothing to do with whether you made good music, but, at that time and in that insular world, people felt that it did. John Niven had most definitely been dropped and I didn't get the impression he fancied sticking around in the music industry.

Some time later while on tour in America, Chris Lombardi showed us a short story that John had written about the night he graduated from university, when he'd taken acid and wandered around the small town he grew up in. John tells the tale of how he thought he'd died and ended up screaming, 'I want to live!' out of his pal's parents' bathroom window. It was printed in the free magazine put together by Heavenly Records, and was without doubt the funniest thing we'd ever read. I got in touch with

John to say that we'd loved it and he should do more of that kind of thing. I think he was already ahead of us on that front.

Over the last few years I'd been told by a number of people that Robert Smith from The Cure had said some nice things about us in interviews. It seemed almost too good to be true, and at a time when the internet was in its infancy and only really a few steps ahead of Teletext, it was hard to verify. In early 2002 I got a call from Mick which stopped me in my tracks. The Cure had invited us to open for them at a gig in Hyde Park in London. This was incredible news.

We were still with PIAS and working on plans for a fourth album, but things were definitely not the same. There wasn't the budget to record with Dave, never mind for going on frivolous trips to New York to record vocals. This time we would record at home in Scotland, revert back to basics and make the record in a few weeks. We decided to do it with Tony Doogan at Cava, a grand old studio built from a converted church next to Kelvingrove Park, not far from where I'd lived with Kenny and Geraldine in Finnieston. To write the music for the album we hired a room in a semi-legal nightclub by the river called Sound Haus, run by a guy called Bruno who drove a fancy car and wore a bandana. He had a bit of pirate vibe and a definite twinkle in his eye. The other people who worked there were all very strange. We'd entertain ourselves by imagining all their backstories. I wonder what they're all up to now? The room we practised in was normally the cloakroom, and it wasn't unusual for us to find random pills on the floor, which brightened up rehearsals no end. We would practise there five days a week, working on the songs that were to become *Happy Songs for Happy People*. We'd acquired some interesting technology and were trying things out, such as a sequencing programme that ran through an old Nintendo Game Boy called Nano Loop. Luke Sutherland, our old friend who'd played on 'Christmas Steps', agreed to collaborate with us on the record and he wrote great looped violin parts for a lot of the songs. I thought the songs we were working on were some of the best we'd ever done, but at the same time I worried about whether people would be that interested. The fashion at the time had gone extremely retro. People were getting very excited by bands like The Strokes, whose music sounded like it was made before they were born. It seemed that musical culture had taken a very retrograde step. I'd always thought that bands whose music was extremely derivative weren't to be taken too seriously, but it seemed as though that had changed.

During the preparation for the record we went to London to open for The Cure. As a lifelong Cure fan, it felt magical. We were the main support band but before us were The Cranes, another band I'd adored as a teenager. Playing big outdoor gigs was still pretty new to us so that added to the nervousness of performing with one of my favourite bands of all time. Grainne came down with us for the gig and she was as excited as me. We got there in time to do a quick soundcheck not long before the doors opened. As we were playing and checking that we could hear ourselves, I looked over to the side of the stage and could see the iconic silhouette of Robert Smith's back-combed hair. I knew that he liked our music – why would he have invited us to play if he didn't? But seeing him actually watching us soundcheck felt unreal. After we finished, he pottered over and said hello and thanked us all for coming to play. I think I was starstruck for about ten seconds before I realised that he was a totally normal guy, obviously a bit eccentric but I think I can count my 'normal' friends more easily than I can the ones who aren't. Robert was great at putting us at ease and seemed genuinely enthused about getting to see us play. His passion for our music was evident. It felt like such a boost after all the upheaval.

Our show that day flew by in the blink of an eye. We used the gig to showcase one of the new songs for the record, written by Barry on vocoder and guitar. It ended up being called 'Hunted By A Freak', named after Jill Dando's still-uncaught killer. We didn't play for very long. We were the support for a band who famously played extremely long sets so that wasn't really any surprise. Robert watched the whole gig and was really complimentary afterwards. There was a big backstage area, more like a festival than a gig, and Grainne met Gary Numan there. We were both big Numan fans and ended up hanging out with him for the whole of The Cure's show. He was lovely and only complemented the unusual nature of the whole night. I still couldn't believe I was on the same bill as The Cure. More than that, I could hardly believe I was getting to see The Cure without buying a ticket. They played a main set that was made up mostly of songs from their dark early albums like *Faith* and *Pornography*, and their latest, *Bloodflowers*. I was in awe when they played 'The Figurehead' and 'The Drowning Man'. It was just like a dream to reference their classic 'Just Like Heaven'.

Afterwards, the weirdness continued backstage. The singer from Coldplay, Chris Martin, was very generous about our music. Coldplay were on the verge of global superstardom and it was nice to see a guy in that position be so down to earth. I spoke to Robert for ages too. He had loads of his family – young nieces and nephews – running around. He clearly enjoyed the social side of playing music. Why wouldn't you? Making music is all about hanging out with your friends. The fact that people (in his case lots and lots of them) want to see you do it is a big bonus. After chatting to Robert for a bit he said he had to go and speak to Steve Severin, his old bandmate from his Banshees days whom he hadn't spoken to for a decade. As if the evening couldn't get any stranger.

Back from London we got on with the task in hand of making our new record with Tony in Glasgow. I would get the train through every day and then the last one back from Edinburgh. I rode my BMX bike up the steep Easter Road Hill every morning and avoided the drunks on Sauchiehall Street as I cycled through the city after we finished. It was our first time recording with Tony and it was evident he was a brilliant engineer. The first album he'd made was *In the Space of a Few Minutes* by Telstar Ponies, which we all adored. He had a masterful use of sound and space which really suited the songs we were working on. One night after we'd almost finished one of the songs, I asked Barry how he was feeling about the music. 'Really happy,' he replied. That was how we came up with the title *Happy Songs for Happy People*. Sarcastic but borne out of something true, like a lot of our titles. The songs that Luke had contributed also turned out great. He was a brilliant guy to be around. Razor sharp, smart and funny as hell, he added a lot to what we did. At this point he had left music mostly to concentrate on his writing. His novels were doing well but you could tell he still enjoyed being involved with music.

With the album recorded but not released until the following year, we spent some time doing sporadic gigs, culminating in a return to Australia for a series of headline gigs as well as being part of the Livid touring festival. Our pals Trail of Dead were doing the festival and playing with us at the side shows. The headliners of the festival were Oasis and Morrissey, and the events were held in sports arenas and fields. It was a strange experience but totally enjoyable. The Trail of Dead boys were our partners in crime and it seemed that whenever we were all together, all kinds of anarchy would ensue. We shared a bill and a tour manager with them on this trip. The tour manager, Noel Kilbride, was a lovely Yorkshireman who'd played in the band A.C. Temple before changing careers. We'd first met on the drunken day in Belgium with Pavement back in 1997. He definitely had his hands full with us both, though, especially with them. Their propensity to smash their equipment up every night led to all sorts of problems, not the least of which was paying for and locating more equipment for subsequent gigs. It'd be fair to say that Noel wasn't best amused by these antics and during one trip which the bands were taking by plane he decided to hire a car and make the journey by road instead. Sadly for Noel, he hit a kangaroo on the drive and came perilously close to being seriously hurt in the crash. So much for some respite.

Also on the tour were the phenomenal Australian band, The Dirty Three. I'd been a huge fan since hearing them at David Keenan's night at The 13th Note and seeing them every day was an absolute pleasure. They were transcendent live. Mick the drummer had the driest sense of humour and was always great to hang out with. Warren the violinist and frontman was hilarious too. They were a good few years older than us and seemed genuinely happy to see a (mostly) instrumental band doing so well. I'm sure when they started out people thought it was completely weird to have a band with no singer. There was great camaraderie on the tour with everyone hanging out and watching the other bands. Except Morrissey. I'm pretty sure he materialised for his gigs then disappeared in a puff of smoke. Andy Bell the guitar player from Ride was playing bass for Oasis and would come and watch us perform most days. He knew that we'd taken a lot of the blueprint of what Ride and bands of that era had done and was glad to see the tradition continuing. At the last Livid show, I told him about our final show in Australia. We were playing a birthday party for our label, Spunk, on a boat that was sailing round Sydney Harbour. Arab Strap were coming over from Scotland especially for the show too, and Andy said that he was going to try to come along for the boat trip. It promised to be quite a night.

The boat gig was to prove as strange as we all imagined it might be. For a start the boat was tiny. I don't know what I was thinking, probably some big yacht from a hip-hop video, but the reality couldn't have been more different. Andy held true to his promise to come and he had somehow convinced the rest of Oasis to come too. I'd never taken Liam Gallagher for a Mogwai fan, so perhaps he liked Arab Strap? Then again, perhaps not. Arab Strap played as a duo, just Aidan and Malcolm. By this point their experiment of signing to a major label had crashed and burnt and they were back on Chemikal Underground. They should probably have never left. I was starting to think that perhaps we shouldn't have either. Anyway, their latest album, *Monday at the Hug and Pint*, was one of their best and they were on phenomenal form. It was just the two of them for most of the gig, though Martin joined them for one song at the end.

About halfway through Arab Strap's set it became abundantly clear that some of the celebrity contingent on board were not quite as prepared for their night of entertainment as others. Liam Gallagher was not feeling Arab Strap one bit and got off the boat at its first stop. Noel, Andy and the others stayed for the whole trip and hung out with us at the end of the night. It'd been a long time since we had actually played a gig with Arab Strap and, with me now living in Edinburgh, I hadn't really hung out with them for a while. It was great to do it again, especially in these weird circumstances: we were literally on the other side of the world, playing our maudlin Scottish music as we sailed past the Sydney Opera House. A world away from home but still with friends, still making music.

The next year everything was centred around the release of *Happy Songs*, our fourth album, and we did a tour of smaller venues around the UK to promote the release. I definitely got the impression that fashion had changed and that this record was a bit of a harder sell than our first three. We weren't asked to do an *NME* interview at all, never mind another cover story. One person who still had our back though was John Peel. John had started doing live sessions with a small audience from the Maida Vale Studios in London and asked us to do one. The only issue was the date. It coincided with the UEFA Cup Final and Celtic were in it. Celtic hadn't been in a European final since before we were born and this was literally a once in a lifetime opportunity. I would dearly have loved to go and see Celtic in Seville but didn't want to let

John Peel down. Martin was not happy about missing the game either but understood what a huge champion of the band John Peel had been. We also weren't in a position to turn down opportunities to promote the record. Playing a full set on national radio was a great way of letting people hear the new songs.

The night itself was straight-up weird, playing to an audience of about fifty people who had applied for tickets. We had arranged to hold off playing until the game finished and we watched it on a TV in the lounge area next to the recording studio. The audience were there too. I'm sure a few liked football but they clearly weren't as invested as we were. The sight of the band they were waiting to watch, screaming at a TV (mostly in despair) must have been very odd. The initial timings were for the normal length of a game (ninety minutes) but of course it went into extra time. My nerves were absolutely shot. Porto got a third goal in extra time and from that second on spent every second flailing around on the ground, wasting time to minimise the chances of Celtic getting an equaliser. The game ended with Celtic losers despite putting on a heroic display. We were all gutted but we had a job to do, and there's no better way to get over disappointment than playing live music on the radio.

We had bought champagne to celebrate if Celtic won, the use of which immediately changed to commiseration. We played a set consisting mostly of new tracks from *Happy Songs* with just one old song, 'Helicon 1'. It was an emotional set after the experience of the final. I would dearly have loved to have been in Seville watching Celtic but I was sure we'd made the right decision. John Peel's influence was one of the reasons I'd picked a guitar up in the first place and his support was a huge factor in us being able to make a living from our music. Once the show finished, John quipped, 'It's been a sad night for football but a great night for music.' We were all having a glass of wine and chatting, and John said me that he was really surprised at how popular we'd become. He said he thought we would always be the kind of band he often played but that no one ever really 'got'. I took that as a huge compliment because it was clear from John's outlook on music that commercial success wasn't really the be-all and end-all. It certainly wasn't for us, either. It would turn out that that night would be the last time we saw John Peel, as he died suddenly on holiday in Peru the following year. After he died, Mary Anne Hobbs played a recording of him on Radio 1 asking her if there was any good Peruvian techno he should check out. She played it over one of our songs from that night. It was one of the most moving things I've ever heard and I wept when I heard it.

I really miss John Peel.

On the home front things were about to change considerably. Grainne had received an offer to work for All Tomorrow's Parties so we would be moving to London, which wasn't something I'd ever considered before, but this was a great opportunity for Grainne – and how bad could it be? Pretty fucking bad it would turn out.

I was really happy for Grainne. It was such a great opportunity for her to be working for one of the most exciting promoters who ran the best festival going. That said, I definitely had a few reservations. London was a great place to visit but I wasn't sure about living there. We were moving into a big place in Swiss Cottage, sharing a living and workspace with Barry from ATP. Barry was a good friend but I'm not sure he would have been at the front of the queue had I been making a list of ideal housemates. By this point me and Grainne had largely put our chemically induced partying days behind us but Barry most definitely had not and there was never a dull moment with him around. Swiss Cottage was a strange place, quite posh (Martin wearily observed that it didn't have a chip shop when I told him I was moving there), but if you scratched the surface there was definitely something dark about it. Not long after we moved in someone was beheaded just a few streets away, then one night when Grainne was in on her own, someone tried to get into the house with a spurious excuse about needing to call an ambulance. It definitely felt a bit weird. We hadn't been there for that long when I started to feel homesick. I would take the big walk to King's Cross station to buy a *Herald* newspaper to get the news from back home and would religiously watch the Scottish news on TV. I'd always loved going to gigs but in London it didn't quite feel the same. People seemed to be there more to be seen that to listen to the music. The living room of the flat was joined onto the office so it felt like there was never any peace. Grainne and Barry are two of the loudest people ever to be born, and that mixed with the frenzied world of gig promoting led to pretty much constant mayhem.

A few years earlier, through Grainne putting their gigs on, I'd become friends with the Texan band Explosions In The Sky and was excited to see them play at the Institute of Contemporary Arts (ICA). I was looking forward to seeing some friendly faces and hanging out with some pals. Barry, Grainne and I got there early for a proper flat night out and we bumped into Kevin Shields in the bar before the show. He was with a small woman with long brown hair, who I thought was his girlfriend as I recognised her. After chatting to Kevin for a bit, I asked her how she was doing and what she was up to. I was sure I'd met her before but she was looking at me with a slightly perplexed look. Oh well, I thought, people in London can be a bit odd. We arranged to meet Kevin after the show and headed in to watch the gig.

To say that people talking during gigs bothered me would be an understatement. I fucking despised it. It was probably born out of frustration at folk yacking away during our gigs (I'd recently kicked someone in the front row in Canada for doing so) and it drove me nuts. Explosions In The Sky, like us, had long quiet passages in their songs and I suspected that people might well use that as an excuse to blether. I was prepared for it but that didn't stop me getting annoyed when it happened. A woman next to me would not shut up during the gig so, already in a bit of a shitty mood, I asked her to stop talking. She completely ignored me and seemed to continue talking but at an even louder volume. By this point, incandescent with fury, I straight-up told her to fucking shut up. This didn't go down well. She looked at me dead in the eyes and poured her entire drink over my head and walked away. To be fair it was a pretty good full stop to the altercation, as there was nothing I could really do other than go to the toilets to dry myself and seethe. I already had a permanent low-level rage about being in London but this had taken it up a notch. After the gig I spoke to my friend Esteban, a lovely Mexican-Texan guy who tours with Explosions. He gave me a bunch of shirts to give to the rest of Mogwai, which I stuffed into the side pockets of my duffel coat. We also met back up with Kevin. From chatting to him it became abundantly clear that the girl he'd been with hadn't been his girlfriend but actually the film director Sofia Coppola, whom he was working with on the soundtrack for *Lost in Translation*. I felt extremely silly. No wonder she thought I was mad. I had recognised her from magazines. What a dumpling.

It seemed very early to call it a night so Kevin suggested a place we could head out to, one of the private members clubs that are all over London. Plebs had to finish their drinks at 11 p.m., but if you were 'someone' you could stay out as late as you wanted. Never ones to turn down a drinking opportunity, we all headed out. The place was down a bunch of dark stairs and felt like somewhere from a bygone age, all dark wood and brass. The clientele were super weird, city boys and people who looked like they worked in the theatre. It was soon after we all got our drinks that we spotted someone familiar at the end of the bar: Steve Diggle from the Buzzcocks! Both me and Kevin were immediately star-struck. He was a hero to both of us and we couldn't pass up the opportunity to go and say hi. Like two shy autograph hunting kids we sheepishly approached him. I doubt Steve had a clue who My Bloody Valentine or Mogwai were but he welcomed us completely. We were in our element chatting to him. He was totally smashed but had it together enough to regale us with amazing stories of his punk heyday and touring with Joy Division and Nirvana. Diggle was a bona fide legend and without doubt one of the reasons that me and Kevin loved the electric guitar so much. Not being as interested in talking to old punk dudes, Grainne ended up speaking to one of the city boys. He was clearly coked up and trying his luck. Grainne was a tough woman and more than capable of handling herself in situations like this. It happened all the time and telling hopeful men to get lost was absolutely in her repertoire. By this point I'd had quite a lot to drink and after the incident at the ICA was in enough of a bad mood to want to tell him to get lost myself. I went up to the slimy suited wanker and informed him, 'That's my wife. You need to fuck off.' He said it was fair enough to tell him it was my wife, but I shouldn't tell him to fuck off, to which I purposefully, deliberately and emphatically replied, 'Fuck. Off.' This did not go down well with the coked-up hedge fund wanker and he shaped up to punch me. Being from a small town in Canada, Grainne was clearly more used to this kind of drama and thought wisely to get the first hit in. Without blinking she punched him as hard as she could in the side of the head, managing to detach his ear lobe somewhat and causing quite a bit of blood to materialise. As the guy held his arm aloft to punch me, I took the opportunity to react first and instinctively took one of the T-shirts from my pockets and whacked him as hard as I could on the other side of his head.

Then all hell broke loose.

In a scene like something from a western it turned into an old-fashioned bar brawl, arms flying everywhere. Diggle saw what was happening and got in on the action straight away, punching city boys left and right with arm movements that suggested he was pretty adept at the front crawl. With bedlam ensuing Kevin got on a chair and pleaded for everyone to calm down. Barry was in the toilet for the whole debacle. Eventually the management from the bar stopped all the nonsense and we were asked to leave. For his part, Diggle immediately made peace with the dudes he'd been punching and stayed drinking with them, while me, Kevin, Barry and Grainne headed back to the flat. Kevin told us more about the Sofia Coppola movie he was scoring, which sounded really cool.

It was becoming clear to me already that London maybe wasn't the place for us: a great city but clearly not a good fit. It wouldn't be long before we headed back up the road to Scotland.

19.

Getting It Together in the Country

Our London experiment was over. Things weren't working out for us so we decided to head back to Scotland. Grainne had always fancied living in the countryside and we found a place not far from where I'd grown up in the picturesque village of Rosebank. It was a terraced three-bedroom house across the road from the hotel where John Peel had bought me dinner all those years before. Basically, we wanted to live somewhere as different from the chaos of London as possible. It wasn't a big house but had enough rooms for me to have my own studio. When we went to look at the house after we bought it, we heard a voice with a familiar bassy tone. It was Robert Gibb, aka Dr Robert, a friend of our accountant David who we both knew from going to gigs. Robert was a psychiatrist and lived in the converted church right next to us. It was a strange but welcome coincidence. Robert was a massive music enthusiast and had the best record collection and stereo of anyone I'd ever met. He'd collected psychedelic and krautrock records all his life and had such a big collection that they were often strewn all over his massive living room. We would spend weekends hanging out and listening to weird and wonderful music until the small hours, drinking and chatting about everything. Robert was a great neighbour and a huge character. His dry wit and enthusiasm for music was infectious. I was introduced to a lot of mind-expanding music by Robert.

Not long after moving into the house we decided to get a dog. We went to the local shelter to check them out and instantly fell in love with a little black staffy whose behaviour was so wild that we thought if we didn't adopt her then no one else would. She was a total nutter but also completely adorable. We named her Princess, after Princess Leia from *Star Wars*. After we'd had her for a few weeks we noticed that no matter how little we fed her she kept getting fatter. She started to look like some kind of mutant kangaroo. Thinking there was something wrong with her we took her to the vets. The vet told us straight away that she was not fat but in fact pregnant. Our house was still a complete riot with piles of boxes everywhere. Having puppies was not on the agenda, but puppies it was. I was on tour when they arrived but it all happened in dramatic fashion during a lightning storm. Grainne was helped with the birth by our pal Valerie who lived nearby. There were five puppies and I fell in love with a little brown and black one that we decided to keep. We named him Rambo, which our friends the Japanese band Afrirampo informed us means 'violence' in Japanese. Despite his name, he was a far gentler soul than his maniac mother. The rest of the pups were adopted by friends once they got a bit bigger. One went to my friend Hubby, and he named him Dee Bone after the singer in the Minutemen. Whenever I was home I'd walk the dogs all over the Clyde Valley countryside. I loved them so much. I love all dogs but those two were very special indeed.

On the music front we were still out promoting our *Happy Songs* album and had a really busy schedule. Despite Grainne leaving ATP (she was by this point putting concerts on under her own name as Synergy Concerts), we remained on great terms with Barry Hogan and he invited us to play at another ATP festival that spring of 2004. We curated a day and had people playing like Sonic Boom, Papa M and Japanese hardcore band Envy, whose music we were releasing on our rejuvenated Rock Action label. We'd taken the decision to revive the label and were putting out records by bands like Errors and Part Chimp. This ATP was way less chaotic than the first one but loads of fun nonetheless. It was great to see the festival thriving and Barry doing so well. Sadly that wasn't to last forever but at the time it was wonderful.

We were also invited to play in the Californian desert at Coachella. We'd heard great things about the festival but the reality wasn't quite as we had imagined. We had a nightmare on stage and our equipment was going haywire. It meant that we had to move the set away from a lot of the newer computer-based songs and revert to songs featuring just guitars, which wasn't ideal. We were also on at the same time as Madonna who was playing at one of the dance tents. Clashing with Madonna had certainly never been a problem I'd envisaged when we started. There was something distinctly weird about the festival itself. People backstage seemed a lot more photogenic and glamorous than usual at a festival. So much so that I asked someone what was going on, and it was explained to me that you could buy a VIP ticket which allowed you to basically hang out with the bands. This was the start of what would become Instagram culture and the whole thing seemed really grotesque to me. Hanging out backstage isn't that much fun to start with, so to see it sold as some kind of commodity seemed incredibly vulgar.

Since Colin had left a few years earlier we'd muddled on without a manager. I'd done a lot of the work but it hadn't been quite as I'd imagined. I was fine making decisions but some aspects of managing the band were either of little or no interest to me, or were simply things I didn't know enough about. A lot of it was getting palmed off to either our lawyer or our accountant and that didn't seem the most sensible way of doing things. It certainly wasn't cost effective. It was then that we were approached by someone offering to manage the band and it seemed too good an offer to turn down.

It was Alan McGee.

I knew Alan a little bit from being around bands that had been on Creation Records, such as Super Furry Animals and Primal Scream. Alan was a larger-than-life character who had been responsible for releasing records that had been pivotal for me, and he had previously managed The Jesus and Mary Chain, one of my favourite bands of all time. Alan wanted to work with us because he loved our music. He also thought we should be doing better than we were. I absolutely agreed with him and decided to take him on. Alan would come up to Glasgow to spend time with us and was always fabulously entertaining company. He'd lived a colourful life in music and always had brilliant stories. Being a Scot in exile he always liked hanging out with other Scots. As a Rangers supporter he loved to wind up Celtic-supporting musicians. That applied to almost everyone because hardly anyone in the arts supports Rangers. Or will admit to it anyway.

One of the first gigs we were offered after Alan became our manager was one that our teenage selves would have killed for: opening for Pixies in Paris. Pixies were one of my favourite bands and one of the few bands that I hadn't managed to see the first time around. Adele had seen them at the Barrowlands and I was eternally jealous of her about that. As I've mentioned, Paris was one of our favourite cities so playing there with Pixies was doubly exciting.

We got the word through a few days before the gig that, as Kim Deal had stopped drinking, the entire backstage was to be alcohol free. Martin was the only member of the band who regularly played gigs sober. To the rest of us, playing a gig straight was absolute anathema. We totally respected what Pixies were doing to help out their struggling bass player but we just couldn't cope with the concept of playing to so many people straight. We had to come up with some kind of plan to get round it.

Alan came to Paris for the show. He had gone through his own substance abuse issues but at this point was still drinking. He would quite often have Long Island Iced Teas, the toxic drink that had felled me so dramatically back in Chicago on our first US tour. Alan arranged to meet us in a restaurant a stone's throw from the enormo-dome that we were to play with Pixies. After the briefest of soundchecks we headed over to meet Alan. He was as fun and gregarious as always, generously buying rounds of drinks on the management credit card (i.e. we were paying for them). By the time we were due to go back to the venue we were fairly inebriated, but that didn't solve the problem of what to do when we actually got to the gig itself. As a solution to this problem we located a small corner shop and bought as much booze as we could possibly conceal and stuffed it into every pocket available. Jeans, jackets, hoodies were all crammed with contraband swally and snuck into the venue. Once we got in, we decanted it all into cups and fizzy drinks bottles. It really was the most tramp-like manoeuvre known to man. I can barely remember our gig at all. I also can't remember watching Pixies, a band I'd literally waited most of my life to see. All because someone said we couldn't do something. An absolute shambles of a situation.

That summer on our normal run of festivals we played two twin festivals in Germany, Hurricane and Southside. On the bill was Alex Kapranos's new band Franz Ferdinand. They had made it big with their debut album and were literally everywhere at this point. It was great to catch up with old Glasgow pals and even better to see them doing so well. Alex and Paul Thompson on drums had been in great bands since before we started, but had never done too much outside of Glasgow, so it was tremendous to see them having such an impact all over the world. I remember our show at Hurricane mostly for the clapping. Germans just love clapping along to music. It's great to see enthusiasm like that, though it can prove a bit tricky with us as quite often the music changes tempo and the clapping can cause a fair bit of confusion. After we played, me and Barry headed off to watch David Bowie. With our passes we could watch him play from the photo pit. Bowie was huge for us. That night Bowie played so many classic songs like 'Station To Station', 'China Girl' and 'Ashes To Ashes'. For his encore he played the incredible trilogy of 'Life On Mars', 'Suffragette City' and 'Ziggy Stardust'. Me and Barry felt so honoured that night and watching him close-up was incredible. This bit of good fortune was only amplified when he cancelled the tour a few days later. It would come to pass in later years that it was the last gig he ever played. It had been such an honour to have seen it.

That summer Robert Smith got back in touch again and asked us if we would join The Cure on their Curiousa tour of America. Also on the bill were Interpol (our old friend Daniel from Jetset's band) as well as other bands like The Rapture, Muse, Melisa Auf der Maur and The Cooper Temple Clause.

Our first gig in America before The Cure tour started was in Jacksonville, Florida. It was a weird show in a town that we'd never been to before and haven't been to since. For the first Cure gig in West Palm Beach, Alanna, a native Floridian came down with her friend, the actress Chloë Sevigny. Before the show Alanna took us to the beach. Me, Barry and Chloë jumped in the sea before heading to the venue for the show. Later that afternoon we played to a smattering of Floridian goths. Most days we would have a half-hour set, meaning that at most we would play three songs. Quite often we would just play the one – 'My Father, My King'. Our set didn't feel like the most important part of the day though. For me that was watching The Cure. Robert knew that quite a few of the band members were big Cure fans and asked us what songs we'd like them to play, graciously indulging us by playing some of them. The gigs were quite often in big natural amphitheatres, and after we played I'd go to the top of the hill to watch the sun go down as Interpol and then The Cure played. After the show one night, Robert Smith told Chloë that the film *Boys Don't Cry* had made him cry. There was great camaraderie among the bands and there would be a party every night after

The Cure played. The Cure had made loads of fans over the years and they would invite them to come to the parties. It felt like a real family. One night on our tour bus, Robert Smith was onboard hanging out with us drinking. He said to me that he thought we should be bigger than we were and insisted that we write a pop song, something simple with a chorus. It took me a long time to actually listen to this, but it was definitely sound advice.

Dominic had taken up a spell of sobriety but the rest of us were wrecked the entire time. John got ill halfway through the tour and ended up staying in Fredonia with Dave Fridmann while David Jack, my best man and guitar tech, ably deputised.

The tour was messy as hell but I was in my element. Being on such a big tour really helped the record as well. America is too vast for fashions to take hold as rapidly as in the UK and people only just seemed to be becoming aware of us. I think it also re-energised The Cure. They'd been through a weird spell where they weren't as popular as they were in the eighties and early nineties, but that seemed to be changing. The internet has had a huge part to play in changing people's perception of music. The entire concept of 'cool' or 'uncool' now seems moribund. People just listen to whatever they want. The tribalism of the era that I'd grown up in seems to have evaporated. People back then were completely defined by what music they liked. It dictated everything about their lives. That just seems quaint now. The internet has decimated the music industry, but as far as music itself, it's probably saved it for a lot of people who in bygone decades would have been cast aside to make space for something newer and shinier.

Once home we were making plans about what to do next. We'd been talking to Tony for ages about getting a studio together and Tony had made plans to actually make it happen. Renting studios didn't make much sense when we could just set up our own place and Tony found us a building to rent and use as a studio in the West End. The building looked like something from a Disney film, quite twee. I jokingly referred to it as the Castle of Doom and that became its name.

We didn't have to wait too long for our next recording project. A friend of mine, the artist Douglas Gordon, was looking for someone to score a film he'd made and asked if we fancied it. Douglas had won the Turner Prize for *24 Hour Psycho*, his slowed-down version of the Hitchcock classic. The film that he wanted us to score was about the French footballer Zinedine Zidane. They'd filmed him with tons of cameras throughout an entire game, with the cinematographer who'd worked on David Fincher's *Seven*. He'd used a song by us, the Surgeon remix of 'Mogwai Fear Satan', to accompany the final scene where Zidane was sent off and it worked incredibly well. The half-time part of the film showed things that had happened that day all over the world. From bombings in Iraq to a *Star Wars* ship selling on eBay. Douglas was making the film with another artist, a Frenchman called Philippe Peron. Douglas is quite an extravagant, eccentric Glaswegian and was very respectful of artistic integrity. He pretty much let us do whatever we wanted. We would come to realise that this attitude is very seldom the case in the film industry. The film, rather than glamorise Zidane, had quite a sombre feel to it, portraying him as a man at work rather than any kind of superstar. It was an unusual but completely engaging film. I was so proud of the music we made for it.

I'd imagined the film would be quite an underground affair but I was totally wrong. It ended up being quite a big deal, helped in no small amount by the fact that the next summer, around the release of the film, Zidane got himself sent off in the World Cup final for headbutting Materazzi. You literally can't buy that kind of coverage.

Just after finishing *Zidane* we got ourselves another film score project to work on. Clint Mansell, the singer from Pop Will Eat Itself, had reinvented himself as a composer for film, making brilliant soundtracks for Darren Aronofsky's *Pi* and *Requiem for a Dream*. I was particularly fond of *Requiem for a Dream* because it is based on a novel by my favourite author, Hubert Selby Jr. Clint's innovative and dramatic scores were what really made the film. I read an interview where Clint mentioned that he wanted his new score for a film called *The Fountain* to sound like Mogwai. On reading this I immediately got in touch with him and offered for us to play on it. Clint, now living in LA, was in London and asked me to meet up with him to chat about it. I'd never met Clint before but we got on well immediately. He said he'd love for us to play on the soundtrack.

A few months later, me and Dominic were invited to watch the film in a hotel room in London. It was really early in the morning and the level of secrecy was unbelievable. We had to sign all kinds of forms before we saw it. The whole scene in the London hotel room at dawn felt shady and weirdly funny. The film itself was a trip. A psychedelic observation on grief and eternal life. We heard some of Clint's themes for it and they were immense. For the recording, Clint and a small army of assistants, musical supervisors and engineers decamped to Glasgow to record us at our studio. The Kronos Quartet were also playing on the soundtrack but did theirs separately at Skywalker Sound in California. As a lifelong *Star Wars* fan, I was pretty jealous of that. It was fascinating to see how things worked in a big movie and it would prove really helpful for us in the years ahead. With our parts done I was excited to hear what The Kronos Quartet would add and to see the finished film. While we were playing our parts, Darren Aronofsky would watch us via Skype on a laptop. The whole thing was very strange but also new and exciting.

With the two soundtracks done we dedicated ourselves to recording a new album, deciding to work with Tony again in our own studio. Since we were recording in our own place, time wasn't an issue. It made the recording process pretty much endless, which brought up a different set of issues, the main one being knowing when something was finished. With no one saying that it had to be finished by a certain date, we ended up spending an awful lot of time on songs and it became pretty stressful. What we ended up with was probably our most polished record. We'd had a lot of hassles translating some of the songs from our most recent records live, and we kept that in mind with these songs because we wanted a record that we could play on tour. We called it *Mr Beast* after a sign we saw in an airport for some unfortunately named chap.

When the record was about to be released, Alan said in an interview that the record was better than *Loveless* by My Bloody Valentine. Alan and Kevin had had issues with each other going all the way back to the release of *Loveless*, and I'm pretty sure Alan was just trying to annoy Kevin as much as I'm sure he was fond of our record. I'm not certain it was that helpful from our end. It's quite a lofty claim after all.

To launch the record, Mick had the idea for us to do a run of gigs at the ICA. Hopefully my return to the venue would be better than my last time there, where I got a drink thrown over me and ended up in bar brawl. We decided that for each of the five nights a different band member would get to choose the opening band and setlist. Normally I'd get lumped with writing it, so it was nice to have a few nights off. The run of shows was a blast and a great way to launch the record. One of the highlights of the week was meeting Martin O'Neill, the ex-Celtic manager who is also a huge music fan. I knew him through his daughter Alanna who went out with a pal of mine. He came backstage and it was brilliant to hang out with him. He entertained us all with stories about Celtic and gigs he'd been to over the years. He's a funny guy.

That year we did a ton of touring, playing 122 shows. One highlight was an ambitious show we played in London at the prestigious Royal Albert Hall. It was by some way the biggest venue we'd ever played and somewhere I'd never even envisaged playing. Mick had suggested it and pretty much everything he came up with had worked out, so we all went along with it. I was quite worried that it wouldn't sell out but amazingly it did. The occasion wasn't lost on our families, all of whom came down. All except mine that is. My folks decided to skip the trip to London when they found out that we were playing in Glasgow the next night.

Wanting to make the gig a bit more special than our usual shows we hatched a plan with our lighting guy, Nick, to make a massive Mogwai Young Team sign out of scaffolding. It's probably the most Spinal Tap thing we've ever done, other than our obsession with volume. All we were missing was the dancing midgets. The venue was as ornate and impressively grand as I'd imagined. We opened the gig with 'Christmas Steps', all of us walking onto the stage one at a time to start the song. It was Barry's dad's birthday and Barry got to wish him a happy birthday and give him a wave from the stage to the fancy box his dad was sitting in at the back of the hall. The gig felt like more of an occasion than a concert and we were all delighted with how it went.

After the show the band all went out to see their families. Because it was such a big deal, lots of people had given us congratulatory bottles of champagne. I suppose playing the Royal Albert Hall is the indie band equivalent of getting married. I was so relieved and happy that it had gone well that I slightly over celebrated with the champagne and ended up completely mortal. I went out to see our friends after the show and found a similarly tipsy Robert Smith. Robert had loved the show. Indeed, he loved it so much that soon afterwards he hired our soundman Michael to mix The Cure. It had been an amazing night. Once the gear was packed down we jumped on the bus because we were playing the Barrowlands the next day. Another incentive to get back to Glasgow was to see the Celtic vs Rangers game that we were going to attend before soundcheck, which had an early kick-off.

I'd got so drunk at the show that I ended up puking on the bus and subsequently felt like death the next morning. We were excited to see the game, though, and rolled out of the bus just in time to make it, if we ran. I remember crawling out of the bus and running up the Gallowgate towards Celtic Park, feeling like my heart was going to burst out of my chest. Old Firm games are tense affairs at the best of times, and with the hangover from hell and the adrenaline still in my system from the Albert Hall gig, I felt like I was levitating with anxiety. Thankfully Celtic won 2–0.

Back at the Barrowlands we all amused ourselves by referring to the Royal Albert Hall gig as the warm-up. The gig that night was fantastic. It always was at the Barrowlands. I was glad to see my family. Clearly an aversion to the capital was a genetic trait.

With the epic year of touring behind us, I got a call from Alan McGee. He'd had a pretty epic fall out with the guy he ran the management company with and was folding the company. He was going to keep on managing bands on his own but said to me that we should just manage ourselves. 'I don't need the money and you guys make all the decisions anyway.' It was one of the straightest conversations I've ever had in the music industry. Having Alan manage us had been a blast. He's a smart guy whose influence on independent music was huge. I'd been happy to have him around for a while but it had come to a natural end.

20.

Low

I've been lucky enough to find myself in some weird and wonderful places over the years. Music has been kind to me, opening doors and taking me to places that I would have only seen
in films. At the start of 2008 I found myself somewhere that I
never imagined possible: in an Austin recording studio with Roky
Erickson of The 13th Floor Elevators.

Roky's music had been a constant in my life. Roky was a sur-
vivor and a total legend of the countercultural underground. His
music has soundtracked my life ever since I became a true fan.
Thinking of different collaborators for our new record, I wanted
to see if we could record a track with him. By this point Roky was
old in years but had come in from the cold and started making
music again and was sounding great. I contacted him through
his brother, Summer, and told him that we'd love to get Roky
on a song. Summer was a great guy and he sent Roky our music
to listen to. Roky wanted to sing but wasn't keen on writing the
lyrics, which left the task up to me. It felt daunting writing for a
bona fide music legend, but I was so excited about the prospect of
Roky singing on a Mogwai song that I got on with it straight away.
I wanted to write in Roky's style, with the horror references, but
also something that made sense from his perspective. Something
really personal. I called the song 'Devil Rides' after the seventies
horror film *The Devil Rides Out*. The lyrics were more heartfelt
than spooky schlock though, and I was proud of it. We recorded
the song at the Castle of Doom with Tony and sent it over to Roky

for him to track the vocal in Austin. I did a rough vocal to give him an idea of how the song went so he could listen before tracking his vocal. When we got the track back, Roky hadn't quite understood what I'd meant and was clearly struggling to get the vocal pattern. Thankfully there was a solution at hand because I was going to Austin with Grainne for the South by Southwest festival the following month.

We had been to South by Southwest a few times before and the trips were a riot. The festival is basically a ton of gigs around the town of Austin, with people flying in from across the world to see all the new bands perform. When we started going, most of the bands were new and emerging acts, but it had mutated into a pretty huge media affair with loads of big bands using it to launch their latest projects. In the past we'd stayed at one of the many big hotels that got booked out with music industry types for the festival, but this time we crashed with a friend of ours, Julianna, who we'd got to know from visiting Austin. Roky held his own mini event as part of SXSW, the 'Roky Erickson Psychedelic Ice Cream Social', where he would perform alongside some other like-minded folks. Since I was in town and going into the studio with Roky, I agreed to play a few songs at it on my own.

Grainne had just started working with a new Scottish band that she was a huge champion of called The Twilight Sad. They were one of the first bands we went to see. They'd played for Grainne in Glasgow, opening for David Pajo, and she said I had to see them play. She wasn't wrong. They were mesmerising. James the singer got completely lost in the music, performing like he was exorcising demons, while Andy the guitar player, who looked about twelve years old, summoned a wild racket with his Jazzmaster guitar and arsenal of pedals. It would be the first of hundreds of times I'd see them. They were a truly special band. There was another familiar face in Austin too, Alan McGee. Alan was over with Dirty Pretty Things, who he was still managing, and he was as entertaining and funny as ever.

The main event was the recording with Roky though. I was so excited about it. Any time I'd mention it to anyone, their eyes would widen. It was so cool that it was scarcely believable. The studio we went into was one that had been used for loads of great records by brilliant Texan bands like Butthole Surfers, Bedhead, and my friends . . . And You Will Know Us by the Trail of Dead. I met Roky and found him to be the sweetest guy, with a great sense of wonder about him. Before we recorded the vocal, Roky wanted to take me to an ice cream parlour that had named a milkshake after him. Grainne came too and we all went and got our Roky milkshakes. He was so proud and happy that they'd done it. When we got into the studio, it didn't take long at all. The way I write lyrics is a bit unusual, with the vocal usually coming in about halfway through a bar as opposed to the start. When I sang it for Roky he got it straight away.

If my teenage self had known while getting lost in the music of The 13th Floor Elevators that a few decades later I'd be in a studio with Roky Erickson, singing a song that I'd written for him, I would probably have exploded.

Back from Austin we were invited to play in London in the grounds of Somerset House. It was a grand setting for a gig set in the heart of the UK government. The only issue we had was that there was a huge Union Jack flag flying above the stage. As proud Scots we couldn't bear to play under the flag of the British Empire so we requested that they remove it. Incredibly, they did. I can't see that happening now. We'd probably end up in jail for such an act of insubordination.

In Paris we played at a festival called Rock en Seine. Also on the bill was MIA, whom I hadn't seen since the Elastica tour. It was great to catch up. We talked about how nuts that trip had been and how our lives had changed in between. It felt like we were totally different people at this point, which I suppose we were.

We started getting on with plans to make a new record, re-
ceiving a hand with management from a pal of ours that we'd
met through All Tomorrow's Parties, a tour manager called
Shaun Kendrick. Shaun had tour-managed us a few times, quite
memorably trying to stop Martin who, when drunk, thought it
would be a good idea to try and climb out of the bus sunroof
while on the motorway. We decided to record in Hamilton back
at Chemikal Underground's studio, Chem 19, with Andy Miller,
with whom we had recorded our 'New Paths To Helicon' single
years back. To mix the album, Shaun suggested Gareth Jones.
Gareth had been an engineer since the eighties and had worked
on loads of amazing albums, most notably with Depeche Mode,
a band we all adored.

That summer we met someone who we'd end up working a
lot with over the next few years, an eccentric French filmmaker
called Vincent Moon. Shaun suggested he come with us to Italy
to film us while we played a rural festival near Florence. Italy is
one of my favourite countries on the planet, mostly because it's
so unpredictable. The trip was eventful largely because we were
assigned drivers who appeared to have a death wish of some sort.
Their driving was so demented that we genuinely thought we
might die. The fact that they were getting stoned while driving
at over 100 miles an hour didn't help our nerves at all. Vincent
captured it all for posterity. He was profoundly entertaining. A
genuine one-off. He lived a nomadic lifestyle, never really living
anywhere, making films about musicians and having fun.

Before we went in to record, we received an offer that I profoundly regret turning down. Lou Reed was organising a festival
in Sydney, Australia, and had asked if we would play at it. Not
only did he want us to play but he wanted to do a noise jam
together too. We were just focused on making our record and
thought it would have disrupted our plans so declined the offer.
When I told my neighbour Robert about it, he thought I'd lost my
mind. As a psychiatrist he would know all about that of course.

It's not the kind of offer that comes every day and Robert knew how important Lou Reed was to me. The only way I can rationalise it now is that we've never been the kind of band to chase after celebrity connection, preferring to be known on our own terms. In this instance, though, I think we called it completely wrong. Lou Reed was literally why I was playing electric guitar every day. Hearing 'Heroin' and 'I Heard Her Call My Name' had genuinely changed me. Lou Reed had shown me how powerful music could be and shown me what being a singular artist meant. The idea that we would not go and play with him when asked just melts my fucking brain. I've no idea what I was thinking.

Around this time, I received a copy of a novel called *Kill Your Friends*. John Niven had indeed done 'more of that kind of thing' and this book was his blowtorch account of his time in the music business. I blinked a few times myself when the narrator, Steven Stelfox, says that any 'Indie Spastic' will love you for telling them your favourite album is *Marquee Moon* . . . which is what John had told me.

In the run-up to the recording we'd been asked to do our first ever full film soundtrack; *Zidane* had been amazing but was more of a documentary than a movie. David Holmes, the DJ and film scorer, had recommended we work with his film agent, and he'd taken us on and got us the job. It was a South American film made by a first-time director. There were issues right from the start, mostly language-based but also to do with the filmmaker's lack of understanding of the music-making process. He'd used temporary music for the film, which he sent to us to illustrate what kind of tone he was looking for. That was fine and totally normal. The issue came when we sent him the demos of pieces we'd written for the film. The recordings were raw and hadn't been mixed. If the director likes the music, then it gets mixed at the final stage. The problem arose as the director had no idea about this process and didn't understand why the demos didn't sound as good as the finished pieces of music that he had in the temporary score. He didn't know what mixing meant and the language barrier made it worse. We were working all hours of the day and getting these pretty rude messages constantly. We were still really green in the film world and hadn't at that point realised that as film scorers you really need to leave your ego at the door. Getting rude messages from film people is something that you just have to get used to. To say that we didn't take it well would be a massive understatement. We got a message suggesting that what we had done was nowhere near good enough and we responded rather vigorously. What we should have done was leave it and let it get sorted out by the people working for us. That was not, however, what happened. We went mental and sent some pretty acerbic replies, burning all bridges in the process. The annoying thing was that the music we'd written was really good. We were left with a ruined relationship with the film score agent that we'd been lucky to procure and out of pocket because we were planning to pay for the studio with fees we were now not going to receive and a bunch of music that we now had no use for.

We did find a solution to the last problem though. We repurposed a lot of the music for the album.

We've never been too much into nostalgia as a band. I always think it's better to look forward than back, but that summer we received an offer to indulge in nostalgia that was too tempting to turn down. We were offered more money than we'd ever been paid to play *Mogwai Young Team* from start to finish at a festival in Spain, Summercase. Barry Hogan had been doing his own shows where bands played the whole of a record called Don't Look Back, which we'd always resisted. Barry was none too pleased when he heard we were doing the shows in Barcelona and Madrid but understood when I told him the fee. Some things, however, are genuinely too good to be true. When we were at the airport and about to get on the plane to Spain, Mick called our tour manager, Simon, and said to hold off getting on the plane because the deposit for the shows hadn't been paid. Hearing that we were on the verge of not coming at all, the promoter paid the 50 per cent deposit and we got on the plane. Playing an old album from start to finish was a weird experience. For a start the album hadn't been designed to be played live and loads of the record was deathly quiet, rendering it pretty useless when performed outdoors. What didn't help matters at all was that the Sex Pistols were playing at the same time as us and drowned out the quiet parts. We were also upset about missing the Sex Pistols, which only rubbed salt in the wounds. After the show in Barcelona we were hanging out with some other bands we knew backstage and we saw John Lydon. He was pretty drunk, getting lairy, being pretty rude to everyone. I suppose I just thought of it as part of his shtick. His entourage were big hooligan thug-type guys and they kept making racist comments to our friend Kele from Bloc Party. Kele later told me that after I'd left they beat him up in what was clearly a racial attack. I've been put off Lydon's music ever since that night and he's since turned into a Trump-supporting, gammon nightmare. You ever get the feeling you've been cheated? John Lydon had been a huge inspiration to me, epitomising anti-establishment values. It was so sad to see him become everything that he used to be against.

As far as the gig went, the other half of the fee never arrived and the promoter fled the country. He was last seen in Brazil.

With the festivals out of the way we got on with the job of making our next album in Hamilton at Chem 19 studios with Andy Miller. Having repurposed a lot of the music from our aborted first attempt at scoring a movie, I felt we were in pretty good shape to record. A lot of the songs had a really spacey soundtrack feel to them. We hadn't booked a massive amount of time and planned on recording as much of it live as possible. At this point Barry was living out in the Clyde Valley not far away from me and Grainne. We would have a great laugh in the car taking turns at driving each other in. We noticed a housing estate in Blantyre, not the most salubrious part of Scotland, called Kings Meadow and became obsessed with singing medieval songs to each other about it. It's hard to explain how absurd it was but it entertained us for a good month or so. The nonsense that Barry and I would come out with was never-ending on those car journeys. That's where song titles like 'The Sun Smells Too Loud' and 'The Precipice' came from. Barry had had a dream about looking over a precipice underneath the sea which really stuck with him. The title of the album, *The Hawk is Howling*, came from an interview we heard with the keyboard player from The Doors, Ray Manzarek, who went off on one describing the early days of the band. We also channelled The Doors for the song 'I'm Jim Morrison I'm Dead', which was something Dominic said randomly, probably while drunk. I don't know what it is about The Doors but we've always found them endlessly amusing. I think their music is pretty good but there's something about the preening and posturing that makes them unbelievably funny. They are The Velvet Underground for Neds.

We had a big American tour booked that autumn, with the album coming out three quarters of the way through, on 27 September. The tour was based around an appearance at the All Tomorrow's Parties curated by My Bloody Valentine. It was a real honour to be asked to play by one of our favourite bands. ATP had spread out all over the world by now, with events in Australia and Japan as well as the States. We were due to play a few days before the album came out. Our old friend Keith Cameron was coming over for the festival to interview us for a feature in *Mojo* magazine. We were all looking forward to it. The line-up was immense, with bands that we all adored such as MBV (obviously), Low and Dinosaur Jr.

Touring with us were a band that we'd become very good friends with, Fuck Buttons, who were two guys called Ben and Andy. A noisy duo who made an incredible and, at times, beautiful racket. On tour, John, who had recorded their first album, did their live sound and made sure that every night they challenged us in the noise stakes. They were fun to tour with and always great to watch. Every time I would see them at a restaurant near the venue, I would tell the waiters that it was Andy's birthday, which would inevitably lead to them bringing him a cake and singing to him. It was a childish prank but one that I never tired of.

After a run of three great shows in Washington DC, New York and Philadelphia we arrived at ATP in good spirits. The venue where the festival was held was an old holiday camp. Known as the Borscht Belt, in years gone by it had been where wealthy American-Jewish families would go on holiday every summer to be entertained by the crooners and comedians of the day.

The ballroom where we were scheduled was incredible. It had the grandeur of an old theatre with the shape of a modern rock venue. We missed the first day of the festival but arrived in time to spend the Saturday there. Fuck Buttons played a blinding set on the main stage and were followed by amazing shows from Steve Albini's Shellac and the incredible two-piece Lightning Bolt, who played on the floor of the venue in a sea of arms and legs. Also playing that day were Low. The week previously, Alan the singer had had a bit of a freak-out at End of the Road Festival and thrown his guitar into the crowd. He was clearly having a hard time and there was talk of them not playing at all. They did play though, and it was one of the best performances I've ever seen from them. Pure raw emotion from a band that clearly live every note and word. When they played 'Murderer', one of their best songs, I was completely overcome by emotion. It was probably a portent of what was to come.

The festival was great apart from one thing, the accommodation. The rooms were like something from a horror film. I'm not a prissy type and will usually sleep anywhere but this was way too much. The rooms were filthy and mouldy, too minging for me to handle, so I slept on the tour bus. I get pretty used to sleeping on a tour bus and quite often find it hard to readjust when tours end and I have to sleep in a stationary bed.

The line-up for the stage we were playing was insane. First on was Robin Guthrie from Cocteau Twins, followed by EPMD, Mercury Rev and Yo La Tengo, then we played and the stage was closed by Dinosaur Jr. and My Bloody Valentine. Doing our sound was a quiet shaven-headed English chap called Stephen. Stephen had played in bands including Mute Drivers, who I'd seen on *Snub TV* in my early teens. A few years later before a tour, Simon told us that Stephen was now called Julia and was transitioning to become a woman. We were surprised but completely accepting and tried to be as supportive as we could as she navigated touring the world as a trans woman. Sadly, Julia died of cancer quite suddenly a few years later. Touring with Julia gave me real insight into the struggles that trans people have to endure; I could see that she faced adversity because of it every day.

That night, Julia was mixing us extremely loud. I've had a few moments while playing music where I've felt like I should pinch myself to see if it was really happening, but I think that playing before Dinosaur Jr. and My Bloody Valentine was a big one. Their music had had such a profound effect on me, not only as a person but also in terms of informing the music we'd made as a band. It was going to be a special night.

During the day we did our interview with Keith and the obligatory photos with a great photographer called Piper. She couldn't remember our names so just called me PE as I was wearing a Public Enemy shirt. The interview with Keith was great; it felt so good to be on the verge of releasing our sixth record and getting to talk about everything that was happening with someone who'd been there supporting us from the start. It felt like everything was right with the world. Martin hadn't been feeling great throughout the tour but wasn't a complainer so none of us had any suspicions that it would be anything too serious. He'd had heart problems since he was a kid and had to have his pacemaker changed every few years, so he was used to his body giving him all kinds of shit. He mentioned that he wasn't feeling too well but none of us paid it that much mind.

When we eventually got onstage I was determined for the show to be a success. Playing before what I consider to be two of the best bands of all time dictated that we had to be good. Not to be would have been all kinds of terrible. Thankfully it all worked out. We ended with 'Batcat', the fairly thunderous track from our new record, and we played 'Mogwai Fear Satan' in the middle of the set. We weren't fucking around.

After the show, feeling exhilarated and relieved we all went back to our rooms (or in my case the bus) to get ready to enjoy the rest of the night. I'd met some pals and was aimlessly wandering around waiting for Dinosaur Jr. to start when I saw a load of people I knew, including Shaun Kendrick and Barry Hogan, running down the corridor. I asked what was going on and was told that Martin's pacemaker had come out of his chest while he was having a shower and they were going to call an ambulance. I know Martin well so was sure that it must be serious for him to want an ambulance. He's the hardest person I know and not someone to want any kind of fuss. I immediately lost it. I thought I was going to lose one of my best friends. Not only that but he'd mentioned to me that he was feeling shit and I hadn't encouraged him to see a doctor or do anything about it. I was wracked with guilt and full of concern for Martin. I was a mess. I ran towards Martin's room but by the time I got there the paramedics had arrived and he was on his way to hospital, accompanied by Simon. There was nothing we could do except wait for news. And drink. It's probably a national failing of sorts that Scottish people use alcohol as a sticking plaster for emotions, but I was as guilty as anyone of doing it that night. I drank and drank. I stood with Michael Brennan at the sound desk watching My Bloody Valentine with Alan from Low. I kept forgetting that Alan was teetotal and kept trying to get him to drink too. I was a mess of emotions, attempting to hold them down with wine. Even the bone-crushing volume of the My Bloody Valentine show couldn't numb me. I was fully prepared to hear that my friend and bandmate hadn't survived. I was thinking about what to tell his folks. It was the worst I've ever felt. What should have been one of our best ever nights, playing with some of our favourite bands, surrounded by loads of friends the night before our album came out, had turned into an absolute nightmare. Martin was more than a bandmate though, he was one of my closest friends and the thought of what he was going through, never mind the possibility that he wouldn't make it, was too much to bear.

Thankfully when the news came it was good. Martin had been seen by a doctor and was comfortable. The doctor had a look at his chest and advised him to go back and see his doctor in Scotland. The price of this advice? THIRTY THOUSAND DOLLARS. It blows my mind that a country as rich as America sees healthcare as a privilege and not a right.

Martin was allowed out the next day, but it was clear that the tour was over. We said bye to Ben and Andy. We all flew home and cancelled the rest of the American tour. The day that Martin got out of hospital to fly home was the day our album came out.

Incredibly, Martin was back playing drums just a few weeks later. What had caused his body to reject his pacemaker was historical though, with loads of wires and detritus stuck in his chest from various procedures over the years. Sadly for Martin, this wouldn't be the end of it. He would be struggling with these issues for the next twelve years.

21.

'Hardcore Will Never Die, but You Will'

With Martin back behind the kit way sooner than any of us expected, we continued to tour.

The five-album deal we had signed with PIAS at the start of the century was about to end and we had a decision to make about what to do next. PIAS themselves were keen on us staying but we had a solution a lot closer to home. In recent years our Rock Action label had grown to the point where it was well established. Records by bands like Errors and Part Chimp achieved national recognition and it had been pointed out to us by David McBride, among others, that the sensible thing to do would be to put our own records out on Rock Action. It was a bit of a leap of faith. For a long time we'd relied on advances from our publisher and record label to pay our wages, and putting our own records out would remove that safety net entirely. If we continued to sell records we'd be better off financially and the label would continue to grow, but the opposite would be pretty catastrophic. We made the decision and left PIAS on good terms, though Kenny Gates would quite often enquire to see if we'd changed our minds.

The first Mogwai record we would release ourselves since the 'Tuner/Lower' single back in 1996 was to be a live album that we were going to record in New York. As well as the record, we had Vincent Moon come and shoot it for a live film that would come with the record. The plan was to record three shows in

Brooklyn at the Music Hall of Williamsburg, with The Twilight Sad opening for us. The venue held 500 people and it was sold out. I was excited about it. I always had a great time in New York, and it was the perfect opportunity to hang out with Alanna and my New York pals.

The New York shows went really well and amazingly I managed to pretty much forget that the shows were being filmed and recorded while on stage. We were staying down the road from the venue and would hang out with our friends till late after every show. It was so great to spend time with Alanna and be back in America after the trauma of how the last tour had ended. I know Martin was relieved too. After every show the five of us would hang out until really late and battle our hangovers the next day.

The tour continued through the year, taking us back to Europe, America and Japan. It was hectic. When I wasn't on tour, though, things weren't so good with Grainne. She was really busy with her business but under a lot of stress, loads of it totally unnecessary, caused by another Glasgow promoter who had made it his life's goal to make her life as difficult as possible. With a frail, fragile male ego and not able to deal with any competition, he'd resorted to making up the most insane nonsense about her in the live music world in order to harm her business. Some of it was so ridiculous that it was almost funny, such as that she had tried to knock his son down with her car. She's not the murderous type for a start, but to add to the absurdity of it all, she can't even drive. All of this was stressful for her, and I think the fact that I wasn't around very much wasn't helping either. Our relationship had deteriorated. We definitely weren't as close and had become quite resentful of each other. Both of us are fiery people and there were a lot of epic arguments. It got to the point where we didn't really talk to each other. It was a weird situation and I don't think either of us really knew what to do about it. I felt really lost and alone and I'm sure Grainne did too.

I found out that we were going to have a Scottish premiere

for our film in Glasgow, at the prestigious Glasgow Film Theatre. When I mentioned it to Grainne, though, she said she wasn't going to come. Something was seriously wrong. Grainne had always been really supportive of me (and I her), so this was not a good sign. Grainne eventually did come but it was clear that something in our marriage had fractured. Not only was our relationship falling apart but I didn't know what to do about it. Unable to cope with my rapidly collapsing marriage, I threw myself into making music. I had a little studio set up and I'd spend all my time in there working on songs. Arthur Baker had asked me to write some music for a fashion show and The Twilight Sad had asked me to do a remix for them. One of my favourite musicians, the guitarist Jack Rose, with whom we'd toured, had died suddenly so I recorded a cover version of an old blues song by Washington Phillips called 'What Are They Doing In Heaven Today?' for a compilation organised to raise money for his family. I also made music as part of a collaboration that the rapper Doseone was putting together with Alan Moore, my favourite comic writer. I was throwing myself into work rather than facing up to what was happening with me and Grainne. Running away from problems has always been one of my favourite moves.

One night after a particularly brutal row we both spoke about how shit we felt and then one of us said, 'I think this is over.' We both took our rings off and Grainne moved into the upstairs bedroom. It was finished. That was it. Almost ten years of marriage over in an instant.

The next months were really strange. We both stayed in the house but wanted to be out as much as possible. We shared the same friends. I was nervous about telling our neighbour Robert about me and Grainne breaking up, but when I went to tell him it turned out she already had. People deal with things differently, I suppose. Robert was a good friend and assured me that everything would be fine. He's a bit older than me and had seen this happen with loads of his friends. I hardly knew anyone who was married, never mind anyone who'd been divorced. Telling my parents was hard but all they cared about was that we were both OK. We weren't really, but would be in time.

A week or so later I went to London with Robert to see the reformed Stooges. It was one of Barry Hogan's Don't Look Back shows where they played their *Raw Power* album from start to finish. The opening band was Suicide playing their first album. I was a fucking mess and this was exactly what I needed. That night taught me a powerful lesson. No matter what is going on in your life, music can transport you away from it. I was going through hell. I felt like I'd let so many people down and was dealing with something I was in no way equipped to deal with, but for the entire time that The Stooges were onstage everything went away. When Iggy came on and sang the opening line, 'Dance to the beat of the loving dead, lose sleep baby stay away from bed', it seemed like a mantra. It felt like I was being exorcised of everything that was making me feel like shit. Iggy was a healer. A preacher. Even just being in the same room as these musicians who'd shaped my life felt energising.

I felt lost all that summer. I was struggling to cope and the only thing that made me forget about it was music. We had started working on our new album and had a plan to record it with Paul Savage. It would be our first time back in the studio with Paul since *Mogwai Young Team* thirteen years previously. It was also going to be the first time we'd released an album on our own label. We all knew that if we were to continue to make a living from music then this album had to do well. We didn't talk about it but with no advance from a label, if the record didn't do well then we were fucked. Things hadn't worked out well with Shaun on the management front, but we stayed on great terms and would tour with him loads over the years to come. I was left as the band's manager. I had my hands full but as my home life was a bin fire I was fine with taking on as much as possible.

As well as working on the music I also went along to several showings of our New York live film *Burning*. It was surreal seeing us play on the big screen but great to meet so many folks who liked the band. Performing at the kind of venues we now usually played meant we met a lot less people than we did when playing in small rooms, and it was really nice to get to know the people whose lives had been touched by our music.

Throughout the summer we recorded with Paul at Chem 19. The sessions were invigorating. It felt like it had been a matter of months since we recorded with Paul rather than over a decade. We all clicked back into it seamlessly. I had a good feeling about the songs we had for this record. There was a lot of variety and everything seemed to be turning out really well. We played a few festivals over the summer and would intersperse trips away with recording back in Scotland. The record was taking shape well and we managed to name it via a typically daft story told to us, this time by Errors drummer James Hamilton. He'd overheard a young Ned in a shop getting turned down for buying booze and his retort for this slight from the shopkeeper was to proclaim: 'Hardcore will never die, but you will.' Perfection.

Around this time I felt really uncentred. I tried to think back to my youth and the things that made me happy. Music was obviously one, but I was already making and playing as much music as humanly possible. The other activity that I thought about was skateboarding. I had pretty much stopped because I was worried about breaking a limb and jeopardising tours. We had a gig booked in LA and my dear friend Alanna Gabin was coming along. She had a bunch of friends she wanted to bring who were skaters. As it had been at the back of my mind, I said of course they could come to the show but would it be possible for them to bring me a board. When I got back to Scotland I built my first skateboard from the component parts and went out skating for the first time in over a decade. I knew straight away that it had been a great decision. It felt amazing. I was so into it that I couldn't fathom why I'd ever stopped in the first place. Like a lot of things, life had got in the way.

In November I went to Birmingham to DJ at Supersonic Festival. It was run by two really cool girls called Lisa and Jenny, and they booked excellent music. My most memorable visit up to that point had been in 2003 with Grainne when the whole festival had to be called off because of a bomb scare. The headliners that night were Psychic TV, and as we were in the same hotel as them we spent the night in their room hanging out with Genesis P-Orridge and their wife, Jane. Grainne talked with Jane about make-up while Genesis shouted belligerently out of the window at the police. This time I went alone, though I had quite a few friends playing and attending, most notably my neighbour, Dr Robert. One of the people that I knew there was Heather Leigh, an American musician who had relocated to Glasgow because she was going out with my friend David Keenan, the musician and writer. There was a communal backstage area where all the people playing would hang out when not watching the other bands. I saw Heather and went to speak to her. She was with another girl called Elisabeth. We immediately got on really well. She was funny, smart and really interesting. I had to leave them to go and DJ but afterwards we met up again to watch the other bands. Michael Rother from Neu! and Steve Shelley from Sonic Youth were playing. I knew them both and we all ended up hanging out with Elisabeth and Heather back at the hotel. It was the first time I'd had fun in a long time. To be honest, I could barely remember the last time I'd had fun at all. The whole year had been utterly wretched, but hanging out with Elisabeth was wonderful. She was studying art and music at university in Brighton and had a young son who she'd had when she was a teenager. She, like Heather, was obsessed with tarot and the occult. She had also recently come out of a relationship. That night we ended up staying up really late talking and listening to music. Even though we'd just met, it felt like we'd known each other forever.

The next morning we had breakfast in the hotel. It felt strange saying goodbye, knowing that we were both heading off to where we lived at opposite ends of the country. I really wanted to see Elisabeth again and hoped that she felt the same way.

We kept in touch over text but I really wanted to meet up again. Elisabeth had told me that she had grown up in France and that Paris was one of her favourite cities, so with that in mind I made quite an audacious offer. I was due to go to Paris for a showing of *Burning* and I decided to ask Elisabeth if she wanted to come with me. She agreed to come, though she did confess to me later that she asked a mutual friend to verify I wasn't a total weirdo. Thankfully I seem to have fallen just on the right side of the weirdo-meter.

In Paris, me and Elisabeth had a wonderful time exploring the city. She asked me if I had voted for David Cameron and looked delighted at the horror on my face at even the mention of such a thing. She came along to the showing of our film and we giggled all the way through it to the annoyance of the other attendees. After the film, Elisabeth and I walked along the Champs-Élysées to find something to eat. In an unsurprising turn of events the best vegetarian option we could find was chips. They were nice chips though. It was a wonderful evening and definitely the start of something special between me and Elisabeth.

For New Year's Eve we went to London. Barry Hogan had booked a show with Sonic Youth, Shellac and Factory Floor and asked me to DJ. The chance to get paid to play some records and watch some of my favourite bands was too good to pass up. Elisabeth's old band, Hush Arbors, had opened for Sonic Youth before so she knew them too. We were very much in the throes of a new romance and that night when I was playing, we were kissing next to the DJ booth whenever I didn't have to change a record. That was all fine and good but when we went out front to watch Sonic Youth, it became abundantly clear that the DJ booth was not tucked away in the wings of the stage as I had thought, but actually pretty much on the stage. Our unintended display of exhibitionism aside, we had amazing time, and even finding out that Mogwai's new album had leaked onto the internet six weeks ahead of release couldn't dampen my spirits. Watching Sonic Youth slay Hammersmith Apollo with 'Brother James' and 'Schizophrenia' with my new girlfriend felt wonderful. What had been a horrendous year had a fairy tale ending.

Little did I know that something was going to happen that would send me crashing back down. My world was about to fall apart.

22.

The Standing Stones

That Christmas, I went down to Hexham in Northumberland to meet Elisabeth's family for the first time. They were extremely welcoming and gloriously eccentric. I also spent time back in Lanarkshire with my parents, Vic and Jared.

It became apparent while there that my dad wasn't feeling too well. Not one to complain, it was a while before he took it seriously. Shoulder pain that had been bothering him for weeks wasn't getting any better and he was looking slightly jaundiced. On my mum's advice he went to the hospital to get checked out.

I was a bit surprised when my mum told me that he was being kept in hospital overnight. My dad had always been the strongest person in my life and the thought of him being very ill had never crossed my mind. My mum called me and my sister to go with her to visit him. I presumed that it was a normal social visit, to cheer him up. Thinking that he might be bored, I picked him up a book compiled from one of our favourite magazines, *Fortean Times*. It was called *A Compendium of Strange Deaths*. My dad hated hospitals. As soon as we got into the ward I sensed that something wasn't quite right. Everyone in the ward looked very sick. It didn't look like the kind of ward where people got taken to have some tests done. My dad didn't waste any time. He told us straight that he had liver cancer and that it wasn't going to get any better. I felt like the ground below me was collapsing. I couldn't believe that my dad was dying. I made a joke about how at least he wouldn't have to stay in the hospital and he made another about being able to assassinate David Cameron and get away with it. My dad didn't seem sad. He said he'd had an amazing life and this was just how it was going to end. He was amused at the book I'd bought him too, which now seemed in remarkably bad taste.

When I left the hospital I walked out into the cold winter air and wept like I've never wept before. My heart was truly broken. That night I called my mum and said that maybe I could donate my liver to help him. My mum thought it was sweet but explained that that wasn't how it works. I just couldn't deal with the fact that there was no way to make him get better.

Soon after finding out, I had to go to Greece to play some shows. Backstage after the first show I told the rest of my band about my dad. I could hardly get the words out of my mouth. The sympathy and support I received from Dominic, Martin, Barry and John was huge in helping me get through that time. They all loved my dad. He'd been a huge support for us and was proud of everything we'd done. I was numb for that whole trip, though being on stage felt like a reprieve from the shock and grief I was experiencing. Our music has a strong sense of nostalgia, and while playing I'd catch myself being reminded of my dad and the fact he wasn't going to be around for much longer, only for the hurt to return.

Music helped, but in this case it couldn't change anything.

The next day my dad went home. I knew that he didn't have much time but I had no idea how little he had. I'd had an offer to go and speak at the MIDEM conference in Cannes and my dad said I should go. I went with Craig, who runs Rock Action. It was a surreal time. I was constantly checking how my dad was, and I felt like a fish out of water anyway at such a business-centred event. My dad urged me to go as he was proud of how well I'd done and didn't want me to miss out on anything because of his illness. In the week I was away though, he deteriorated really quickly. If I'd known how rapid his illness would be, I would never have gone. He was in bed on constant medication and was spending most of the time asleep. My sister and Jared were help-ing him sort out his affairs. Quite a few of my dad's friends came to see him but he couldn't really handle the emotion of it all. He was completely at peace with dying and I suppose having to deal with everyone else's emotions was a burden that he didn't really need. He was surrounded by all of his favourite poetry books but told me that he had memorised them all anyway. My mum, my sister, my aunt Catherine and me would sit with him in shifts, making sure he was never alone. I remember sitting with him when he was finding it hard to speak and he looked at me with the kindest expression and said, 'Tell everyone that I love them.' It was a beautiful thing to say and one that just perfectly encap-sulates who he was. A wonderful, kind person.

One morning I got the call that I'd been dreading. It was 5 February, Victoria's birthday of all days. My sister called and told me that he had gone. I felt numb but not overly sad. My dad had an amazing life and died the way he wanted to. He'd often said he didn't want to wither away in a nursing home and he definitely hadn't done that. How quickly he deteriorated was a shock to me but much better than being desperately ill for a long time. No one wants to die, but at home surrounded by those who love you is the way to do it.

My dad's funeral was a sad but wonderful affair. His saltire-draped coffin was heralded by a jazz band. It reminded me of the time I called him from a payphone in New Orleans to let him hear one at a funeral on one of my first visits to the city. Jared, who had ordained himself as a minister a few years earlier because he found out it was a possibility, conducted the service beautifully. He spoke of my dad's many lives, as an astronomer, a telescope builder, a fierce champion of Scottish independence and, in his later life, as an internet troll who would take great mischievous delight in winding up right-wing conservative Christians online. He was a kind man too, though, and I learnt after his death that many of his close friends had polar opposite views to him.

It didn't matter to him, he just loved people. He also loved debate and arguing, which meant it was a handy thing to have people around who he disagreed with. As the band played while my dad made his final journey in the crematorium, I was struck by how loved he was. What a difference he'd made to so many people's lives. He was my dad but he was so many things to so many people. Elisabeth held me close that day. Her love and support was invaluable to me. Even though we hadn't been together for long, it was clear we had a bond that was special and true.

After my father's death I moved in with my mum. I think I told myself it was so I could look after her but I'm sure the opposite was closer to the truth. It also meant Grainne could stay at our house while we sorted everything out with the divorce.

I'd dream about my dad a lot after he died. I still do. Always there. Always kind. For my whole adult life my dad would always pick me up from the airport and drive me home. Even when I lived in Edinburgh, which for him would be an almost three-hour trip. He'd be waiting at departures for me, smiling and pleased to see me. On the drive home he'd ask about my trip and tell me everything that he had going on. Every time after he was gone I'd dread going through those airport doors knowing he would no longer be there to greet me. I felt that way for a long time, though the feelings have softened now and I just think gladly of how lucky I was to have him there to meet me for all those years. He was a wonderful man and I'm blessed to have had him as my father.

I spoke to my dad all the time when he was alive, but I was amazed by the amount of things I found out about him after he died and what an incredible life he had led. He'd been on *Tomorrow's World* with his telescopes, driven a taxi, stood for parliament and sung in the folk scene. The Reagan administration even unsuccessfully tried to recruit him to work on the ill-fated Star Wars missile system. He lived more in some decades of his life than many people manage in the entirety of theirs. One thing that my dad was immensely proud of, that I was aware of but hadn't looked at too closely, were 'the standing stones'. I knew he'd been part of erecting some standing stones in Glasgow when I was very young but didn't know too much about them. After his departure I would become all too aware of them as they were in danger and I knew that my dad would want them to be saved.

In the late seventies, before Margaret Thatcher's hated reign began, Glasgow City Council ran a competition for every kid in Glasgow for ideas for a park in the Sighthill area of the city. Sighthill was a deprived area, cut off by the M8 motorway and largely neglected in all aspects. The winning entry was for an astronomically aligned stone circle to be built in Glasgow. The first to be built on Scottish soil for thousands of years, since the pre-Christian time of the druids. Obviously, this was a mammoth task which would require the knowledge and expertise of astronomers. My dad and his friend, Duncan Lunan, were brought on board to oversee the project. This all happened when I was a toddler, but I recall the excitement around it. There was a chance that the project would never get to be completed as the Thatcher government tried to put a stop to it. Public money being spent on deprived areas was anathema to Thatcher and her gang of capitalist vultures. The fact that Thatcher's will was thwarted made the stones even more special for my dad. The stones themselves were literally massive. Handpicked by my dad and Duncan from a quarry in nearby Kilsyth, they were lifted into the park in Sighthill by massive army Chinook helicopters. The day that they were airlifted in, every school kid in Glasgow got the day off to see it happen. Over the years the stones were used by astronomers on dates like the solstice and equinox. It wasn't just stargazers who used them though. The druid and occult community would use them too. They were really special to my dad and he spoke of them fondly and proudly.

The year after my dad's death, news came through that felt like a spit in the face of his memory. Sighthill was to be completely redeveloped and the council had no plans for the standing stones. As it stood, they were to be destroyed and chucked in a fucking skip. I was completely distraught when I heard this. The area the stones were in had been neglected and it had reached the point where to see them you needed to make a bit of effort, but they were still being used and continued to hold huge cultural and historical importance. No one since that time had built one; they were still the only ones that had been built for thousands of years. Astronomers and druids still gathered there. The locals were fond of them too, though many probably didn't know about their history. They were just a local oddity in the park but still thought of affectionately.

The news of their imminent destruction shocked me to my core. I had to do something about it. I just couldn't let it happen. I spoke to Duncan who was already on the case and said that I would do literally anything to make sure they weren't destroyed. I said that I would shackle myself to a bulldozer if need be, and I fucking meant it. The stones were a little piece of magic in an urban jungle. They represented everything about my dad and what he stood for. Wonder. Magic. Science. History.

With Duncan's blessing I organised a gig with as many of my friends as I could round up to bring attention to the cause. Alun from Chemikal Undergound was booking the music at a great arts venue called Platform in Easterhouse, another deprived part of the city, and they agreed to host the gig. Aidan Moffat, The Twilight Sad and Eugene from The Vaselines all offered to play. I did a short set on my own. The artist David Shrigley did a really cool poster to promote the event. It was such a special night. I was so touched by how many of my friends and peers stepped up to help. I also found out that other friends like David Keenan and Heather Leigh knew the stones anyway because of their adventures walking around the lesser-known parts of the city. As well as the gig, I made myself available to talk about the stones and their plight to whoever would have me. I ended up on the TV and radio speaking about them. It was an obsession. I even enlisted the Arch Drude himself, Julian Cope, who lent his significant antiquarian heft to the campaign. Calling him was a wonderful and surreal experience. He was beyond kind and it felt great finding out that someone whose music and books had meant so much to me was an equally lovely person.

Gerry Braiden, a journalist who covered local stories for the *Herald* newspaper and had some connection to the council, was giving me the inside scoop on what was happening, and the jungle drums seemed to be good on the subject. It seemed as much as mine and Duncan's efforts had helped in bringing attention to their plight, it was actually the druids who in the end saved the stones. Apparently local politicians are scared of druids. This amused me greatly as the druids I'd met had been exceedingly nice people and not in the slightest scary. Scary enough though, it would seem. In the aftermath of the gig the fantastic news came through that the stones were saved! As I write this, the stones are now pride of place in the redeveloped Sighthill. Where they actually stand now was apparently the first choice for where to put them back in the seventies. My dad would have been so proud. The way that the music community rallied round to help me and also save a bit of Glaswegian cultural history was really special.

My father had taught me so much when he was around. He taught me to follow my passions and to value what really mattered: people, art and culture. His worlds and mine were very different. One day he'd suggested to me that I should call a record 'The Piper At The Gates Of Dawn', genuinely unaware that Pink Floyd had beaten him to it by half a century. He showed me that by turning away from materialism and greed that your life becomes far richer, even if not in wealth, than that of those obsessed by it. The standing stones meant a lot of different things to a lot of different people. To me they represented so much of what was special about my dad and it felt truly wonderful to have used what had guided me in my life – music – to make sure that they remained in Glasgow, intact, hopefully for generations to come.

A perfect convergence of sound and the stars.

I reflected a lot after the loss of my father. I looked back on the life that he had led, and at my own life. Our journeys had been so different, but were in many ways the same – we had both taken our own paths and found peace in doing exactly what we wanted to do, never compromising and yet somehow managing to get to exactly where we wanted despite that. I was heartened that my efforts had ensured that the standing stones he'd help create were to remain in Glasgow for generations to come.

Losing my father felt like losing a part of myself. I was grateful to my bandmates for their support, and my family were wonderful as ever. With Elisabeth by my side, I could look forward. Grief can be all-consuming and losing someone so important hit me hard. In time though, the pain began to subside and is gradually replaced by gratitude for having had him in my life in the first place.

I'm lucky to have had such a great father. I'm lucky too to have so many wonderful people in my life and to have found a way to make a living doing exactly what I would be doing whether I was being paid to do it or not. I'm not sure I would have been able to if it hadn't been for my dad.

And for that, I'm eternally grateful.

Acknowledgements

Thanks to Lee Brackstone, Keith Cameron, Jennifer Otter-Bickerdike and John Niven for holding my hand through writing this book.

Thanks to Adele Bethel, Victoria Braithwaite, Kate Braithwaite, Nicola Smith, Jaffa, Neale Smith, Mick Griffiths, Colin Hardie, Craig Wallace, Grainne Vedimanikam, Barry Hogan, Alex Kapranos, Paul Thompson, Mog, Kevin McCrorie, Martin Bulloch, Dominic Aitchison, Barry Burns, Colin Kearney, Kenny MacLeod, David Jack, Lisa Archibald, David Robertson, Keiron Mellote and Kiko for your help with jogging my memory and giving me photos to use.

In loving memory of John Braithwaite, Alanna Gabin and Mick Griffiths.

Picture Credits

All photos are from the author's personal collection, except for the following, which are printed by kind permission of:

Lisa Archibald: plate 3 (*bottom*)
Adele Bethel: plate 4 (*top*), plate 6 (*middle, bottom*)
Victoria Braithwaite: plate 3 (*top*), plate 8 (*top*)
Martin Bulloch: plate 6 (*top*)
Barry Burns: plate 7 (*top*)
Steve Gullick: plate 7 (*bottom*)
David Jack: plate 2 (*bottom right*)
James Jarvie: plate 5 (*bottom*)
Graham Kemp: plate 5 (*top*)
Keiron Mellote: plate 4 (*bottom left, bottom right*)
Elisabeth Oswell: plate 8 (*bottom*)